ANGELS TO ZEPPELINS

UNITED STATES OF AMERICA

ANGELS TO ZEPPELINS

A Guide to
the Persons, Objects,
Topics, and Themes
on United States
Postage Stamps,

1847-1980

DONALD J. LEHNUS

GREENWOOD PRESS
WESTPORT, CONNECTICUT • LONDON, ENGLAND

Library of Congress Cataloging in Publication Data

Lehnus, Donald J., 1934-
  Angels to Zeppelins.

  Bibliography: p.
  Includes index.
    1. Postage-stamps—United States—History.   2. Post-
age-stamps—Collectors and collecting—United States.
I. Title.
HE6185.U5L34   769.56973   82-918
ISBN 0-313-23475-2 (lib. bdg.)   AACR2

Library of Congress Catalog Card Number: 82-918
ISBN: 0-313-23475-2

First published in 1982

Greenwood Press
A division of Congressional Information Service, Inc.
88 Post Road West
Westport, Connecticut 06881

Printed in the United States of America

10 9 8 7 6 5 4 3 2 1

Copyright Acknowledgments

The Scott Catalogue Numbers are used herein under license from Scott Publishing Company,
the copyright owner. All rights thereto are reserved under the Pan American and Universal
Copyright Conventions. Copyright 1980 by Scott Publishing Company.

Minkus Numbers are used in this publication by permission of Minkus Publications, Inc.

With love and gratitude
this book is dedicated to my parents,
Carl H. Lehnus and Maude Proffitt Lehnus

Contents

Illustrations

The Illustrations consist of photographs of topical groupings of U.S. postage stamps.

Tables

Part I. THE STAMPS AND THE STUDY

1 Couriers and Forerunners

Systems of one type or another for the sending of messages by courier have existed since ancient times, but the use of postage stamps as we know them today only dates back to the nineteenth century.

Great Britain was the forerunner in many aspects of postal history, and, because the United States was part of the British Empire until 1776, our postal history is closely entwined with that of Great Britain. In 1710, the postal act of Queen Anne was passed; this act regulated the mails and set up uniform postal rates throughout the Empire. A few years later Benjamin Franklin began his long experience in postal matters when he was appointed postmaster general of Philadelphia in 1737. In 1753, Franklin and William Hunter were appointed joint deputy postmasters general for all the colonies.

The postal system in England was already well established by the end of the eighteenth century. During the early years of the nineteenth century the British post office began having financial problems due to misuse of the franking privilege and also because postage was not prepaid, but rather collected on delivery. Because of this, letters were often refused by the addressee and the government had to return the letter to the sender. Thus the government delivered the same letter to two different addresses with nothing being paid for either delivery. A system for the prepayment of mail was put into effect in 1840; letters were one penny if prepaid and twopence if paid when delivered. The British government issued stamped envelopes and wrappers for letters and papers and also printed adhesive stamps in the denominations of one penny and twopence that bore the likeness of Queen Victoria. These were the first adhesive postage stamps printed by any country and were issued in England on May 6, 1840.

Other countries soon adopted the use of postage stamps to show that postage had been prepaid. Brazil issued its first stamps in 1843, the United States in 1847, France in 1848, Belgium in 1849, and Spain in 1850. Thus began the use of the postage stamps to indicate that prepayment of postage had been made by the sender. Stamps are now issued by all politically independent countries in the world, and the collecting of these small bits of paper has become one of the world's most popular hobbies—philately.

THE FIRST UNITED STATES POSTAGE STAMPS

Americans of the eighteenth century realized the importance of a good postal system for the development of the country. One of the first acts of the Continental Congress was to establish a United States Post Office. This was done on July 26, 1775, almost a year before the adoption of the Declaration of Independence. On that date the Continental Congress named Benjamin Franklin as the first Postmaster General of the United States. It is not surprising that Franklin was chosen as he had been a postmaster for many years, during which he had made many improvements, and he was also well aware of the importance of an excellent mail system for the new country. His role in the development of the United States Post Office is indubitably the reason why he was chosen to appear on the first postage stamp of the United States.

Postal rates had always been very expensive from the very inception of the United States Post Office in 1775. It was not until 1845 that Congress approved an act which reduced the postage rates to a point where the use of the mails would be more accessible to everyone. This Act of March 3, 1845, established the rate of five cents for a letter conveyed in the mail for any distance less than 300 miles; for distances greater than 300 miles the charge was ten cents. Every letter or parcel not exceeding half an ounce was deemed a single letter, and each additional weight of half an ounce was charged an additional single postage.[1]

This act still did not provide for any kind of postage stamp to be used on the letters. Some postmasters took it upon themselves to supply postage stamps as a convenience to the public to indicate prepayment of postage. The first to do so was the postmaster of New York City, Robert H. Morris, who began to issue stamps in July 1845. Postmasters in other cities, such as Annapolis, Baltimore, Providence, and Saint Louis, also issued stamps. Some were adhesive stamps, and others were printed or stamped on the envelope, and often the initials or the signature of the postmaster were added. These are the forerunners of United States postage stamps and are known as "postmasters' provisionals."

POSTAL SERVICES

It was two years after Congress reduced the postage rates that an act was passed which authorized the Postmaster General to issue postage stamps that were to be sold at any United States Post Office. This Act of March 3, 1847, stated "that, to facilitate the transportation of letters in the mail, the Postmaster-General be authorized to prepare postage stamps, which, when attached to any letter or packet, shall be evidence of the payment of the postage chargeable on such letter."[2] The act authorized the use of U.S. Post Office stamps to begin on July 1, 1847, which would supersede the postmasters' provisionals. The bank note engraving firm, Rawdon, Wright, Hatch & Edson, was contracted by the Post Office Department to print the first United States stamps.[3]

Stamps were printed in two denominations, distributed to various post offices, and put into use in July 1847. One was a five-cent stamp, red brown in color, depicting Benjamin Franklin, the first Postmaster General of the United States and "Father of the American Postal System." The other was a black ten-cent stamp bearing a portrait of George Washington, the first President of the United States and "Father of His Country." The likeness of Franklin was adapted from a work by the engraver Louis B. Longacre, and the portrait of Washington was taken from a painting by Gilbert Stuart. These first two stamps (Scott Numbers 1 and 2) are also the only ones ever issued with the inscription, "U S Post Office" in the stamp design.

Thus in 1847 was begun the 134-year history of the issuance of postage stamps by the United States government, which are the subject of this study.

NOTES

1. Act to Reduce the Rates of Postage, March 3, 1845. U.S., *Statutes at Large*, vol. 5, chap. 43, sec. 1, p. 733.

2. Act to Establish Certain Post Routes and for Other Purposes, March 3, 1847. U.S., *Statutes at Large*, vol. 9, chap. 63, sec. 11, p. 201.

3. In April 1858 the firm of Rawdon, Wright, Hatch & Edson consolidated with four other bank note engraving companies to become the American Bank Note Company.

2 The Study: Its Purpose, Scope, Methodology, and Terminology

Since 1847, when the first United States stamps were issued bearing the likenesses of Franklin and Washington, the United States has issued many stamps honoring and depicting persons, events, organizations, anniversaries, and a wide variety of topics. This study deals with the postage stamps issued during the 134-year period, 1847-1980, by the U.S. government as prepayment of postage for letters and all other materials sent by mail. These include regular and commemorative stamps (Scott Numbers 1-1851); air mail stamps (Scott Numbers C1-C100); special delivery stamps (Scott Numbers E1-E23); parcel post stamps (Scott Numbers Q1-Q12); and the air mail special delivery stamp (Scott Number CE1). Explicitly excluded from this study are stamps of the following categories: postage due, official, special handling, registration, and certified mail. Also excluded are stamped envelopes and postal cards.

Many philatelists are interested in and collect variations of the same stamps which often result due to printing errors, flaws in printing plates, reprintings, different types or colors of paper, absence or presence of grill marks, watermarks, the number of perforations or the lack thereof, different colors or shades of ink used in printing, and slight changes in the design caused by a redrawing. The purpose of this study is to analyze the persons, themes, and objects that have been used on U.S. postage stamps, and even though philatelists may consider variations of stamps caused by the factors listed above as different stamps they have been disregarded by this author. Stamps of the same design but of variant denominations are considered here as distinctly different; for example, the one- and two-cent stamps portraying George Washington issued in 1912 (Scott Numbers 405 and 406) are identical in design and only vary in denomination and color; but those of the same design and denomination which were reprinted in a different color or shade are considered to be the same stamp, for example, the seven-cent air mail stamp issued as a blue stamp in 1958 and two years later printed in red with no change in design or denomination (Scott Numbers C51 and C60). The word stamp used in this study refers to a single design used on U.S. postage stamps according to the criteria given above.

Appendix I lists in numerical order by Scott Numbers the 1,355 stamps which were considered to be distinct according to these criteria. Each Scott Number is accompanied by the corresponding Minkus Number for those philatelists who use Minkus Numbers. These 1,355 stamps are the constituents of this analysis of U.S. postage stamps.

Each stamp was studied and examined very carefully (often with a magnifying glass and/or a small microscope) to determine the objects and details in the design of the stamp. In most cases the actual stamp was used, but in those instances where the stamp was not available a reproduction was used. Descriptions of the stamps were carefully read and perused, such as those that appear in stamp catalogs, journals, and publications of the United States Postal Service.[1]

The dates, 1847 to 1980, were chosen because the first U.S. stamps were issued in 1847, and the writing of this study began in 1980; therefore, it was decided to include all stamps issued from the very first one to the last one of 1980.

The purpose of the study is to point out new and different data, and by means of a thorough analysis to discover facts about the stamps of the United States that heretofore have never been determined or written about. Some of the questions that arise when one examines a collection of U.S. postage stamps are: Which individuals have been honored most frequently? What professions are represented by the persons honored on stamps? Are women, blacks, or foreigners depicted on many stamps? How many stamps have honored living persons? Who has been honored almost immediately after death? What items or objects are most often found in the designs? Which stamps have depicted clocks? wristwatches? ropes? dolphins? eyeglasses? What are some of the other unusual objects to be found on stamps? How are the denominations usually indicated; for example, are they written in words, arabic numerals, roman numerals, or combinations thereof? In what denominations have stamps been issued; for example, was there ever a twenty-three cent stamp? How many three-dollar stamps are there? What inscription is used most often to indicate that the stamps are issued by the United States? Are there any trends in the type of inscriptions used?

The following analyses of United States postage stamps will answer all these questions, and many more, about the persons, themes, and objects which have been on our stamps.

NOTE

1. *Minkus New American Stamp Catalog*, 1981 ed. (New York: Minkus Publications [1980]), 390 pp.; *Minkus Stamp Journal* (New York: Minkus Publications, 1966-) (title was changed to "Minkus Stamp & Coin Journal" in 1980); *Scott Specialized Catalogue of United States Stamps, 1981* (New York: Scott Publishing Company, 1980), 762 pp.; *Scott's Monthly Stamp Journal* (New York: Scott Publishing Company, 1920-); U.S., Postal Service, *Stamps & Stories: The Encyclopedia of U.S. Stamps* (Washington, D.C.: U.S. Postal Service, 1980), 264 pp.; U.S., Postal Service, Philatelic Affairs Division, *United States Postage Stamps: An Illustrated Description of all United States Postage and Special Service Stamps* (Washington, D.C.: U.S. Government Printing Office, 1972-).

3   The Stamps

According to the criteria established in the preceding chapter, the United States has issued 1,355 different stamps during the past 134 years. For the purposes of the various analyses of this study, this 134-year span (1847-1980) has been divided into thirteen periods. Each period covers ten years, except for the first one which contains fourteen years. This permitted each of the twelve subsequent periods to cover exactly a decade. So few stamps were issued during the first fourteen years of U.S. postage stamp history that it is felt that this slight deviation will not skew any conclusions drawn from the analyses. The inclusive dates of the thirteen periods, the number of different stamps for each period, and their Scott Numbers are given in Table 1. The use of inclusive Scott Numbers in Table 1 to indicate the stamps of each period does not signify that each numbr in that range is included in the study, but rather that the stamps covered in this study fall within that range of Scott Numbers. For a complete list of all the 1,355 stamps on which this study is based please refer to Appendix I which lists all the stamps by Scott Number with the corresponding Minkus Number.

Table 1 points out some interesting facts about the number of stamps issued. During the five periods of the nineteenth century (1847-1900) only eighty-eight stamps (6.5 percent of the total) were issued, but during the last two periods (1961-80) 649 stamps (47.9 percent, or almost one-half) appeared. The number of stamps that came out in the past ten years (1971-

Table 1
The Thirteen Periods and Their Stamps

Period	Scott Numbers	Number of Stamps	Percentage
1. 1847-60	1-39	10	0.74
2. 1861-70	63-148, 150-155	30	2.21
3. 1871-80	149 and 179	2	0.15
4. 1881-90	205-224	12	0.89
	E1, E2		
5. 1891-1900	225-293	34	2.51
6. 1901-10	294-372	46	3.39
	E6, E7		
7. 1911-20	397-550	39	2.88
	C1-C3		
	Q1-Q12		
8. 1921-30	551-689	71	5.24
	C4-C15		
	E12-E14		
9. 1931-40	690-902	164	12.10
	C17-C24		
	CE1		
10. 1941-50	903-997	115	8.49
	C25-C45		
	E17, E18		
11. 1951-60	998-1143, 1145-1173	183	13.50
	C46-C59		
	E20, E21		
12. 1961-70	1144, 1174-1393	223	16.46
	1405-1422		
	C62-C76		
	E22		
13. 1971-80	1393D-1400, 1423-1851	426	31.44
	C77-C100		
	E23		
Total		1,355	100.00

80) is almost double that of the preceding decade. If this increase continues at the present rate, philatelists can expect almost 800 stamps to come out in the decade 1981-90. The quantity of stamps issued during each ten-year period has been increasing consistently since 1911. The only exception is Period 10 (1941-50), during which time World War II occurred; throughout the first half of this period the nation's interests were concentrated on the war effort, and it seems likely that the planning and issuance of new postage stamps would have had a low government priority.

Tables 2 and 3 group the stamps into five fundamental categories based on use and purpose: (1) regular postal issues, (2) commemoratives, (3) air mail, (4) special delivery, including air mail special delivery, and (5) parcel post. The category of commemoratives is based on the special group of separately numbered stamps that appear in the section entitled "Commemorative Issues" of the stamp catalog of Minkus Publications, Inc.[1] The Scott Publishing Company catalog has no special section for commemorative stamps, and its numbering system makes no distinction between the regular postal issues and the commemorative stamps; they are grouped together in a section called "General Issues."[2] Table 2 lists the number of stamps in each of the five categories and distributes them according to the thirteen periods. Table 3 gives the percentages of the stamps that were issued during each of the thirteen periods.

The information given in Table 2 shows that more than two-thirds (69.08 percent) of the stamps are classed as commemoratives, while less than one-fourth of them (22.43 percent) are regular issues. Since the 1930s, the number of commemoratives issued in each period has been more than four times the number of regular issues, and the total number of commemoratives is more than three times greater than the number of regular stamps. Few commemoratives were issued prior to the time when James A. Farley became the Postmaster General under President Franklin D. Roosevelt in 1933. From 1847 to 1930, only seventy-nine commemoratives came out, but in the 1930s more than one hundred were issued. This seems to have started a trend that has continued to the present. In fact, 857 (91.56 percent) of the commemoratives have been issued in the past fifty years (1931-80). Even though the number of stamps issued each period has greatly increased since the 1930s, a glance at Table 3 shows that the percentage of commemoratives has remained constant at close to 75 percent of each period's production of stamps. The percentage of commemoratives issued during Period 5 (1891-1900) was also almost 75 percent of that decade's stamps. This is due to the two large series of stamps that came out in 1893 and 1898; the Columbian Exposition set of commemoratives (Scott Numbers 230-245) consisted of sixteen stamps, and the Trans-Mississippi Exposition issue (Scott Numbers 285-293) had nine stamps.

The stamps can also be categorized into two groups according to the topic or theme, namely, (1) subject stamps and (2) stamps depicting or honoring persons. A subject stamp is one that has no identifiable person or a personal name in the design. Any stamp with a likeness of a real person is considered a "person stamp." This likeness may be an original portraiture, a reproduction of a painting, drawing, sculpture, statue, or any other art form, or any means through which the person's likeness appears in the design and was either identifiable by this author or identified in the various publications of the United States Postal Service, Scott Publishing Company, and Minkus Publications, Inc.

Table 2
Number of Stamps in the Five Basic Categories

Period	Regular	Commemo- rative	Air Mail	Special Delivery	Parcel Post	Total
1. 1847-60	10	0	0	0	0	10
2. 1861-70	30	0	0	0	0	30
3. 1871-80	2	0	0	0	0	2
4. 1881-90	10	0	0	2	0	12
5. 1891-1900	9	25	0	0	0	34
6. 1901-10	27	17	0	2	0	46
7. 1911-20	16	8	3	0	12	39
8. 1921-30	27	29	12	3	0	71
9. 1931-40	33	122	8	1	0	164
10. 1941-50	0	94	19	2	0	115
11. 1951-60	27	141	13	2	0	183
12. 1961-70	43	167	12	1	0	223
13. 1971-80	70	333	22	1	0	426
Total	304	936	89	14	12	1,355
Percentage	22.43	69.08	6.57	1.03	0.89	100.00

Table 3
Percentage of Stamps in the Five Basic Categories for Each of the Thirteen Periods

Period	Regular	Commemo- rative	Air Mail	Special Delivery	Parcel Post	Total Percentage
1. 1847-60	100.00	—	—	—	—	100
2. 1861-70	100.00	—	—	—	—	100
3. 1871-80	100.00	—	—	—	—	100
4. 1881-90	83.33	—	—	16.67	—	100
5. 1891-1900	26.47	73.53	—	—	—	100
6. 1901-10	58.70	36.96	—	4.34	—	100
7. 1911-20	41.03	20.51	7.69	—	30.77	100
8. 1921-30	38.03	40.85	16.90	4.22	—	100
9. 1931-40	20.12	74.39	4.88	0.61	—	100
10. 1941-50	—	81.74	16.52	1.74	—	100
11. 1951-60	14.75	77.05	7.10	1.10	—	100
12. 1961-70	19.28	74.89	5.38	0.45	—	100
13. 1971-80	16.43	78.17	5.17	0.23	—	100

All stamps which include a personal name are also considered to be "person stamps." The person's likeness may not appear on the stamp, but if the name is included in the design, then it is assumed that the stamp honors that person. Examples of this type of "person" stamps are:

1. Those that obviously honor individuals, such as the one commemorating the centenary of the birth of Booker T. Washington (Scott Number 1074); the Lindbergh stamp of 1927 (Scott Number C10); the Jefferson Memorial stamp with the signature of Thomas Jefferson prominently displayed (Scott Number 1510); the stamps depicting homes of famous men which also include the name of the person, for example, Wheatland, the home of James Buchanan (Scott Number 1081) and Gunston Hall, the home of George Mason (Scott Number 1108). Stamps with famous homes that did not include the name of the person were not considered as person stamps, for example, Mount Vernon (Scott Number 1032) and Monticello (Scott Number 1047).
2. Stamps which include the name of the artist whose work is reproduced on the stamp, for example, Winslow Homer (Scott Number 1207), Jan van Eyck (Scott Number 1363), Josef Albers (Scott Number 1833), and Alexander J. Davis (Scott Number 1841).
3. Stamps that contain a quote from a person's writings or speeches and include the name of the author, for example, Thomas Carlyle (Scott Number 1082), Benjamin Franklin (Scott Number 1140), and John Donne (Scott Numbers 1530, 1532, 1534 and 1536).

Stamps whose designs contain buildings, structures, geographical features, or any other item named after a person were not considered as "person stamps." Examples of this type of subject stamp are Lincoln Memorial (Scott Number 571), Popham Colony (Scott Number 1095), Verrazano-Narrows Bridge (Scott Number 1258), and Gadsby's Tavern (Scott Number C40).

Table 4 tabulates the number of "subject" stamps and "person" stamps which have been issued during each period. The number of subject stamps has increased greatly since the first one came out in 1869 (Scott Number 113). During the past twenty years, there have been 449 subject stamps; this is almost 60 percent of all subject stamps ever issued. The total production of subject stamps is 770, or 57 percent of the 1,355 stamps emitted since 1847, but the total number of person stamps has been only 585, or 43 percent.

Table 5 lists the thirteen periods and the percentage of each period's stamps that were subject stamps and person stamps. It is obvious from the ever-increasing trend of issuing a larger percentage of subject stamps each period that, if the present rate of increase continues, the issuance of stamps portraying or honoring persons will almost cease.

Table 4
Subject Stamps and Stamps with Persons

Period	Subject Stamps		Person Stamps		Total Number of Stamps
	No.	%	*No.*	%	
1. 1847-60	0	—	10	1.71	10
2. 1861-70	5	0.65	25	4.27	30
3. 1871-80	0	—	2	0.34	2
4. 1881-90	2	0.26	10	1.71	12
5. 1891-1900	7	0.91	27	4.62	34
6. 1901-10	10	1.30	36	6.16	46
7. 1911-20	21	2.73	18	3.08	39
8. 1921-30	37	4.80	34	5.81	71
9. 1931-40	55	7.14	109	18.63	164
10. 1941-50	78	10.13	37	6.32	115
11. 1951-60	106	13.77	77	13.16	183
12. 1961-70	141	18.31	82	14.02	223
13. 1971-80	308	40.00	118	20.17	426
Total	770	100.00	585	100.00	1,355

Table 5
Percentage of Subject and Person Stamps for Each of the Thirteen Periods

Period	Subject Stamps	Person Stamps	Total Percentage
1. 1847-60	—	100.00	100
2. 1861-70	16.66	83.34	100
3. 1871-80	—	100.00	100
4. 1881-90	16.66	83.34	100
5. 1891-1900	20.59	79.41	100
6. 1901-10	21.74	78.26	100
7. 1911-20	53.85	46.15	100
8. 1921-30	52.11	47.89	100
9. 1931-40	33.54	66.46	100
10. 1941-50	67.83	32.17	100
11. 1951-60	57.92	42.08	100
12. 1961-70	62.23	36.77	100
13. 1971-80	72.30	27.70	100

SUMMARY

Since 1847, the total output of different U.S. stamps has been 1,355; this is an average of only ten stamps per year during the 134-year history of United States postage stamps. Even though the average is only ten per year, it should be noted, however, that during the last ten years there were 426 stamps issued. This is almost one-third of the total output for the entire 134 years.

A categorization of the stamps into five groups according to purpose and use shows that more than two-thirds of all the stamps can be classed as commemoratives and less than one-fourth are regular issues. Less than 7 percent are air mail stamps; special delivery and parcel post stamps combined make up less than 2 percent of all stamps.

A bifurcation of the stamps into two groups, subject stamps and person stamps, points out that there are 770 subject stamps with no identifiable person on them and 585 stamps that depict or honor one or more persons. Forty percent of all subject stamps have appeared in the past ten years (1971-80), and during this decade almost three-fourths of the stamps issued were subject stamps. This indicates that the percentage of person stamps is rapidly diminishing.

NOTES

1. *Minkus New American Stamp Catalog*, 1981 ed. (New York: Minkus Publications [1980]), pp. 67-175.

2. *Scott Specialized Catalogue of United States Postage Stamps, 1981* (New York: Scott Publishing Company, 1980), pp. 5-241.

4 Inscriptions and Overprints

An inscription on a stamp consists of the letters and numbers that are a part of the stamp design. Inscriptions may be categorized into two parts. One is the denomination which appears on almost all stamps and indicates the face value. The denomination may be written in words, numerals, or a combination thereof. The other part consists of all other words and numerals included in the stamp design and may consist of three distinct types of legends. Of these three types, none, one, two, or all three may be present in the inscription. The three types are: (1) a word, phrase, abbreviation, or other device that identifies or denotes the issuing country, (2) a word or phrase that indicates the use for which the stamp is intended, for example, air mail, special delivery, postage, parcel post, and (3) a word, groups of words, dates, numerals, or a phrase that identifies, explains, describes, or gives any other information about the person, event, organization, object, theme, quotation, or anything else that the stamp commemorates, honors, promotes, or publicizes.

Richard Cabeen wrote that three elements are considered necessary in stamp design: the name of the country, the use of the stamp, and the denomination.[1] U.S. postage stamps have been issued which have all of the above elements, some with two, and others with only one element. All U.S. stamps have at least one of the three elements.

How many different legends have been used to identify the United States as the issuing country? Which legend has been the most frequently used? Which ones are currently used more often? What different legends are found on the stamps to indicate the use for which they were intended? Does the word "postage" always appear on U.S. stamps? These are just a few of the quesions that are answered in this chapter on the inscriptions that have been on U.S. stamps.

The analyses and discussion in this chapter principally treat the parts of the inscriptions that deal with the identification and denotation of the issuing country and the word or phrase that indicates the intended use.

Table 6 lists the four distinct country denotations of U.S. stamps. There have been ten stamps printed without any country denotation at all. The most frequently used is that consisting of the two initials, "U.S.," which appears on 530 stamps, or almost 40 percent of all U.S. stamps.[2] The other often employed is "United States"; it has been used on 484 stamps, or a little more than 35 percent of the stamps. "USA" is the denotation that has come into use the past few years, and, in the last ten years (1971-80), it was

Table 6
Country Denotations on All U.S. Stamps

Period	U.S.	USA	United States	United States of America	None	Total
1. 1847-60	10	0	0	0	0	10
2. 1861-70	25	0	1	5	0	31*
3. 1871-80	2	0	0	0	0	2
4. 1881-90	1	0	11	0	0	12
5. 1891-1900	0	0	9	25	0	34
6. 1901-10	16	0	0	30	0	46
7. 1911-20	36	0	0	0	3	39
8. 1921-30	16	0	56	0	0	72*
9. 1931-40	46	0	117	4	0	167*
10. 1941-50	29	0	73	13	1	116*
11. 1951-60	96	2	77	7	1	183
12. 1961-70	111	2	105	1	5	224*
13. 1971-80	142	250	35	0	0	427*
Total	530†	254	484	85	10	1,363*
Percentage	38.88	18.64	35.51	6.24	0.73	100.00

*Eight stamps have two different country denotations, therefore the totals are eight more than the number of stamps covered in the study. These eight are: Scott Numbers 115, C12, C17, C19, C24, and C38 (U.S. and United States), and C75 and C81 (USA and United States).

†Twelve air mail stamps (Scott Numbers C79, C89-C96, and C98-C100) have the inscription, "USAirmail," which can be read either as US Airmail or USA Airmail; in this study it is considered as US Airmail. The Mazzei stamp (Scott Number C98) has "USA" in red and the letters "irmail" in black, thus pointing out the double purpose of the letter A.

used on almost 60 percent of the stamps issued. This indicates a new trend which undoubtedly will continue into the future. The full name, "United States of America," has only been used on a little more than 6 percent of the stamps; however, it was used on almost 70 percent of the stamps issued from 1891 to 1910, but since that time it was hardly been used at all. In fact, it has only been used once in the past twenty years; it last appeared on the Patrick Henry credo stamp of 1961 (Scott Number 1144). "United States" appeared on almost 57 percent of all stamps issued between 1921 and 1970, but in the last ten years it was only on slightly more than 8 percent of the stamps.

The following chart containing data extracted from Table 6 indicates the country denotation that predominated in each of the thirteen periods. During sixty-four years (1847-80, 1911-20, and 1951-70) the abbreviation, "U.S.," was the one most often used. The one used for the next longest period of time was "United States," which predominated for forty years (1881-90 and 1921-50).

1847-80	U.S.
1881-90	United States
1891-1910	United States of America
1911-20	U.S.
1921-50	United States
1951-70	U.S.
1971-80	USA

Tables 7, 8, and 9 list the exact phrases that appeared on the stamps of each period which indicate the issuing country and the intended use of the stamp. Table 7 gives the legends used on regular and commemorative postage stamps, that is, those not intended for a specific use such as air mail, special delivery, or parcel post (Scott Numbers 1-1851). Table 8 displays the phrases that have been on air mail stamps (Scott Numbers C1-C100). Because the first air mail stamp was issued in 1918, Table 8 excludes the first six periods, 1847-1910. Table 9 lists the wordings found on special delivery, parcel post, and air mail special delivery stamps (Scott Numbers E1-E23, Q1-Q12, and CE1). This table begins with Period 4, 1881-90 because the first stamp in this group was not issued until 1885.

Even though the regular and commemorative issues comprise almost 92 percent of the total, there have been only twelve different legends used for this group. Air mail stamps make up only 6.5 percent of U.S. stamps; yet nineteen different wordings have been used on them. The other group of special delivery and parcel post stamps represents a little less than 2 percent, with seven different phrases on them.

There are well-defined trends in the wording of the legends that have appeared on the regular postage stamps. Table 7 shows that only the first two stamps (Scott Numbers 1 and 2) used the words "U.S. Post Office." For exactly one hundred years, from 1861 to 1960, all but five regular postage stamps contained the word "postage" in combination with some form of the name of the country. (These five stamps, Scott Numbers 548-550, 947, and 1017, will be discussed later in this chapter with five others which were issued without country denotations.) The words "postage," "post office," or "postal service" have been included in the design of more than 62 percent of all the regular and commemorative stamps, but the trend now is to omit any such term from these two classes of stamps. During the first eleven periods, 1847-1960, there were only four regular stamps on which none of these terms appeared (Scott Numbers 548-550 and 947). These four stamps comprise slightly more than one-half of 1 percent of the 706 stamps issued in the United States in those 114 years! During Period 12, 1961-70, ninety-one stamps (42.33 percent) were printed without any such term. But during the last decade, 1971-80, the percentage of regular and commemorative stamps issued without any of these terms zoomed way up: 374 stamps, or almost 93 percent, came out with no mention of postage, post office, or postal service. During this same decade, 1971-80, there were just eighteen stamps (4.48 percent) that used the word postage, and eleven (2.74 percent) that included in its design the new term, postal service. "Postal service" came into use during this period because on July 1, 1971, the original U.S. Post Office Department became the United States Postal Service, a quasi-independent nonprofit government corporation, and the Postmaster General ceased to be a member of the President's Cabinet. A glance at Table 7 reveals that the use of "U.S.," "USA," and "United States" without any mention of postage or postal service did not come into use until the 1960s, and this practice greatly increased during the 1970s. During the past decade, the use of "United States" diminished significantly, and the abbreviations "U.S." and "USA" were used almost exclusively without any such term as "postage" or "postal service."

The data in Table 8 point out that all but nine of the eighty-nine air mail stamps have legends which include "air mail" or "airmail." Of these nine stamps, four were designed expressly for mail carried by the *Graf Zeppelin* in the early 1930s (Scott Numbers C13-C15 and C18). Three of these included the words *Graf Zeppelin* in the design in addition to the phrase United States of America. The other one (Scott Number C18) had the *Graf Zeppelin* as its central design, but did not include the name in its legend. The legend reads: "United States Postage—A Century of Progress Flight." The other five stamps that did not include the words "air mail" or "airmail" simply stated, "U.S. Postage." Three of these were the first air mail stamps which came out in 1918 (Scott Numbers C1-C3) and depicted the Curtiss Jenny airplane. The airplane in the stamp design is the only clue to the intended use—air mail postage—but these stamps were valid for ordinary postage also. Even though these were the first air mail stamps, they were not the first ones to depict an airplane. The first stamp to depict an airplane came out exactly six years earlier in 1912. This first "airplane stamp" was the twenty-cent parcel post stamp (Scott Number Q8). Exclusive of this parcel post stamp, only air mail stamps depicted airplanes until the International Civil Aeronautics Conference stamps (Scott Numbers 649 and 650) were issued in 1928. One of these pictured *Flyer I*, the plane the Wright Brothers used at Kitty Hawk in 1903, and the other used a modern monoplane as its central design. The other two stamps with no mention of "air mail" came out in 1923; one depicted an airplane radiator and a propeller (Scott Number C4), and the other had the DeHavilland biplane as its central design (Scott Number C6).

Besides the *Graf Zeppelin* stamps, only four others have included such a prescribed use in their legends; three of these are the Trans-Pacific air mail stamps of 1935 and 1937 (Scott Numbers C20-C22) which were intended primarily for mail to Hawaii, Guam, and the Philippines. The legend on each of these reads: "U.S. Postage—Trans-Pacific Air Mail." The other one is the Trans-Atlantic air mail stamp of 1939 (Scott Number C24); its legend states, "United States Postage—Trans-Atlantic U.S. Air Mail."

The air mail stamp commemorating the fiftieth anniversary of U.S. air mail service in 1968 (Scott Number C74) is the only one that did not include a country denotation in its inscription. (This stamp is discussed in detail later in this chapter.)

An interesting feature of the air mail stamps is the introduction of "airmail" written as a single word. This first occurred in 1973 (Scott Number C79) and has now been used on sixteen stamps.

The information in Table 9 shows that all fourteen special delivery stamps (including the one air mail special delivery stamp) have country denotations, and all except the first two include the phrase special delivery. The first two (Scott Numbers E1 and E2) used the phrase "special postal delivery" to indicate their intended use. The first one included the explanation that it "secures immediate delivery at a special delivery office," and the second one stated that it "secures immediate delivery at any post office." Only four of the special delivery stamps have used the word "postage"; three of these were issued in the 1920s (Scott Numbers E12-E14), and the other is the air mail special delivery stamp of 1934 (Scott Number CE1).

There are only twelve parcel post stamps, and they comprise a single series that came out in 1912 and 1913; all have the same inscription, "U.S. Parcel Post," which identifies the country and the use. All twelve have the same border design varying only in the denomination. The first eight in the series depict some aspect of postal service; the ninth one, manufacturing; and the last three have agricultural themes in the designs.

There are ten stamps (three-fourths of 1 percent of the 1,355 stamps) that

Table 7
Country and Use Denotations on Regular and Commemorative Stamps

Denotation	Period													Total	Percentage
	1 1847-60	*2* 1861-70	*3* 1871-80	*4* 1881-90	*5* 1891-1900	*6* 1901-10	*7* 1911-20	*8* 1921-30	*9* 1931-40	*10* 1941-50	*11* 1951-60	*12* 1961-70	*13* 1971-80		
Postage	0	0	0	0	0	0	0	0	0	0	1	1	0	2	0.16
Postage USA	0	0	0	0	0	0	0	0	0	0	1	0	0	1	0.08
U.S.	0	0	0	0	0	0	0	0	0	0	0	32	102	134	10.81
USA	0	0	0	0	0	0	0	0	0	0	0	1	247	248	20.00
U.S. Post Office	2	0	0	0	0	0	0	0	0	0	0	0	0	2	0.16
U.S. Postage	8	24	2	1	0	15	21	10	38	22	84	72	11	308	24.84
U.S. Postal Service	0	0	0	0	0	0	0	0	0	0	0	0	10	10	0.81
United States	0	0	0	0	0	0	0	0	0	0	0	55	25	80	6.45
United States of America Postage	0	0	0	0	25	29	0	0	4	5	7	1	0	71	5.73
U.S. Postage United States	0	1	0	0	0	0	0	0	0	0	0	0	0	1	0.08
United States Postal Service	0	0	0	0	0	0	0	0	0	0	0	0	1	1	0.08
Unites States Postage	0	5	0	9	9	0	0	46	113	66	75	45	7	375	30.24
None	0	0	0	0	0	0	3	0	0	1	0	3	0	7	0.56
Total	10	30	2	10	34	44	24	56	155	94	168	210	403	1,240	100.00

Table 8
Country and Use Denotations on Air Mail Stamps

Denotation	Period 7 1911-20	8 1921-30	9 1931-40	10 1941-50	11 1951-60	12 1961-70	13 1971-80	Total	Percentage
Air Mail	0	0	0	0	0	1	0	1	1.12
USA Air Mail	0	0	0	0	1	0	0	1	1.12
USA Airmail	0	0	0	0	0	0	3	3	3.37
USAirmail	0	0	0	0	0	0	12	12	13.48
USA United States Air Mail	0	0	0	0	0	1	1	2	2.25
U.S. Air Mail	0	0	0	0	7	7	5	19	21.35
U.S. Airmail	0	0	0	0	0	0	1	1	1.12
U.S. Air Mail Postage	0	0	0	0	1	0	0	1	1.12
U.S. Postage	3	2	0	0	0	0	0	5	5.62
U.S. Postage Air Mail	0	1	1	6	2	0	0	10	11.24
U.S. Postage Trans-Pacific Air Mail	0	0	3	0	0	0	0	3	3.37
U.S. Postage U.S. Air Mail	0	1	0	0	0	0	0	1	1.12
United States Air Mail	0	0	0	0	0	3	0	3	3.37
United States of America Air Mail	0	0	0	8	0	0	0	8	9.00
United States Postage	0	0	1	0	0	0	0	1	1.12
United States Postage Air Mail	0	4	0	4	2	0	0	10	11.24
United States Postage Graf Zeppelin	0	3	0	0	0	0	0	3	3.37
United States Postage Trans-Atlantic U.S. Air Mail	0	0	1	0	0	0	0	1	1.12
United States Postage U.S. Air Mail	0	1	2	1	0	0	0	4	4.50
Total	3	12	8	19	13	12	22	89	100.00

Table 9
Country and Use Denotations on Special Delivery, Air Mail Special Delivery, and Parcel Post Stamps

Denotation	Period										Total	Percentage
	4 1881-90	5 1891-1900	6 1901-10	7 1911-20	8 1921-30	9 1931-40	10 1941-50	11 1951-60	12 1961-70	13 1971-80		
U.S. Postage Special Delivery	0	0	1	0	1	0	0	2	0	0	4	15.38
United States of America Special Delivery	0	0	1	0	0	0	0	0	0	0	1	3.85
United States Postage Special Delivery	0	0	0	0	2	0	2	0	0	0	4	15.38
United States Special Delivery	0	0	0	0	0	0	0	0	1	1	2	7.69
United States Special Postal Delivery	2	0	0	0	0	0	0	0	0	0	2	7.69
U.S. Postage Air Mail Special Delivery	0	0	0	0	0	1	0	0	0	0	1	3.85
U.S. Parcel Post	0	0	0	12	0	0	0	0	0	0	12	46.16
Total	2	0	2	12	3	1	2	2	1	1	26	100.00

were printed with no express country denotation. The first time the country denotation was ommitted occurred in 1920 when the three Pilgrim Tercentenary stamps (Scott Numbers 548-550) were issued. These included in the inscriptions the denominations, the phrase "Pilgrim Tercentenary—1620-1920," but there was nothing to indicate that these were postage stamps or that the United States was the issuing country. The one-cent stamp depicted a ship identified as the *Mayflower* by the legend under the ship. The two-cent stamp showed a rowboat and people with a ship in the background and under the picture, "Landing of the Pilgrims." The third one in the series was a five-cent stamp reproducing a painting by Edwin White entitled "Signing of the Compact," and this title appeared under the reproduction. Max Johl remarked that these stamps, which did not bear any words indicating the country of origin, created considerable comment among both collectors and the public.[3] Acting Third Assistant Postmaster General William J. Barrows wrote a letter about the Pilgrim Tercentenary stamps in which he stated that they "are a departure in several respects from conventional designs, although precedent exists in previous American and foreign issues. There is no necessity for the name, as the stamps are fully authenticated in a notice. . . . Any additional lettering would have overcrowded designs which required all of the spaces assigned to them."[4]

The next one without a country denotation (Scott Number 947) came out in 1947 to commemorate the centenary of the first postage stamps issued by the United States government. The legend reads: "1847-1947—U.S. Postage Stamp Centenary," and the denomination appears in either upper corner. The stamp depicts George Washington and Benjamin Franklin, as well as an airplane, a ship, two trains, and a pony express rider. The legend does imply that it is a U.S. postage stamp, but that is not expressly stated.

The stamp issued in 1953 to honor the National Guard of the United States (Scott Number 1017) also has a legend implying that the issuing country is the United States, but it lacks a phrase such as "U.S. Postage." The entire inscription reads: "The National Guard of the U.S.—In Peace—In War—The Oldest Military Organization in the U.S.—3 ¢ Postage."

It was not until 1962 that another stamp (Scott Number 1193) came out without a precise reference to the issuing country, but again it was implied, and no mention of postage was included. The inscription on this stamp to honor the first orbital flight of an American astronaut simply says: "U.S. Man in Space—Project Mercury—4 ¢."

On January 7, 1963, the new first class postage rate for letters was increased from four to five cents, and on January 9, a new red, white, and blue five-cent stamp was issued (Scott Number 1208). Depicted in the foreground of the stamp is the fifty-star American flag and in the background is the White House. In the lower left-hand corner is printed the denomination, "5 ¢"; no other letters or numbers are on the stamp. The flag undoubtedly identifies it as a U.S. stamp, but no legend whatsoever is included. This is the only U.S. postage stamp that has no inscription except for the denomination.

The stamp to commemorate the twenty-fifth anniversary of U.S. Savings Bonds and to honor American servicemen was issued in 1966 (Scott Number 1320). The central design contains the Statue of Liberty and the American flag. The inscription is: "We Appreciate Our Servicemen—United States Savings Bonds—25th Anniversary—5¢." No country denotation is included, nor does the word "postage" appear on the stamp, but it may be inferred from either the design or the legend that it is a U.S. stamp.

The register and vote stamp of 1964 (Scott Number 1249) depicts the American flag with the inscription: "Register—Vote—5¢ Postage." From the prominent American flag one may infer that it is a U.S. stamp, but nowhere is that so stated on the stamp.

The air mail stamp of 1968 issued to commemorate the fiftieth anniversary of air mail service (Scott Number C74) also had no country denotation, except for that implied by the inscription, "50th Anniversary—U.S. Air Mail Service—10¢ Air Mail." This is the only air mail stamp that has no precise country denotation.

Even though these ten stamps do not have a precise legend to indicate the issuing country, five of them contain either "U.S." or "United States" in their legends which explain what the stamp honors or commemorates. Two make no mention whatsoever of the country, but the American flag is the most prevailing and conspicuous feature of the designs, and from this it can be deduced that they are U.S. stamps. The other three, the Pilgrim Tercentenary stamps, have no mention of the United States in any form, and there is no feature in their design from which one may infer that they are American stamps, unless one is familiar with the history of the Pilgrims, the *Mayflower*, and the Compact, and then the country that issued them can only be assumed, that is, of course, if one did not know already.

"Overprint" is a term used in philately to signify a printed marking, such as a number, date, name, or inscription, that has been added to a stamp already printed to alter the original denomination, locality, purpose, or to commemorate an event or honor a person. U.S. stamps have been overprinted for various reasons; most of these overprints, however, have indicated that they were to be used in the territories and possessions (Canal Zone, Cuba, Guam, Philippines, and Puerto Rico). In 1929, a few others were overprinted with the abbreviations, "Kans." and "Nebr.," as a measure to prevent losses from post office thefts. No U.S. postage stamps have been overprinted to alter the face value or the intended purpose of the stamp, but in 1928 three overprints were issued instead of specially designed commemoratives.

The Hawaiian Historical Society wanted a stamp issued in 1928 to commemorate the sesquicentennial of the discovery of the Hawaiian Islands by

Captain James Cook in 1778, but the Postmaster General at that time, Harry S. New, was not in accord. New felt that such a commemorative stamp would be only of local interest and would have little national significance. The delegate in Congress from Hawaii, Victor S. K. Houston, finally induced the Postmaster General to issue two stamps overprinted with the phrase, "Hawaii — 1778-1928." The stamps used were the two-cent Washington and the five-cent Theodore Roosevelt (Scott Numbers 634 and 637). These two overprints (Scott Numbers 647 and 648) came out in August 1928 and were valid for postage in the forty-eight states and all U.S. territories and possessions. These two overprints, the first ever used in the United States, however, did cause problems as many postal employees mistook them for precanceled stamps and either refused letters with them or attached postage due stamps.

Also during that same year, 1928, Congressman Harold G. Hoffman of New Jersey made efforts to have a stamp issued to commemorate the sesquicentennial of the Battle of Monmouth and to portray Molly Pitcher, the heroine of the battle, as the central feature of the stamp. The Postmaster General, Harry S. New, would not give his approval for the stamp, but did concede to have another overprint. "Molly Pitcher" was overprinted on the two-cent Washington (Scott Number 634), thereby creating the Molly Pitcher stamp (Scott Number 646). The Molly Pitcher and Hawaii stamps of 1928 are the only U.S. overprints honoring a person and commemorating an event.

SUMMARY

All U.S. stamps have at least one of the three elements considered necessary in stamp design, and most have all three. The most common country denotation appearing on U.S. stamps consists of the initials "U.S.," and it appears on almost 40 percent of them. The other one frequently used is "United States," and it has been on more than 35 percent of all the stamps. However, the trend in the past decade (1971-80), using "USA" on almost 59 percent of the stamps, suggests that those of the future will also use "USA" instead of "U.S." Another interesting feature of the stamps of the past decade is that 374, or almost 93 percent, of the regular and commemorative stamps contained only the name of the country and made no mention of their intended use. Thus, one might deduce that the regular postage stamps of the next decade will be identified by the initials "USA," and no mention of postage or postal service will be included in their designs.

There are seven stamps that have neither a precise word or phrase to indicate the country nor anything to state their intended purpose (Scott Numbers 548-550, 947, 1193, 1208, and 1320). Three stamps lack only the country denotation, but include in their design an indication of their intended use. One is the air mail stamp which included the phrase "air mail'' (Scott Number C74); the other two (Scott Numbers 1017 and 1249) use the word "postage."

Only nine (10.47 percent) of the eighty-nine air mail stamps do not mention air mail in one form or another. All special delivery and parcel post stamps include both the name of the country and their intended use in the design.

There have been very few overprinted U.S. stamps, and in almost all cases these were overprinted for use in the various territories and possessions. But in 1928, three overprints were issued as commemoratives: two to commemorate the discovery of the Hawaiian Islands and one to commemorate the Battle of Monmouth and to honor Molly Pitcher, the heroine of the battle.

NOTES

1. Cabeen, Richard M., *Standard Handbook of Stamp Collecting*, new revised ed. (New York: Thomas Y. Crowell, Publishers, 1979), p. 261.

2. No distinction was made between the instances in which the initials were followed by periods and those cases where there were no periods.

3. Johl, Max G., *The United States Commemorative Stamps of the Twentieth Century* (New York: H. L. Lindquist, Publisher, 1947), vol. 1, p. 75.

4. Barrows, William J., *Mekeel's Weekly Stamp News*, February 12, 1921. Quoted in: Max G. Johl, *The United States Commemorative Stamps of the Twentieth Century* (New York: H. L. Lindquist, Publisher, 1947), vol. 1, p. 75.

5 Denominations and Rates

The denomination of a stamp is its face value which has usually been printed conspicuously on the stamps and is considered one of the necessary elements of stamp design. All U.S. stamps, except three, have included the denomination in their designs. Regardless of the fact that a stamp may not have a specific denomination included in its design, it does have a precise face value assigned to it.

The three U.S. stamps printed without denominations were issued at times when postage rate increases were imminent, but the exact amount of increase or the effective dates were not yet determined. Post offices must maintain ample supplies of stamps of the most popular denomination, which is the first class letter rate. When new rates are not approved with sufficient anticipation to permit a large enough quantity of stamps to be printed and distributed before the new rates become effective, then other measures must be taken. One of these measures is to print stamps without any face value included in the design.

This course of action has been used by the U.S. Postal Service only two different times. This first occurred in October 1975, when two Christmas stamps (Scott Numbers 1579 and 1580) came out, with no face value indicated on the stamps. The assigned face value was ten cents, which was the current first class letter rate, and had been in effect since March 2, 1974. In the fall of 1975, it was known that a postage rate increase was soon to take place, but it was not known what the new rate might be or the effective date; therefore, the Christmas stamps were printed without denomination in case the new rate became effective before Christmas. This is quite understandable when one considers that the Christmas stamps are printed in quantities of approximately two billion each year. The new rate of thirteen cents did not go into effect until December 31, 1975.

The only other stamp without a denomination is the "Eagle A" stamp of 1978 (Scott Number 1735). The color is a bright orange and it depicts an eagle with the inscription "A—U.S. Postage." The letter A represents the face value. Quantities of this stamp had been printed in 1975 and 1976 and then stored for contingency use.[1] The "Eagle A" was issued on May 22, 1978, with an assigned value of fifteen cents, the new first class letter rate that became effective a week later on May 29.

Throughout the 134 years of U.S. postage stamp history, stamps have been issued with fifty-six different face values ranging from one-half cent to five dollars. Table 10 lists the fifty-six denominations and the number of different stamps of each denomination issued during each of the thirteen periods.

The face value of the 1,355 different stamps issued between July 1, 1847 and December 31, 1980 is $207.27. If one had been able to purchase just one of each new stamp as it came out, the investment of slightly more than two hundred dollars would be worth many, many times that today.

Several denominations have not been issued in recent years; three of these (90¢, $3.00, and $4.00) have not been used in the twentieth century. Others that have not appeared in the past fifty years are 65¢, 75¢, $1.30, and $2.60.

There are twenty (36 percent) of the fifty-six denominations that have been used on a single stamp (see Table 11). One-half of these single-stamp denominations have come out in the past ten years, and, of these, six have values that include fractions of a cent. These fractional-cent stamps were designed to accommodate the special rates for bulk mailings and nonprofit organizations.

Twenty-two (39.3 percent) of the fifty-six denominations were issued only on stamps during a single period. These include the twenty single-stamp denominations of Table 11, plus the two 28-cent stamps and the nine 31-cent stamps issued only in Period 13 (1971-80).

Thirteen (23.21 percent) of the denominations have been issued during at least eight of the thirteen periods. The denominations issued throughout the greatest number of years are those of one, three, five, and ten cents, which have been used on new stamps in twelve of the thirteen periods. One-, three-, and ten-cent stamps were issued in every period except for Period 3 (1871-80). In fact, a minimum of two ten-cent stamps came out during each of the twelve periods. At least one five-cent stamp appeared in each of the first twelve periods (1847-1970), but there has been no new five-cent stamp since the issuance of the Mississippi statehood sesquicentennial stamp of 1967 (Scott Number 1337).

Two- and six-cent stamps were issued in all but the first and third periods (1847-60 and 1871-80).

Ten of the thirteen periods have seen new fifteen- and thirty-cent stamps. Neither of these denominations was used on a new stamp in Periods 3 and 4 (1871-90). No fifteen-cent stamp came out in the first period (1847-60), and there was no thirty-cent stamp in Period 6 (1901-10).

Three denominations appeared during nine of the thirteen periods. New eight- and fifty-cent stamps have been printed in every period since the first ones came out in 1893 (Scott Numbers 225 and 240). No four-cent stamp was printed during the first three periods (1847-80); the first one was issued in 1883 (Scott Number 211). Since then, at least one four-cent stamp has come out every period, except for Period 10 (1941-50).

One- and five-dollar stamps were first issued in 1893 (Scott Numbers 241 and 245), and at least one of each of these two denominations has appeared in every period since then, except for Period 10 (1941-50) when neither a one- nor a five-dollar stamp came out.

Very few stamps have been issued which have had a higher value than the first class letter rate. Some of the data presented in Table 10 have been summarized to make Table 12. This table shows that of the 1,355 stamps issued since 1847 less than 12 percent have a value higher than fifteen cents, and more than 88 percent have denominations ranging from one-half cent to fifteen cents. From the information provided in Tables 10 and 12, it can be seen that during the past 134 years there were 523 stamps (39 percent) with a value of less than three cents, but only forty-three stamps (3.17 percent) had a value of sixty cents or higher. Of the 706 stamps issued during the first eleven periods (1847-1960), 331 stamps (46.88 percent) had a face value of three cents or less.

Table 12 points out that few stamps have higher values than the first class letter rates used over the course of U.S. postage stamp history. Table 13 proves that those denominations used for the first class letter rates are also the most frequently issued. The denominations from Table 10 are listed in Table 13 in rank order according to the number of stamps issued with each denomination. The first nine denominations listed in this table are also the only ones ever used as first class letter rates. There have been 1,097 stamps (80.96 percent of the 1,355 stamps) issued with these nine denominations. There can be little doubt that any denomination used as the first class letter rate will also be among those denominations with the largest number of stamps issued.

A perusal of Table 10 shows that there are twelve instances in which more than twenty stamps of the same denomination were issued during a single period. The data concerning these twelve instances were extracted to form Table 14, which lists the denominations, the number of stamps, and the

Table 10
The Denominations and the Quantity Issued during Each Period

Denomi-nation	Period													Total
	1 1847-60	2 1861-70	3 1871-80	4 1881-90	5 1891-1900	6 1901-10	7 1911-20	8 1921-30	9 1931-40	10 1941-50	11 1951-60	12 1961-70	13 1971-80	
½¢	0	0	0	0	0	0	0	1	2	0	1	0	0	4
1¢	1	3	0	2	2	5	4	3	14	2	2	2	1	41
1¼¢	0	0	0	0	0	0	0	0	0	0	1	1	0	2
1½¢	0	0	0	0	0	0	0	2	2	0	1	0	0	5
2¢	0	3	0	2	2	9	4	23	18	2	1	1	5	70
2½¢	0	0	0	0	0	0	0	0	0	0	1	0	0	1
3¢	1	3	0	1	1	3	2	1	57	73	76	1	1	220
3.1¢	0	0	0	0	0	0	0	0	0	0	0	0	1	1
3.5¢	0	0	0	0	0	0	0	0	0	0	0	0	1	1
4¢	0	0	0	2	2	3	1	2	5	0	55	31	1	102
4½¢	0	0	0	0	0	0	0	0	1	0	1	0	0	2
5¢	2	1	1	2	2	5	3	8	15	20	3	83	0	145
6¢	0	2	0	1	1	2	1	1	5	4	3	76	6	102
6.3¢	0	0	0	0	0	0	0	0	0	0	0	0	1	1
7¢	0	0	1	0	0	0	1	1	3	0	5	0	1	12
7.7¢	0	0	0	0	0	0	0	0	0	0	0	0	1	1
7.9¢	0	0	0	0	0	0	0	0	0	0	0	0	1	1
8¢	0	0	0	0	3	3	1	2	4	1	14	7	74	109
8.4¢	0	0	0	0	0	0	0	0	0	0	0	0	1	1
9¢	0	0	0	0	0	0	1	1	3	0	1	0	2	8
10¢	2	3	0	2	3	6	3	4	10	3	3	4	61	104
11¢	0	0	0	0	0	0	1	1	1	0	1	1	5	10
12¢	1	3	0	0	0	0	1	1	1	0	1	1	0	9
13¢	0	0	0	0	0	2	1	1	1	1	0	2	132	140
14¢	0	0	0	0	0	0	0	1	1	0	0	0	1	3
15¢	0	3	0	0	2	2	2	4	1	3	2	2	84	105

	10	30	2	12	34	46	39	71	164	115	183	223	426	1,355
16¢	0	0	0	0	0	0	1	0	2	0	0	0	2	5
17¢	0	0	0	0	0	0	0	1	1	1	0	0	1	4
18¢	0	0	0	0	0	0	0	0	1	0	0	0	8	9
19¢	0	0	0	0	0	0	0	0	1	0	2	0	1	2
20¢	0	0	0	0	0	0	2	3	2	1	0	3	0	13
21¢	0	0	0	0	0	0	0	0	1	0	0	0	4	5
22¢	1	3	0	0	0	0	0	0	1	0	0	0	0	1
24¢	0	0	0	0	0	0	1	1	1	0	2	0	6	13
25¢	0	0	0	0	0	0	1	1	2	2	0	1	3	12
26¢	0	0	0	0	0	0	0	0	0	0	0	0	1	1
28¢	0	0	0	0	2	0	0	0	0	0	0	0	2	2
29¢	1	3	0	0	0	0	0	0	2	0	2	0	1	15
30¢	0	0	0	0	0	0	1	1	0	1	0	1	1	9
31¢	0	0	0	0	0	0	0	0	0	0	0	0	9	1
35¢	0	0	0	0	0	0	0	0	0	0	1	0	1	3
40¢	0	0	0	0	0	0	0	0	0	0	0	0	1	1
45¢	0	0	0	0	3	2	0	0	3	0	1	1	0	15
50¢	0	0	0	0	0	0	2	1	0	1	0	1	1	1
60¢	0	0	0	0	0	0	0	0	0	0	0	0	1	1
65¢	0	0	0	0	0	0	0	1	0	0	0	0	0	1
75¢	0	0	0	0	0	0	1	0	0	0	1	0	0	1
80¢	0	0	0	0	1	0	0	0	0	0	0	0	0	5
90¢	1	3	0	0	3	2	0	1	1	0	1	2	1	13
$1.00	0	0	0	0	0	0	2	1	0	0	0	0	0	1
$1.30	0	0	0	0	3	1	0	1	1	0	0	0	1	8
$2.00	0	0	0	0	0	0	1	0	0	0	0	0	0	1
$2.60	0	0	0	0	1	0	0	0	0	0	0	2	1	1
$3.00	0	0	0	0	1	0	0	0	0	0	0	0	0	1
$4.00	0	0	0	0	2	0	0	0	0	0	0	0	0	1
$5.00	0	0	0	0	0	1	1	1	1	0	1	1	1	9
Total	10	30	2	12	34	46	39	71	164	115	183	223	426	1,355

Table 11
Single-Stamp Denominations

Denomination	Date of Issue	Scott Number
2½¢	June 17, 1959	1034
3.1¢	October 25, 1979	1613
3.5¢	June 23, 1980	1813
6.3¢	October 1, 1974	1518
7.7¢	November 20, 1976	1614
7.9¢	April 23, 1976	1615
8.4¢	July 13, 1978	1615C
22¢	November 22, 1938	827
26¢	January 2, 1974	C88
29¢	April 14, 1978	1605
35¢	December 30, 1980	C100
45¢	November 21, 1969	E22
60¢	May 10, 1971	E23
65¢	April 19, 1930	C13
75¢	December 18, 1912	Q11
80¢	March 26, 1952	C46
$1.30	April 19, 1930	C14
$2.60	April 19, 1930	C15
$3.00	January 2, 1893	243
$4.00	January 2, 1893	244

Table 12
Summary of the Fifty-six Denominations Issued from 1847 to 1980

Denomination	Number of Stamps	Percentage
½¢ to 5¢	594	43.84
6¢ to 10¢	339	25.02
11¢ to 15¢	267	19.70
16¢ to 50¢	112	8.27
60¢ to $5.00	43	3.17
Total	1,355	100.00

periods in which they were issued and compares them to the years during
which these denominations were the first class letter rates. The dates for the
different postage rates are taken from Table 15. There were 1,182 stamps
issued during Periods 8 through 13 (1921-80), and at least 825 (70 percent)
had a face value equivalent to the first class letter rate at the time of issuance.

Table 13
Rank Order of the Denominations According to the Number of Stamps Issued with Each Denomination

Number of Stamps	Denomination	Percentage	Number of Stamps	Denomination	Percentage
220	3¢	16.24	9	18¢	0.66
145	5¢	10.70	9	31¢	0.66
140	13¢	10.33	9	$5.00	0.66
109	8¢	8.04	8	9¢	0.59
105	15¢	7.75	8	$2.00	0.59
104	10¢	7.68	5	1½¢	0.37
102	4¢	7.53	5	16¢	0.37
102	6¢	7.53	5	21¢	0.37
70	2¢	5.16	5	90¢	0.37
41	1¢	3.02	4	½¢	0.29
15	30¢	1.11	4	17¢	0.29
15	50¢	1.11	3	14¢	0.22
13	20¢	0.96	3	40¢	0.22
13	24¢	0.96	2	1¼¢	0.15
13	$1.00	0.96	2	4½¢	0.15
12	7¢	0.89	2	19¢	0.15
12	25¢	0.89	2	28¢	0.15
10	11¢	0.74	20	—*	1.48
9	12¢	0.66	1,355		100.00

*There are twenty denominations of which only one stamp was ever issued. These are listed in Table 11.

From the information found in Table 14, one may infer that each time more than twenty stamps of the same denomination were issued in any ten-year period that was a precise reflection of the cost to mail a first class letter during that time.

Postage rates have changed numerous times since the U.S. Post Office Department was established in 1775. They have not always been increased; they have been reduced on several occasions! It has been pointed out that the postal rates affect the denominations used on stamps because logically stamps have been available in the denominations that have been used most frequently.

From the end of the eighteenth century until 1863, rates for letters and packets were dependent on distance, as well as the number of sheets of paper in a letter or the weight of a packet. In 1792, rates were established allowing a letter of one sheet of paper, called a "single letter," to be mailed for six cents if the distance was not over thirty miles; eight cents for distances

Table 14
Denominations of Which More Than Twenty Stamps Were Issued in a Single Period Compared to the Years in Which That Denomination Was the First Class Letter Rate

Denomination	Number of Stamps	Period	Years the Rate Was in Effect
2¢	23	8 (1921-30)	1919-32
3¢	57	9 (1931-40)	1932-58
3¢	73	10 (1941-50)	1932-58
3¢	76	11 (1951-60)	1932-58
4¢	55	11 (1951-60)	1958-63
4¢	31	12 (1961-70)	1958-63
5¢	83	12 (1961-70)	1963-68
6¢	76	12 (1961-70)	1968-71
8¢	74	13 (1971-80)	1971-74
10¢	61	13 (1971-80)	1974-75
13¢	132	13 (1971-80)	1975-78
15¢	84	13 (1971-80)	1978-80
Total	825		

of 31 to 60 miles; ten cents for 61 to 100 miles; twelve and a half cents for 101 to 150 miles; 151 to 200 miles, fifteen cents; 201 to 250 miles, seventeen cents; 251 to 350 miles, twenty cents; 351 to 450 miles, twenty-two cents; and twenty-five cents for all distances over 450 miles. These "single letter" rates were doubled for letters of two sheets, trebled for three sheets, and quadrupled for letters of four sheets. Packets were charged the quadruple rate for each ounce because four sheets of paper actually weigh one ounce.[2]

The rates established in 1792 remained basically the same until 1845 when Congress approved the Act of March 3, 1845, which reduced the postage rates. This act stated:

For every single letter, in manuscript, or paper of any kind by or upon which information shall be asked for or communicated in writing, or by marks and signs, conveyed in the mail, for any distance under three hundred miles, five cents; and for any distance over three hundred miles, ten cents; and for a double letter there shall be charged double these rates; and for a treble letter, treble these rates; and for a quadruple letter, quadruple these rates; and every letter or parcel not exceeding half an ounce in weight shall be deemed a single letter, and every additional weight of half an ounce, or additional weight of less than half an ounce, shall be charged with an additional single postage. And all drop letters, or letters placed in any post office, not for transmission by mail, but for delivery only, shall be charged at the rate of two cents each.[3]

These new rates determined the denominations of five and ten cents for the first U.S. stamps that were issued in 1847 (Scott Numbers 1 and 2).

Four years after the issuance of the first stamps Congress simplified the rate structure and again reduced postage rates. The Act of 1851 set the rate for a single letter ". . . conveyed in the mail for any distance between places within the United States, not exceeding three thousand miles, when the postage upon such letter shall have been prepaid, three cents, and five cents when the postage thereon shall not have been prepaid; for any distance exceeding three thousand miles, double those rates. . . . And all drop letters or letters placed in any post-office, not for transmission, but for delivery only, shall be charged at the rate one cent each."[4]

In 1851, three new stamps were issued with the denominations of one, three, and twelve cents (Scott Numbers 5, 10, and 17), which conformed to what would be needed for the new rates.

Until 1855, prepayment of postage was not required for sending a letter, but the Act of March 3, 1855 made it compulsory. The act stated that "upon all letters passing through or in the mail of the United States, excepting such as are to, or from a foreign country, the postage as above specified shall be prepaid."[5] This act also raised the rate from six to ten cents for letters mailed to points at a distance greater than 3,000 miles. The rate for letters traveling less than 3,000 miles remained at three cents. That same year the Post Office Department issued a ten-cent stamp (Scott Number 13) to be used on letters traveling distances over 3,000 miles.

Table 15
First Class Domestic Mail Rates, 1863 to 1981

Period	Rate
July 1, 1863-September 30, 1883	3¢ per one-half ounce
October 1, 1883-June 30, 1885	2¢ per one-half ounce
July 1, 1885-November 2, 1917	2¢ per one ounce
November 3, 1917-June 30, 1919	3¢ per one ounce
July 1, 1919-July 5, 1932	2¢ per one ounce
July 6, 1932-July 31, 1958	3¢ per one ounce
August 1, 1958-January 6, 1963	4¢ per one ounce
January 7, 1963-January 6, 1968	5¢ per one ounce
January 7, 1968-May 15, 1971	6¢ per one ounce
May 16, 1971-March 1, 1974	8¢ per one ounce
March 2, 1974-December 30, 1975	10¢ per one ounce
December 31, 1975-May 28, 1978	13¢ per one ounce
May 29, 1978-March 21, 1981	15¢ per one ounce
March 22, 1981-	18¢ per one ounce

Prior to 1863, different classes of mail, such as first class, second class, or third class, did not exist. The Act of March 3, 1863, categorized all mailable items into three classes. It was enacted "that mailable matter shall be divided into three classes, namely: first, letters; second, regular printed matter; third, miscellaneous matter."[6] Fourth class for merchandise was not established as a separate category until 1879. This same act also eliminated charging postage according to the number of sheets in a letter as done previously when rates were defined in terms of single, double, treble, and quadruple letters. Thereafter, rates were based solely on weight, and the distance factor for domestic mail was abolished. The new rate for domestic letters was then three cents per one-half ounce and three cents for each additional half-ounce or fraction thereof. Drop letters were two cents per one-half ounce or fraction thereof.

First class postage rates changed twelve times from 1863 to 1980. Table 15 lists the various first class letter rates from 1863 to 1981 and their effective dates.[7] The Act of March 3, 1885, changed the weight factor from one-half ounce to one ounce, which is still in use. Some day the U.S. Postal Service will probably use a weight factor of twenty-five grams (one ounce is equal to 28 grams). The data in Table 15 also point out that the rate of two cents per ounce was in effect longer than any other rate in history—a total of forty-five years, 1885 to 1917 and 1919 to 1932. The rate of three cents per ounce was in effect twenty-eight years, from 1917 to 1919 and 1932 to 1958. Since 1958 there have been seven increases, and none was in effect for more than five years. The first occurred in 1958 when postage was raised from three to four cents, then there were two increases in the 1960s, and in the 1970s the rates increased four times.

It is not surprising that more three-cent stamps have been issued than any other denomination. Since 1847 the basic letter rate of three cents was in effect for sixty years (1851-83, 1917-19, and 1932-58), or almost half of the 134-year history. It must be pointed out, however, that 206 (93.64 percent) of the three-cent stamps were issued during the years 1931 to 1960. In comparison, it may seem odd that so few two-cent stamps have been issued when one considers the fact that the letter rate was two cents for forty-seven years (1883-1917 and 1919-32), and drop letters were two cents during the years 1917-19 and 1932-58. But when one reexamines the total in Table 10 and sees that during the first eight periods (1847-1930) only 244 different stamps (18 percent of the 1,355) came out, the low number of two-cent stamps is not so astonishing.

There are more than a hundred different stamps of each of the denominations of 4, 5, 6, 8, 10, 13, and 15 cents. This is not unexpected when one notes that these denominations were the first class letter rates in the last three periods, 1951 to 1980, during which time 832 stamps (61.4 percent of the 1,355) were issued. Also, it should be noted that prior to the 1930s few commemoratives were issued. Only seventy-nine commemorative stamps came out from 1847 to 1930, but in the 1930s more than a hundred were issued. The great increase in the number of commemoratives began when James A. Farley was Postmaster General from 1933 to 1940. Since the days of Farley, the number of commemoratives has continued to grow, and a majority of the commemoratives are issued with the current first class postage rate, thus accounting for the large numbers of stamps with the denominations of 4, 5, 6, 8, 10, 13, and 15 cents.

Up to this point only the face value of the denomination has been discussed, and nothing has been said about the manner in which it was printed on the stamp. Denominations may be written in a variety of ways: arabic numerals, roman numerals, words, or any combination thereof. Table 16 indicates the different forms that have been used and in which periods. Arabic numerals have been used on 1,328 stamps (98 percent of the total). Of these, 156 have the denomination in words in addition to the arabic numerals.

During the first five periods (1847-1900), the denomination always appeared in words; of these eighty-eight nineteenth century stamps, there are six that have denominations in words only, two in roman numerals and words, and eighty stamps that have both arabic numerals and words. But only ninety (7.1 percent) of the 1,267 stamps issued since 1900 have the denomination written in words. During Periods 6 through 13 (1901-80) most stamps were issued with arabic numerals only; in fact, 1,172 (92.5 percent) of the 1,267 stamps issued in the twentieth century have the denomination in arabic numerals only. During the past forty years (1941-80), the percentage of stamps exclusively with arabic numerals has risen to 98.3 percent. Thus the trend is to use only arabic numerals to indicate the face value.

Only four stamps have denominations in roman numerals. Two (Scott Numbers 2 and 13) are ten-cent stamps portraying George Washington with the words "ten cents" as well as the roman numeral X. The other two are the only ones whose denominations are expressed only in roman numerals; they are the one- and three-cent stamps issued in 1933 to commemorate the Century of Progress International Exhibition and the incorporation of Chicago as a city (Scott Numbers 728 and 729).

Just twenty stamps use only words to indicate the face value; of these ten came out during Period 10 (1961-70). In the first period (1847-60), six stamps used words only (Scott Numbers 5, 10, 12, 17, 37, and 39); Period 6 (1901-10) had three stamps with words only (Scott Numbers 331, 332, and 367); in Period 9 (1931-40) the only stamp with a "words only" denomination was the one to commemorate Mother's Day (Scott Number 737). After the Mother's Day stamp of 1934 there were no stamps with "words only" denominations until 1966 when two such stamps (Scott Numbers 1295 and 1306) were issued. Eight more (Scott Numbers 1294, 1371, 1386, 1391, and 1410-13) came out in the last four years of Period 12 (1967-70). In Period 13

Table 16
Numerals and Words Used to Indicate the Values of the Denominations

Numerals and Words	Period													Total	Percentage
	1 1847-60	*2* 1861-70	*3* 1871-80	*4* 1881-90	*5* 1891-1900	*6* 1901-10	*7* 1911-20	*8* 1921-30	*9* 1931-40	*10* 1941-50	*11* 1951-60	*12* 1961-70	*13* 1971-80		
Arabic numerals only	0	0	0	0	0	11	39	62	129	113	182	213	423	1,172	86.49
Arabic numerals and words	2	30	2	12	34	32	0	9	32	2	1	0	0	156	11.51
Words only	6	0	0	0	0	3	0	0	1	0	0	10	0	20	1.48
Roman numerals only	0	0	0	0	0	0	0	0	2	0	0	0	0	2	0.15
Roman numerals and words	2	0	0	0	0	0	0	0	0	0	0	0	0	2	0.15
None	0	0	0	0	0	0	0	0	0	0	0	0	3	3	0.22
Total	10	30	2	12	34	46	39	71	164	115	183	223	426	1,355	100.00

(1971-80) only stamps with arabic numerals were printed, excepting of course the three stamps without any denominations which were discussed at the beginning of this chapter.

Not only have the face values been expressed in different ways, but also the use of symbols and words to indicate cents and dollars in the denominations has varied greatly during the course of 134 years. Tables 17 and 18 list the symbols and words that have been used and distribute this information by period so that trends can be detected. During the first four periods, the highest denomination issued was that of ninety cents, and the word "cent" or "cents" appeared on every stamp. The first stamp ever issued with the cent sign (¢), instead of the word cents, was the ten-cent special delivery stamp of 1908 (Scott Number E7); the next one was the sixty-five cent *Graf Zeppelin* air mail stamp of 1930 (Scott Number C13). Then in the 1930s when James A. Farley was the Postmaster General, a new trend started which used only the cent sign (¢). The first came out in 1933: the National Recovery Administration (NRA) stamp (Scott Number 732) and the Kosciuszko stamp (Scott Number 734). In 1934, eight stamps were issued with the cent sign (Scott Numbers 739-741 and 744-748). There have been only two stamps with the cent sign and the word cents; they came out in 1934 and 1940 (Scott Numbers 746 and 898). Since Farley's time, the word cent or cents has hardly appeared on stamps; of the 939 stamps issued since 1940 with face values of less than one dollar, only 85 (9.05 percent) have been printed with the word cent or cents. The data in Table 17 also point out that the trend moved from the word cent or cents in the 1930s to the cent sign (¢) in the 1940s when 75 percent of the stamps used the cent sign. Beginning in the late 1950s, the trend evolved to using just the letter "c" instead of the cent sign; during the past twenty years (1961-80), 643 stamps were issued with face values less than one dollar, with 481 (75 percent) using the letter "c" to indicate cent or cents.

Nine stamps with values of less than one dollar have had no cent sign, letter "c," or the word cents. The forty-five cent special delivery stamp of 1969 (Scott Number E22) was the first stamp to be issued without a cent sign, the letter "c," or the word cents. In 1970, the four Christmas stamps depicting toys of yesteryear (Scott Numbers 1415-1418) had only the numeral 6 to indicate the value. The last six-cent stamp to be issued was the blood donor stamp of 1971 (Scott Number 1425); it also had just the numeral 6 without any cent sign, letter "c," or the word cents. The other three of the nine stamps are those that have no denomination whatsover included in their designs (Scott Numbers 1579, 1580, and 1735) and were treated at the beginning of this chapter.

The dollar sign ($) was used on the first thirteen stamps that had face values of one dollar or more. These were issued between 1893 and 1903, and all had the word dollar or dollars in addition to the dollar sign, but since then not a single stamp has used the word as well as the sign. In 1909, the first dollar stamp was issued without the dollar sign (Scott Number 342).

Table 17
Symbols and Words Used to Indicate Cents in the Denominations

Period	Cent Cents	¢ Cents	¢	C	None	Total
1. 1847-60	10	0	0	0	0	10
2. 1861-70	30	0	0	0	0	30
3. 1871-80	2	0	0	0	0	2
4. 1881-90	12	0	0	0	0	12
5. 1891-1900	24	0	0	0	0	24
6. 1901-10	41	0	1	0	0	42
7. 1911-20	35	0	0	0	0	35
8. 1921-30	65	0	0	1	0	66
9. 1931-40	109	2	50	0	0	161
10. 1941-50	33	0	82	0	0	115
11. 1951-60	4	0	137	40	0	181
12. 1961-70	27	0	77	111	5	220
13. 1971-80	21	0	28	370	4	423
Total	413	2	375	522	9	1,321
Percentage	31.26	0.15	28.39	39.52	0.68	100.00

Table 18
Symbols and Words Used to Indicate Dollars in the Denominations

Period	Dollar Dollars	$ Dollar $ Dollars	$	None	Total
1. 1847-60	0	0	0	0	0
2. 1861-70	0	0	0	0	0
3. 1871-80	0	0	0	0	0
4. 1881-90	0	0	0	0	0
5. 1891-1900	0	10	0	0	10
6. 1901-10	1	3	0	0	4
7. 1911-20	4	0	0	0	4
8. 1921-30	3	0	2	0	5
9. 1931-40	0	0	3	0	3
10. 1941-50	0	0	0	0	0
11. 1951-60	0	0	2	0	2
12. 1961-70	2	0	1	0	3
13. 1971-80	0	0	0	3	3
Total	10	13	8	3	34
Percentage	29.41	38.24	23.53	8.82	100.00

During Periods 7 through 12 (1911-70), exactly seventeen stamps had face values of one dollar or more; nine used the word dollar or dollars, and eight had only the dollar sign. In Period 13 (1971-80), three stamps with face values of one, two, and five dollars were issued (Scott Numbers 1610-1612), and none used either the dollar sign or the word dollar.

SUMMARY

Postage stamps of the United States have been issued with fifty-six different denominations, and twenty of these denominations have been used on a single stamp. The denominations used most often are those which are first class letter rates. The current first class letter rate can always be detected when there are more than twenty different stamps of the same denomination issued in a ten-year period. Very few stamps have denominations greater than fifteen cents, and almost 40 percent of all stamps have denominations of less than three cents. Stamps with denominations of sixteen cents or more account for less than 12 percent of all stamps ever issued.

Denominations can be printed in a variety of ways, but arabic numerals are the most commonly used. During the nineteenth century, the denomination always appeared written in words, and most often the words were also accompanied by arabic numerals; only six stamps of the nineteenth century used words without arabic numerals. In the twentieth century, the trend has been to use only arabic numerals; of the 1,267 stamps issued since 1900, almost 93 percent have used only arabic numerals.

Another obvious trend in the printing of the denomination is to use the letter "c" instead of the word, cent or cents, or the cent sign (¢). Before the 1930s, only two stamps with face values of less than a dollar were printed without the word cent or cents on them. From the 1930s until the end of the 1950s, the cent sign was on almost all stamps, but during the past twenty years, the letter "c" has been used much more frequently than the cent sign or the word cent or cents.

The information included in the denomination has evolved to a very brief form, that is, just arabic numerals and the letter "c." This is similar to the trend pointed out in the previous chapter in which the country denotation has been reduced to just US or USA, and the word postage rarely appears on a stamp.

If these trends continue, the stamps of the next decade will only use arabic numerals and the letter "c" to indicate the face value, the country denotation will be simply US or USA, and the word postage will not appear at all.

NOTES

1. "American New Issue News," *Minkus Stamp Journal*, vol. 13, no. 4, 1978, p. 48.

2. U.S. Postal Service, Office of Rates, *Domestic Mail Rate History* (Washington, D.C.: U.S. Postal Service, 1976), p. 22.

3. Act to Reduce the Rates of Postage, March 3, 1845. U.S., *Statutes at Large*, vol. 5, chap. 43, sec. 1, p. 733.

4. Act to Reduce and Modify the Rates of Postage in the United States, March 3, 1851. U.S., *Statutes at Large*, vol. 9, chap. 20, sec. 1, p. 587-88.

5. Act Further to Amend the Act Entitled, "Act to Reduce and Modify the Rates of Postage in the United States," March 3, 1855, U.S., *Statutes at Large*, vol. 10, chap. 173, sec. 1, pp. 641-42.

6. Act to Amend the Laws Relating to the Post-Office Department, March 3, 1983. U.S., *Statutes at Large,* vol. 12, chap. 71, secs. 19 and 23, pp. 704-5.

7. U.S. Postal Service, Office of Rates, *Domestic Mail Rate History* (Washington, D.C.: U.S. Postal Service, 1976), p. 1.

Part II. THE PEOPLE

AMERICAN NOTABLES

W.C. FIELDS

Performing Arts USA 15c

Contributors To The Cause...

Haym Salomon   *Financial Hero*

STATESMAN SOLDIER
GEORGE C. MARSHALL
UNITED STATES
20¢

U.S. 10¢

ONE DOLLAR
EUGENE O'NEILL
UNITED STATES
PLAYWRIGHT

STEVENSON

U.S.
5
CENTS

Carl Sandburg
USA 13c

GEORGE M. COHAN
Yankee Doodle Dandy

Performing Arts USA 15c

U.S. 10¢
Robert Frost
AMERICAN POET

JOHN DEWEY
UNITED STATES

30 CENTS

UNITED STATES POSTAGE

3 CENTS   3

LaGuardia 14¢   U.S.

UNITED STATES POSTAGE

ANDREW W. MELLON
3¢

15¢
OLIVER WENDELL HOLMES

FRANK LLOYD WRIGHT

2¢
U.S. POSTAGE

6¢
US

DOUGLAS MacARTHUR

Einstein
USA 15c

Thomas Paine

U.S. 40¢

FRANCIS PARKMAN AMERICAN HISTORIAN U.S. POSTAGE

3¢

ATOMIC ENERGY ACT
PEACEFUL USES

4   U.S. POSTAGE   BRIEN McMAHON

UNITED STATES POSTAGE

JOHN FOSTER DULLES

4¢

MOVIEMAKER   US 10¢

D.W. GRIFFITH

6 Person Stamps

The criteria used for differentiating "person stamps" from "subject stamps" were presented and explained in Chapter 3. According to those criteria, there are 585 person stamps, or 43.17 percent of the 1,355 stamps covered by this study.

The 585 person stamps honor a total of 873 persons because there are ninety-one stamps (15.56 percent) which have two or more persons on them. The number of persons honored on individual stamps ranges from one to forty-eight. The information presented in Table 19 details how many stamps have one person, two persons, three persons, and so forth; the table also indicates the percentage of person stamps with any given number of persons. Table 19 points out that 494 stamps (84.44 percent) honor only a single individual; seventy-nine stamps (13.51 percent) honor two, three, or four persons; and just twelve stamps (2.05 percent) have five or more persons on them.

The data from Table 19 concerning the number of persons on each stamp are distributed according to the periods in which they were issued and presented in Table 20. This tabulation of the data points out the trend in recent years to include two or more persons on a single stamp. In just the past ten years (1971-80), there were thirty-four stamps with two or more persons; this is more than 37 percent of the ninety-one stamps honoring two or more persons. More than one-half (53.85 percent) of these stamps were issued

Table 19
Number of Persons on Each Stamp

Number of Persons	Number of Stamps	Percentage of All Person Stamps	Total Number of Persons
1	494	84.44	494
2	40	6.84	80
3	29	4.96	87
4	10	1.71	40
5	3	0.52	15
6	2	0.34	12
8	1	0.17	8
9	2	0.34	18
15	1	0.17	15
16	1	0.17	16
40	1	0.17	40
48	1	0.17	48
Total	585	100.00	873

during the past thirty years (1951-80), but, if the calculation is done for the past fifty years (1931-80), since the 1930s when James A. Farley was the Postmaster General, the percentage of stamps with two or more persons is slightly more than 80 percent. During the Farley years (1933-40), fourteen stamps were issued honoring two or more persons, in contrast to sixteen such stamps which were issued in the preceding eighty-six years (1847-1932). The data presented clearly demonstrate a strong trend to honor more than one person on a single stamp.

Table 21 groups the stamps with two or more persons according to the number of individuals on each one and lists them in numerical order by Scott Numbers.

SUMMARY

Less than one-half of all U.S. postage stamps have honored or portrayed persons. There are 585 stamps honoring a total of 873 persons. The number of persons on each stamp ranges from one to forty-eight. A vast majority of the stamps classified as person stamps only honor a single individual, and only ninety-one honor or portray two or more persons. Of these ninety-one stamps, thirty-four were issued in the last ten years (1971-80), and there were only fifty-seven that came out during the first 124 years of U.S. postage stamp history.

Table 20
Number of Persons on the Stamps of Each Period

Number of Persons on Each Stamp	Number of Stamps in Each Period													Total
	1 1847-60	*2* 1861-70	*3* 1871-80	*4* 1881-90	*5* 1891-1900	*6* 1901-10	*7* 1911-20	*8* 1921-30	*9* 1931-40	*10* 1941-50	*11* 1951-60	*12* 1961-70	*13* 1971-80	
1	10	23	2	10	16	34	18	31	94	28	71	73	84	494
2	0	0	0	0	4	1	0	2	9	6	1	3	14	40
3	0	1	0	0	7	1	0	0	4	1	2	5	8	29
4	0	0	0	0	0	0	0	0	0	1	3	1	5	10
5	0	0	0	0	0	0	0	1	0	0	0	0	2	3
6	0	0	0	0	0	0	0	0	0	1	0	0	1	2
8	0	0	0	0	0	0	0	0	0	0	0	0	1	1
9	0	0	0	0	0	0	0	0	1	0	0	0	1	2
15	0	0	0	0	0	0	0	0	0	0	0	0	1	1
16	0	0	0	0	0	0	0	0	0	0	0	0	1	1
40	0	0	0	0	0	0	0	0	1	0	0	0	0	1
48	0	1	0	0	0	0	0	0	0	0	0	0	0	1
Total no. of stamps	10	25	2	10	27	36	18	34	109	37	77	82	118	585
Total no. of persons	10	74	2	10	45	39	18	40	173	53	91	98	220	873

Table 21
Stamps with Two or More Persons Listed by Scott Numbers

Number of Persons	Scott Numbers
2	230, 239, 241, 244, 372, 646, 683, 776, 785, 786, 788, 790-792, 795, 856, 906, 941, 947, 964, 982, 1115, 1251, 1273, 1356, 1523, 1534, 1537, 1551, 1563, 1564, 1687b, 1704, 1722, 1753, 1824, 1842, C45, C91, C92
3	118, 231, 234-238, 243, 328, 703, 787, 793, 796, 959, 1020, 1123, 1321, 1335, 1336, 1361, 1408, 1507, 1530, 1536, 1579, 1687a, 1687d, 1768, 1799
4	956, 1004, 1011, 1063, 1414, 1444, 1686e, 1687e, 1701, C88
5	644, 1686d, 1687e
6	929, 1728
8	1694
9	854, 1693
15	1691
16	1692
40	798
48	120

7 Individuals and Persons: Women, Children, and Men

It has been established that there are 585 stamps honoring a total of 873 identifiable persons. The number of persons on each stamp ranges from one to forty-eight, thus explaining why there are 288 more persons than there are "person stamps." Among these 873 persons, there are many "individuals" who appeared on more than one stamp. In those cases where a person's likeness was reproduced two or more times on the same stamp, the person was considered as having appeared just once. Examples of this are the stamps portraying Will Rogers, W. C. Fields, and Benjamin Banneker (Scott Numbers 1801, 1803, and 1804).

Even though the terms "person" and "individual" are synonymous, they are used with different meanings in this study. Each person who appeared more than once was counted as a "person" each time he or she was honored on a stamp, but as an "individual" when referred to by name. For example, George Washington was on seventy-four stamps and was counted as seventy-four persons; when referred to by name, he is considered as a single individual. Washington is an "individual" who accounts for 8.48 percent of the 873 "persons" who were on the 585 "person stamps." A count of the names of the "persons" who are on the 585 "person stamps" reveals that exactly 464 "individuals" comprise the 873 "persons." Washington is just one of the 464 individuals, but he accounts for seventy-four of the 873 persons.

As each stamp was examined, a file card was made for every identified person. Every time the same individual appeared, a new file card was made. Each of the 873 cards contains the following information: (1) name, as commonly known, (2) birth and death dates, (3) the length of time elapsed between the date of death and the issuance of the stamp, (4) profession, occupation, principal positions held during the lifetime, and/or the reason for being on a stamp, (5) birthplace, (6) nationality, (7) the Scott Number and the Minkus Number of the stamp, and (8) other biographical data concerning the person such as sex and race.

All biographical data were gathered from standard reference sources, namely, biographical dictionaries and directories, general and specialized encyclopedias, biographies, indexes, newspapers, periodicals, and other such publications. Two other very important reference sources frequently consulted were the stamp catalogs of the Scott Publishing Company and Minkus Publications, Inc. Whenever there were conflicts among different sources in any biographical datum, the most prevalent was used.

No distinction has been made in this study for persons who are depicted on a stamp and for those who are honored by just having their names included in the design. In most cases a person honored on a stamp is also depicted, but in some instances the person's name appears without any portraiture. Therefore, the verb "honor" is used to indicate that the person is either depicted on the stamp or that the person's name is included in the inscription.

Women have appeared on stamps less frequently than men; only forty female individuals have been honored on U.S. postage stamps. These forty individuals (8.62 percent of the 464 individuals) appeared a total of fifty-nine times; thirty-five were on just one stamp, and five were on two or more. Mary, mother of Jesus, has been portrayed more than any other female; she has been on ten Christmas stamps since 1966 (Scott Numbers 1321, 1336, 1414, 1444, 1507, 1579, 1701, 1768, 1799, and 1842); Isabella the Catholic, Queen of Castile and Aragon, was depicted on seven stamps of the Columbian Exposition issue of 1893 (Scott Numbers 234, 236-238, 241, 243, and 244); Martha Washington, the first First Lady, was the subject of three stamps in three different series of regular stamps and never on a commemorative stamp (Scott Numbers 306, 556, and 805); Susan B. Anthony, advocate of woman suffrage, was portrayed on two stamps (Scott Numbers 784 and 1051); and Pocahontas, the Indian princess who married John Rolfe, was depicted on two stamps of the 1907 series commemorating the Jamestown Exposition (Scott Numbers 328 and 330).

The thirty-five women who were honored only once are listed below in alphabetical order:

Addams, Jane   Barton, Clara
Alcott, Louisa May   Bissell, Emily P.

Blackwell, Elizabeth	Moses, "Grandma" Anna Mary
Cassatt, Mary	Mott, Lucretia C.
Cather, Willa	Perkins, Frances
Catt, Carrie C.	Pitcher, Molly
Copley, Elizabeth C.	Roosevelt, Eleanor
Dare, Eleanor White	Ross, Betsy
Dare, Virginia	Sacajawea
Dickinson, Emily	Scott, Blanche Stuart
Douglas, Mrs. John	Stanton, Elizabeth
Earhart, Amelia	Stone, Lucy
Keller, Helen	Sullivan, Anne M.
Low, Juliette G.	Tubman, Harriet
Ludington, Sybil	Wharton, Edith
Maass, Clara	Whistler, Anna Mathilda
Madison, Dolley	Willard, Frances E.
Michael, Moina	

The pictures of all but three of the forty females were portrayed. The three who had only their names on stamps are: Mary Cassatt, nineteenth-century artist, whose painting, *The Boating Party*, was used as the central design of the stamp (Scott Number 1322); a portion of the painting, *July Fourth*, honored the modern primitive painter, "Grandma" Moses (Scott Number 1370); and Molly Pitcher, Revolutionary heroine of the Battle of Monmouth, was honored by simply having her name overprinted on a stamp portraying George Washington (Scott Number 646). (See Chapter 5 for more detailed information on the Molly Pitcher overprint.)

Tables 22 and 23 tabulate data by period and sex concerning the 873 persons honored on stamps. Table 22 lists the number and percentage of men and women who were honored on stamps during the entire 134-year history, as well as the total number of person stamps issued since 1847. Table 23 gives the number and percentage of women and men who appeared on stamps during each of the thirteen periods. From Table 22 it can be seen that no female was honored on a stamp during the Periods 1 to 4 (1847-90) and Period 7 (1911-20), but men were on stamps during every period. A comparison of the percentage of males and the percentage of person stamps for each of the periods shows that there is a strong correlation between these two groups of data, but, when one compares the percentage of females with the percentage of person stamps for each period, one finds that there is no correlation. A glance at Table 22 shows that more than one-half of all the women on stamps appeared in Periods 12 and 13 (1961-80), from which one might infer that there was an upsurge in the past two decades to honor more women on stamps. It is quite true that more women have been honored in the past twenty years than ever before, but, when one checks Table 23 and sees that the percentage of women in each of these two decades is less than 10 percent of all persons, it is obvious that the upsurge occurred in the total

WOMEN

Emily Dickinson
American Poet

HELEN KELLER
ANNE SULLIVAN

LUCY STONE

CLARA MAASS
She gave her life

Edith Wharton

number of persons on stamps and not in the percentage of women as compared to men.

The fifty-nine female persons account only for 6.76 percent of the 873 persons who have been honored on U.S. stamps. Only males were honored on stamps until Isabella the Catholic was depicted on seven stamps in 1893. No other woman was honored on a stamp until Martha Washington appeared on an eight-cent stamp in 1902, and later Pocahontas was depicted on two stamps in 1907. From 1907 to 1923, no other woman was so honored. In 1923, another stamp was issued portraying Martha Washington, and in 1928 the Molly Pitcher overprint came out. These four are the only women honored on U.S. stamps during the first eight periods (1847-1930). During Period 9 (1931-40), eight women were portrayed on seven stamps. Almost 200 stamps were issued during Periods 10 and 11 (1941-60), yet only seven of these stamps honored women, with one of these stamps portraying three women. Mary, mother of Jesus, appeared on three stamps in Period 12 (1961-70); and six other women were on one stamp each, including Amelia Earhart, the first woman to be on an air mail stamp (Scott Number C68). In the past ten years (1971-80), there were fifteen different women who were on twenty stamps. Mary, the mother of Jesus, was on seven stamps; Helen Keller and Anne Sullivan were portrayed on the same stamp (Scott Number 1824). The twenty-one portraitures of women during Period 13 (1971-80) account for more than one-third (35.59 percent) of all women on stamps, but, when compared to the total number of persons honored on stamps during this period, one sees that less than 10 percent were women.

The fifty-nine females were honored on fifty-five different stamps. Several of these stamps honor men as well as women; for example, Mary was always portrayed with Baby Jesus and sometimes with Joseph, her husband; and Betsy Ross was depicted with George Washington, Robert Morris, and her husband's uncle, George Ross. However, there are only three instances when two or more women were honored on the same stamp. Two stamps honored two females each: Virginia Dare, her mother, Eleanor White Dare, and her father, Ananias Dare, were portrayed together (Scott Number 796); and Helen Keller and Anne Sullivan were pictured on the same stamp (Scott Number 1824). Three women's rights activists—Carrie Chapman Catt, Lucretia Coffin Mott, and Elizabeth Cady Stanton—were depicted on a stamp issued in 1948 commemorating a century of progress of American women (Scott Number 959).

Although children and youths have been depicted on many stamps, there are only fifteen stamps with identifiable children and youths, and ten of these portray the same child, Baby Jesus. Of the six identifiable individuals who can be considered as children or youths, four are female and two are males. The four females depicted are: Elizabeth Clarke Copley, whose portrait was extracted from the group painting, *The Copley Family*, and

Table 22
Number of Women and Men Honored on Stamps during the 134-Year History

Period	Women		Men		Total Number of Persons	Person Stamps	
	No.	%	*No.*	%		*No.*	%
1. 1847-60	0	—	10	1.23	10	10	1.71
2. 1861-70	0	—	74	9.09	74	25	4.27
3. 1871-80	0	—	2	0.25	2	2	0.34
4. 1881-90	0	—	10	1.23	10	10	1.71
5. 1891-1900	7	11.86	38	4.67	45	27	4.62
6. 1901-10	3	5.09	36	4.42	39	36	6.16
7. 1911-20	0	—	18	2.21	18	18	3.08
8. 1921-30	2	3.39	38	4.67	40	34	5.81
9. 1931-40	8	13.56	165	20.27	173	109	18.63
10. 1941-50	6	10.17	47	5.77	53	37	6.32
11. 1951-60	3	5.09	88	10.81	91	77	13.16
12. 1961-70	9	15.25	89	10.93	98	82	14.02
13. 1971-80	21	35.59	199	24.45	220	118	20.17
Total	59	100.00	814	100.00	873	585	100.00

used on a stamp to honor her father, John Singleton Copley, an early American painter (Scott Number 1273); Virginia Dare, the first child born in America of English parents, was shown with her mother and father on a stamp issued in 1937 (Scott Number 796); Helen Keller, blind and deaf since the age of nineteen months, was depicted as a young girl with her teacher, Anne Sullivan (Scott Number 1824); and Sybil Ludington, Revolutionary War heroine, who at the age of sixteen rode through the countryside announcing to the local militia that the British had sacked Danbury, was portrayed on a stamp issued in 1975 (Scott Number 1559). The two males depicted are the Baby Jesus, who was on the same ten Christmas stamps that also portrayed his mother, Mary, and Peter Francisco, young hero of the Revolutionary War (Scott Number 1562).

SUMMARY

Throughout the history of U.S. postage stamps, a total of 585 have honored or depicted 873 persons. This group of 873 persons is comprised of only 464 individuals because there are several who have been on more than one stamp. The group of 873 persons contains fifty-nine females and 814 males. The 464 individuals are mostly men; 424 (91.38 percent) are men and forty (8.62 percent) are women. Seventy-four stamps have honored George Washington, but only fifty-five stamps have had identifiable women on them. Among the forty females honored on stamps, thirty-five were on just one stamp, one was portrayed on ten stamps, one was on seven, another was depicted on three, and two women had their likenesses appear on two stamps each. No woman was honored on a stamp until Isabella the Catholic was portrayed on seven stamps in 1893. Between 1893 and 1933, only three other women were so honored, namely, Martha Washington, Pocahontas, and Molly Pitcher. More than one-half of all the females who have been on stamps appeared in the last twenty years (1961-80), but during neither of these decades did the percentage of women reach 10 percent of the identifiable persons on stamps. The number of women has risen in the past few years, but, when compared to the total number of persons on the stamps, one sees that the number of men has risen to such an extent that the percentages of the two sexes remain about the same. Only six of the identifiable individuals are children or youths, four females and two males. Only one of these, Baby Jesus, was on more than one stamp; he was on ten Christmas stamps with his mother, Mary.

Table 23
Percentage of Women and Men Honored on Stamps for
 Each of the Thirteen Periods

Period	Women		Men		Total	
	No.	%	No.	%	No.	%
1. 1847-60	0	—	10	100.00	10	100
2. 1861-70	0	—	74	100.00	74	100
3. 1871-80	0	—	2	100.00	2	100
4. 1881-90	0	—	10	100.00	10	100
5. 1891-1900	7	15.55	38	84.45	45	100
6. 1901-10	3	7.69	36	92.31	39	100
7. 1911-20	0	—	18	100.00	18	100
8. 1921-30	2	5.00	38	95.00	40	100
9. 1931-40	8	4.62	165	95.38	173	100
10. 1941-50	6	11.32	47	88.68	53	100
11. 1951-60	3	3.30	88	96.70	91	100
12. 1961-70	9	9.18	89	90.82	98	100
13. 1971-80	21	9.55	199	90.45	220	100

8 Nationality
and Birthplace

The 464 individuals honored on U.S. postage stamps can be classified into two major groups: Americans and foreigners. The Americans may be subdivided into two categories: the native-born and the foreign-born. Native-born Americans are those born in what is now the United States;[1] the foreign-born are those who were born elsewhere, immigrated to the United States and either became naturalized citizens or remained here for the rest of their lives.

Some of the early foreign explorers, colonists, and military people came to America and then returned to their native lands. An example of this is James Oglethorpe who is considered as a foreigner because he was born in London, came to Georgia in 1733, and founded Savannah, but returned permanently to England in 1743 and died there in 1785. Others who came here and remained for the rest of their lives are considered as foreign-born Americans. Such is the case of Peter Stuyvesant, a Dutch colonial officer who arrived in New Amsterdam in 1647. After he surrendered New Amsterdam to the English in 1664, he lived the rest of his life on a farm in present-day Manhattan where he died in 1672.

Tables 24, 27, and 28 include the names of all 464 individuals arranged by birthplace. Table 24 lists the seventy-three foreigners according to their nationality or country of birth. Table 27 includes the fifty-four foreign-

FOREIGN NOTABLES

Copernicus 1473-1973

8¢ US

Alaska 1778
Capt.ⁿ *James Cook*
13c USA

UNITED 3 STATES

CHURCHILL

U.S. 5 CENTS

USA 15c

Gen. Bernardo de Gálvez
Battle of Mobile 1780

CHAMPION OF LIBERTY

SIMON BOLIVAR THE LIBERATOR

8¢

UNITED STATES POSTAGE

國民 華中

SUN YAT-SEN

4¢

UNITED STATES

SHAKESPEARE

5

ARRIVAL OF LAFAYETTE IN AMERICA · 1777

3¢

U.S. POSTAGE HAWAII

Letters
mingle souls

Donne

Raphael

10c US

CHAMPION OF LIBERTY

4¢

UNITED STATES POSTAGE

CHAMPION OF LIBERTY

KOSSUTH-GOVERNOR OF HUNGARY

4¢

UNITED STATES POSTAGE

CHAMPION OF LIBERTY

4¢

UNITED STATES POSTAGE

DAG HAMMARSKJOLD

SECRETARY-GENERAL
of the
UNITED NATIONS

4¢

UNITED STATES POSTAGE

CHAMPION OF LIBERTY

4¢

UNITED STATES POSTAGE

Table 24
Foreigners Honored on U.S. Postage Stamps

ARGENTINA
San Martín, José de

BIBLICAL PALESTINE
Jesus
Joseph, husband of Mary
Mary, mother of Jesus

BRITISH ISLES
England
Burgoyne, John
Charles II, King
Churchill, Winston
Cook, James
Cornwallis, Charles
Donne, John
Douglas, Mrs. John
Gainsborough, Thomas
Hudson, Henry
Oglethorpe, James E.
Phillips, William
Shakespeare, William
Scotland
Carlyle, Thomas
Forbes, John

CANADA
Joliet, Louis

CHINA
Sun, Yat-sen

CZECHOSLOVAKIA
Masaryk, Tomas G.

FINLAND
Mannerheim, Carl Gustaf

FRANCE
Barbé-Marbois, François
Cadillac, Antoine
Chardin, Jean
Grasse, François de
Lafayette, Marquis de
Louis XVI, King
Marquette, Jacques
Nicolet, Jean
Rochambeau, Comte de

GERMANY
Gutenberg, Johann
Reuter, Ernst

HAWAII
Kamehameha I

HUNGARY
Kossuth, Lajos

INDIA
Gandhi, Mahatma

ITALY
Columbus, Christopher
Dante Alighieri
Della Robbia, Andrea
Garibaldi, Giuseppe
Ghirlandaio, Domenico
Giorgione
Lotto, Lorenzo
Marconi, Guglielmo
Mazzei, Philip
Michelangelo Buonarroti
Raphael

JAPAN
Hokusai

NETHERLANDS
David, Gerard
Eyck, Jan van
Master of the St. Lucy Legend
Memling, Hans
Terborch, Gerard

NORWAY
Erikson, Leif

PHILIPPINES
Magsaysay, Ramón

POLAND
Copernicus, Nicolaus
Kosciuszko, Thaddeus
Paderewski, Ignacy Jan

SPAIN
Balboa, Vasco Núñez de
Coronado, Francisco Vázquez de

Table 24—*Continued*

SPAIN *(continued)*	SWEDEN
Ferdinand the Catholic	Hammarskjold, Dag
Gálvez, Bernardo de	SWITZERLAND
Goya, Francisco de	Liotard, Jean Etienne
Isabella the Catholic	VENEZUELA
Noriega, Antonio	Bolívar, Simón
Ortega, José Francisco de	
Pérez, Juan	
Pinzón, Martín Alonso	
Pinzón, Vicente Yáñez	
Triana, Rodrigo de	

born Americans and groups them by their native lands. Table 28 is comprised of the 337 native-born Americans who are listed according to the state in which each was born.

The fourteen individuals from the British Isles comprise almost 20 percent of the seventy-three foreigners listed in Table 24 and form the largest group of aliens honored on U.S. stamps. This is not surprising when one takes into account our language and cultural heritage. John Burgoyne, Charles Cornwallis, and William Phillips fought to squelch the American Revolution. James Cook and Henry Hudson were explorers. Thomas Carlyle, John Donne, and William Shakespeare are authors of great literary works. John Forbes captured Fort Duquesne in 1758 and renamed it Fort Pitt (now Pittsburgh). King Charles II granted the Carolina Charter in 1663; James Oglethorpe founded Savannah, Georgia and governed it for several years; and Winston Churchill was one of Britain's most noted prime ministers. Mrs. John Douglas was the subject of a painting by Gainsborough that was the central design on a stamp.

Spain has been very well represented on our stamps. Ten of the twelve Spanish persons were related to the discovery, exploration, and colonization of the New World. Antonio Noriega was the subject of a painting by Goya that appeared on a stamp.

Five of the eleven Italians were honored by having a work of art reproduced on a U.S. stamp. The other six were honored for various reasons: Christopher Columbus discovered America; Dante Alighieri wrote the masterpiece, *Divine Comedy*; Giuseppe Garibaldi was a leader in the unification of Italy; Marconi invented the wireless telegraph; Philip Mazzei is considered as a patriot of the American Revolution; and Michelangelo Buonarroti was the subject of a painting by Raphael used on a stamp.

Statesmen and military men of the eighteenth century account for six of the nine individuals from France. A painting by Jean Chardin was used as a stamp design. Jean Nicolet explored the region of the Great Lakes; Jacques Marquette traveled down the Mississippi with Louis Joliet, a French-Canadian.

The five men from the Netherlands, the Japanese, and the Swiss were honored by having an art work reproduced on U.S. stamps. Aside from their native land, the three Poles have nothing in common. Nicolaus Copernicus was a sixteenth-century astronomer; Thaddeus Kosciuszko served in the Continental Army during the American Revolution; and Ignacy Paderewski was a pianist and statesman who dedicated himself to the restoration of Poland as a nation. Germany is represented by Johann Gutenberg who invented the printing press and by Ernst Reuter who was mayor of West Berlin after World War II.

The figures who date back further than any of the others classified as foreigners are the three biblical personages who have been honored by being depicted on Christmas stamps and Leif Erikson, who had explored the North American coast around the year 1000.

The men from Argentina, China, Czechoslovakia, Finland, Hawaii, Hungary, India, the Philippines, Sweden, and Venezuela were honored on U.S. stamps as "champions of liberty" or because of their prominent political positions.

Tables 25 and 26 distribute the seventy-three foreigners according to professional categories and regions where they were born. Table 25 points out that more than one-half of the foreigners were either explorers and colonizers or were in politics and government. Ten of the politicians were engaged in political activities in the late 1800s and the twentieth century; the other nine were active before 1850. The nineteen explorers and colonizers all lived before 1800, implying that these foreigners were honored on stamps because of their early activities in the exploration and colonization of the New World. Artists and painting subjects account for almost one-fourth of

Table 25
Professions of the Foreigners

Profession	Number	Percentage
Politicians and statesmen	19	26.03
Explorers and colonizers	19	26.03
Artists and painting subjects	17	23.28
Military	8	10.96
Writers	4	5.48
Scientists and inventors	3	4.11
Biblical personages	3	4.11
Total	73	100.00

Table 26
Summary of the Birthplaces of the Foreigners

Birthplace	Number	Percentage
Europe	62	84.93
Asia	4	5.48
Biblical Palestine	3	4.11
South America	2	2.74
Canada	1	1.37
Hawaii	1	1.37
Total	73	100.00

the foreigners; these artists have been honored because their works were chosen to be the central design on several stamps. This group consists of six Italians, five Dutch, two British, two Spanish, one Japanese and one Swiss artist.

Considering the heritage and cultural background of the United States, it seems reasonable that almost 85 percent of the foreigners are from Europe and only four are Asians, as the data in Table 26 point out.

The largest number of foreigners came from the British Isles, and for the same underlying reasons, common language and cultural heritage, the majority of the foreign-born Americans who were honored on stamps immigrated to the United States from Britain. A count of the names listed under British Isles in Table 27 will reveal that thirty-two, or almost 60 percent, of the foreign-born Americans were emigrants from England, Ireland, Scotland, and Wales. Canada and the Island of Nevis belong to the British Commonwealth, and seven individuals, or almost 13 percent, have come from these two places. Thus it can be seen that a total of thirty-nine individuals, or almost three-fourths of the 54 foreign-born Americans honored on U.S. stamps, emigrated from various parts of the British Commonwealth. Aubudon, the only foreign-born American from the Western Hemisphere not born a British subject, was born in Haiti.

The remaining fourteen Americans who were born abroad are from nine different European countries. No foreign-born American honored on stamps has come from Central or South America, Africa, Asia, or Polynesia.

Of the 464 individuals who have been honored on U.S. stamps, 337 are native-born Americans. Thirty-eight states and the District of Columbia are the birthplaces of these individuals. The states listed alphabetically in Table 28 include the names of those born in that state, or born within what are now its present boundaries. Among these individuals are some who are never associated with the state where they were born, for example, Robert

Table 27
Foreign-born Americans Honored on U.S. Postage Stamps

BRITISH ISLES

England
Blackwell, Elizabeth
Carteret, Philip
Dare, Ananias
Dare, Eleanor White
Daye, Stephen
Gates, Horatio
Gompers, Samuel
Jackson, William
Latrobe, Benjamin Henry
Morris, Robert
Paine, Thomas
Penn, William
Smith, John
West, Joseph
Williams, Roger

Ireland
Barry, John
Butler, Pierce
FitzSimons, Thomas
Harnett, William M.
Herbert, Victor
McHenry, James
Paterson, William
St. Gaudens, Augustus
Thomson, Charles

Scotland
Bell, Alexander Graham
Carnegie, Andrew
Jones, John Paul
Muir, John
St. Clair, Arthur
Wilson, James
Witherspoon, John

Wales
Lewis, Francis

BRITISH WEST INDIES
Nevis (Leeward Islands)
Hamilton, Alexander

CANADA
Charbonneau, Toussaint
Comstock, Henry
Lee, Jason
McLoughlin, John
Naismith, James A.
Sandham, Henry

FRANCE
Chanute, Octave

GERMANY
Albers, Josef
Einstein, Albert
Steuben, Friedrich Wilhelm von

GREECE
Papanicolaou, George

HAITI
Audubon, John James

HUNGARY
Pulitzer, Joseph

NETHERLANDS
Stuyvesant, Peter

POLAND
Prang, Louis
Pulaski, Casimir
Salomon, Haym

PORTUGAL
Francisco, Peter

SWEDEN
Ericsson, John

SWITZERLAND
Bouquet, Henry
Gallatin, Albert

Frost and William Owen "Buckey" O'Neill. Frost lived most of his life in New England where his family had been rooted for generations, and much of his poetry reflects the region and its heritage. Even though Frost is

Table 28
Birthplaces by State of the 337 Native-born Americans

ALABAMA
Handy, William C.
Keller, Helen

ARIZONA
Hayes, Ira Hamilton

ARKANSAS
MacArthur, Douglas

CALIFORNIA
Frost, Robert
Giannini, Amadeo Peter
Patton, George Smith
Steinbeck, John
Stevenson, Adlai E.

CONNECTICUT
Allen, Ethan
Baldwin, Abraham
Cutler, Mannasseh
Grosvenor, Thomas
Hale, Nathan
Huntington, Samuel
Ingersoll, Jared
Johnson, William S.
McMahon, James O.
Salem, Peter
Trumbull, John
Trumbull, Jonathan
Webster, Noah
Williams, William
Wolcott, Oliver

DELAWARE
Bissell, Emily P.
Broom, Jacob
Macdonough, Thomas
Moore, John Bassett
Pyle, Ernie
Ross, George

DISTRICT OF COLUMBIA
Dulles, John Foster
Sousa, John Philip

FLORIDA
Powhatan

GEORGIA
Fremont, John Charles
George, Walter Franklin
Harris, Joel Chandler
King, Martin Luther, Jr.
Lanier, Sidney
Long, Crawford W.
Low, Juliette Gordon
Michael, Moina

IDAHO
Sacajawea

ILLINOIS
Addams, Jane
Disney, Walt
Sandburg, Carl

INDIANA
Riley, James Whitcomb
Wiley, Harvey W.
Wright, Wilbur
Yohn, Frederick C.

IOWA
De Forest, Lee
Hoover, Herbert

KANSAS
Earhart, Amelia
Masters, Edgar Lee
White, William Allen

KENTUCKY
Blair, Montgomery
Davis, Jefferson
Griffith, D. W.
Jones, Casey
Lincoln, Abraham
Sousley, Franklin R.

LOUISIANA
Richardson, Henry Hobson

MAINE
King, Rufus
Longfellow, Henry W.
Whipple, William

Table 28—*Continued*

MARYLAND
Banneker, Benjamin
Bassett, Richard
Carroll, Charles
Carroll, Daniel
Chase, Samuel
Decatur, Stephen
Dickinson, John
Douglass, Frederick
Few, William
Jenifer, Daniel of St. Thomas
Key, Francis Scott
Paca, William
Peale, Charles Willson
Read, George
Schley, Winfield Scott
Tubman, Harriet

MASSACHUSETTS
Adams, John
Adams, John Quincy
Adams, Samuel
Anthony, Susan B.
Appleseed, Johnny
Bartlett, Josiah
Barton, Clara
Bulfinch, Charles
Burbank, Luther
Cobb, David
Copley, Elizabeth Clarke
Copley, John Singleton
Currier, Nathaniel
Dickinson, Emily
Eliot, Charles Wilson
Emerson, Ralph Waldo
Franklin, Benjamin
Gerry, Elbridge
Goddard, Robert H.
Gorham, Nathaniel
Hancock, John
Holmes, Oliver Wendell
Homer, Winslow
Hooper, William
Hopkins, Mark
Howe, Elias

Kennedy, John F.
Kennedy, Robert F.
Knox, Henry
Lincoln, Benjamin
Lowell, James Russell
Mann, Horace
Morse, Samuel F. B.
Mott, Lucretia C.
Otis, Samuel Allyne
Paine, Robert Treat
Parkman, Francis
Perkins, Frances
Poe, Edgar Allen
Poor, Salem
Prescott, William
Putnam, Rufus
Revere, Paul
Sargent, Winthrop
Sherman, Roger
Stevens, Ebenezer
Stone, Lucy
Sullivan, Anne M.
Thoreau, Henry David
Warren, Joseph
Whistler, James A. M.
Whitney, Eli
Whittier, John G.

MICHIGAN
Ford, Henry
Lindbergh, Charles A.

MINNESOTA
Mayo, Charles Horace
Mayo, William James

MISSISSIPPI
Rodgers, Jimmie

MISSOURI
Benton, Thomas Hart
Carver, George Washington
O'Neill, "Buckey" William Owen
Pershing, John Joseph

Table 28—*Continued*

MISSOURI (*continued*)

    Russell, Charles M.

    Truman, Harry S

    Twain, Mark

NEW HAMPSHIRE

    French, Daniel Chester

    Gagnon, Rene A.

    Gilman, Nicholas

    Greeley, Horace

    Langdon, John

    Pierce, Franklin

    Stone, Harlan Fiske

    Sullivan, John

    Webster, Daniel

NEW JERSEY

    Brearley, David

    Clark, Abraham

    Cleveland, Grover

    Cooper, James F.

    Dayton, Jonathan

    Hewes, Joseph

    Kearny, Stephen Watts

    Maass, Clara

    Marshall, James Wilson

    Morgan, Daniel

    Pitcher, Molly

    Stockton, Richard

    Strickland, William

    Washington, John P.

NEW YORK

    Biglin, Bernard

    Biglin, John

    Clinton, George

    Curtiss, Glenn Hammond

    Davis, Alexander Jackson

    Eastman, George

    Fillmore, Millard

    Floyd, William

    Gershwin, George

    Goethals, George Washington

    Goode, Alexander D.

    Herkimer, Nicholas

    Hughes, Charles Evans

    Irving, Washington

NEW YORK (*continued*)

    Ives, James Merritt

    Jay, John

    LaGuardia, Fiorello

    Livingston, Philip

    Livingston, Robert R.

    Livingston, William

    Ludington, Sybil

    MacDowell, Edward A.

    Morris, Gouverneur

    Morris, Lewis

    Moses, "Grandma" Anna Mary

    O'Neill, Eugene G.

    Powell, John W.

    Remington, Frederic

    Renwick, James

    Roosevelt, Eleanor

    Roosevelt, Franklin D.

    Roosevelt, Theodore

    Sampson, William Thomas

    Scott, Blanche Stuart

    Seward, William Henry

    Sheridan, Philip Henry

    Smith, Alfred E.

    Stanton, Elizabeth

    Van Buren, Martin

    Wharton, Edith

    Whitman, Walt

    Willard, Frances

NORTH CAROLINA

    Blount, William

    Dare, Virginia

    Johnson, Andrew

    Madison, Dolley

    Polk, James K.

    Spaight, Richard Dobbs

    Whistler, Anna Mathilda

OHIO

    Armstrong, Neil A.

    Dunbar, Paul Laurence

    Edison, Thomas Alva

    Garfield, James Abram

    Grant, Ulysses S.

    Harding, Warren G.

Table 28—*Continued*

OHIO *(continued)*

Harrison, Benjamin (1833-1901)
Hayes, Rutherford B.
McKinley, William
Norris, George William
Ochs, Adolph Simon
Poling, Clark V.
Sherman, William Tecumseh
Stanton, Edwin M.
Taft, Robert A.
Taft, William Howard
Wright, Orville

OKLAHOMA

Rogers, Will

OREGON

Joseph, chief of the Nez Percé

PENNSYLVANIA

Alcott, Louisa May
Bedford, Gunning
Boone, Daniel
Buchanan, James
Cassatt, Mary
Clymer, George
Eakins, Thomas
Fields, W. C.
Foster, Stephen C.
Fox, George L.
Fulton, Robert
Furness, Frank Heyling
Hopkinson, Francis
Jeffers, Robinson
McKean, Thomas
Marshall, George C.
Mellon, Andrew William
Mifflin, Thomas
Nevin, Ethelbert W.
Peary, Robert Edwin
Peto, John Frederick
Porter, David Dixon
Ross, Betsy
Rush, Benjamin
Sloan, John
Stewart, Walter
Strank, Michael

PENNSYLVANIA *(continued)*

Tanner, Henry Ossawa
Wayne, Anthony
West, Benjamin
Williamson, Hugh
Willing, Thomas

RHODE ISLAND

Cohan, George M.
Ellery, William
Greene, Nathanael
Hopkins, Stephen
Perry, Matthew C.
Perry, Oliver Hazard
Stuart, Gilbert Charles

SOUTH CAROLINA

Heyward, Thomas
Jackson, Andrew
Laurens, John
Lynch, Thomas
Middleton, Arthur
Pinckney, Charles
Pinckney, Charles Cotesworth
Rutledge, Edward
Rutledge, John
Shadoo

TENNESSEE

Crockett, Davy
Farragut, David
Hull, Cordell
Rayburn, Sam
Sequoyah

TEXAS

Block, Harlan H.
Eisenhower, Dwight D.
Johnson, Lyndon B.
Post, Wiley

VERMONT

Arthur, Chester Alan
Coolidge, Calvin
Dewey, George
Dewey, John
Douglas, Stephen Arnold

Table 28—*Continued*

VIRGINIA
    Austin, Stephen Fuller
    Blair, John
    Byrd, Richard E.
    Cather, Willa
    Clark, George Rogers
    Clark, William
    Clay, Henry
    Harrison, Benjamin (1726-1791)
    Harrison, William Henry
    Henry, Patrick
    Houston, Sam
    Jefferson, Thomas
    Lee, Richard Henry
    Lee, Robert E.
    Lewis, Meriwether
    McCormick, Cyrus Hall
    McDowell, Ephriam
    Madison, James
    Marshall, John
    Mason, George
    Monroe, James

    Nelson, Thomas
    Pocahontas
    Reed, Walter
    Scott, Winfield
    Sevier, John
    Taylor, Zachary
    Tyler, John
    Walton, George
    Washington, Booker T.
    Washington, George
    Washington, Martha
    Wilson, Woodrow
    Wythe, George

WEST VIRGINIA
    Jackson, "Stonewall," Thomas J.

WISCONSIN
    Bradley, John Henry
    Catt, Carrie Chapman
    Wright, Frank Lloyd

---

considered a New Englander, he was born in San Francisco. Buckey O'Neill was born in St. Louis, Missouri, raised in Washington, D.C., and migrated to Arizona at the age of nineteen, where he became a famous frontier sheriff. When the Spanish-American War broke out, he volunteered for the Rough Riders and went to Cuba. There he was captain of Troop A of "Teddy's Terrors," and Theodore Roosevelt developed a strong liking for him. He was killed on San Juan Hill in the summer of 1898.

Other individuals were born, raised, and lived all their lives in the place where they were born, such as William Allen White and Thomas Eakins. White was born and raised in Emporia, Kansas where he published a newspaper, and he died in Emporia. Eakins was born and educated in Philadelphia and later taught at the Pennsylvania Academy of Fine Arts; he died in Philadelphia at the age of seventy-two. Thus, it can be seen that one's birthplace may not necessarily indicate the state or region with which an individual is closely related or the place where the person gained fame. The information in Table 28 is based solely on the places in which these 337 Americans were born.

Massachusetts is the leading state as a birthplace for native-born Americans honored on stamps; fifty-three (15.73 percent) of native-born Americans were born there. Only three other states can claim to be the birthplace of more than twenty of these individuals: New York was the birthplace of forty-two people; thirty-four were born in Virginia; and thirty-two in Pennsylvania. Together these four states are the birthplaces of 161 people, or almost one-half of the 337 native-born Americans! Although this may be related in part to the fact that many stamps have honored persons of the Revolutionary period and the early years of the American republic, still, many born in these states have lived during the nineteenth and twentieth centuries.

The states where these individuals were born are classified by geographic region in Table 29. The data presented in this table point out that the further west the region, the fewer the number of individuals born there. New England and the East Central region account for the birthplaces of 205, or almost 61 percent, of these 337 Americans. Only twelve individuals were born in the West. There are twelve states which cannot claim to be the birthplaces of any of these 337 individuals, namely, Alaska, Colorado, Hawaii, Montana, Nebraska, Nevada, New Mexico, North Dakota, South Dakota, Utah, Washington, and Wyoming. This in no way implies that persons prominent in the political, cultural, and economic history of these states have not been honored on U.S. stamps; it only signifies that no one honored on a stamp was born in any of these twelve states.

The fifty states and the District of Columbia are listed in Table 30 according to the period in history when they were admitted to the Union. The first group includes the thirteen original states and the District of Columbia, whose present area was carved out of Maryland, one of the original states. The second group is composed of the thirteen states that entered the Union between 1791 and 1844; the third group is made up of the ten states admitted to the Union between 1845 and 1863; the last group consists of the fourteen states admitted after 1863.

A glance at Table 30 shows that 255, or more than three-fourths of these 337 Americans, were born in the original thirteen states. This is quite a contrast to the three individuals who were born in those states entering the Union after 1863 and who account for less than 1 percent of the 337. The following statements summarize the data presented in Table 30: 225 individuals (75.67 percent) were born in the original thirteen states; fifty-seven (16.19 percent) have their birthplaces in states entering the Union between 1791 and 1844; twenty-two (6.53 percent) in states admitted in the years 1845 to 1863; and only three (0.89 percent) were born in places attaining statehood after 1863.

A large percentage of the individuals honored on stamps lived during the eighteenth century and were active in exploration, colonization, and the development of the United States as a nation (see Tables 38 and 39 in Chapter 10). In view of this and the fact that the history of our country began on

Table 29
Geographic Distribution of States and the Number of Individuals
  Born in Each State

Region and State	Number of Individuals		Percentage
	State	*Region*	
NEW ENGLAND		92	27.30
Connecticut	15		
Maine	3		
Massachusetts	53		
New Hampshire	9		
Rhode Island	7		
Vermont	5		
EAST CENTRAL		113	33.53
Delaware	6		
District of Columbia	2		
Maryland	16		
New Jersey	14		
New York	42		
Pennsylvania	32		
West Virginia	1		
SOUTH		76	22.55
Alabama	2		
Arkansas	1		
Florida	1		
Georgia	8		
Kentucky	6		
Louisiana	1		
Mississippi	1		
North Carolina	7		
South Carolina	10		
Tennessee	5		
Virginia	34		
MIDDLE WEST		44	13.06
Illinois	3		
Indiana	4		
Iowa	2		
Kansas	3		
Michigan	2		
Minnesota	2		
Missouri	7		
Ohio	17		
Oklahoma	1		
Wisconsin	3		

Table 29—*Continued*

Region and State	Number of Individuals		Percentage
	State	*Region*	
WEST		12	3.56
Arizona	1		
California	5		
Idaho	1		
Oregon	1		
Texas	4		
Total		337	100.00

the Atlantic Coast, it seems only natural that a majority of the 337 native-born Americans would have been born in the thirteen original states.

SUMMARY

The 464 individuals honored on U.S. stamps may be divided into three categories: foreigners, foreign-born Americans, and native-born Americans. Of the 464 individuals, seventy-three (15.73 percent) were foreigners, fifty-four (11.64 percent) were born in foreign lands but came to America to live, and the remaining 337 (72.63 percent) were born within the boundaries of the United States.

Tables 31, 32, and 33 list the various birthplaces of the 464 individuals and indicate the number born in each place. An examination of Tables 31 and 32 reveals that 108, or 85 percent, of the 127 foreigners and foreign-born Americans were born in Europe, illustrating our strong historical and cultural ties with Europe. Of these 108 Europeans, forty-six (42.6 percent) were born in the British Isles. When one considers our language and heritage, this is not at all surprising. The group of foreigners consists of just eleven who are not Europeans; these are four Asians, three biblical personages, two South Americans, one Canadian, and one Hawaiian. The eight foreign-born Americans who are not Europeans are from the Western Hemisphere, namely six Canadians and two from islands in the West Indies.

The data in Table 33 show that there are just four states, Massachusetts, New York, Pennsylvania, and Virginia, which are the birthplaces of 161 (47.77 percent) of the 337 native-born Americans. These four are among the original thirteen states which are the birthplaces of 255, or more than three-fourths, of the native-born Americans. The history of our country began on the eastern shores and a large portion of the persons honored on U.S. stamps lived in the eighteenth century, so therefore it is quite reasonable that such a large percentage of these Americans were born in the thirteen

Table 30
Chronological Grouping of States by Year of Admission to the Union
   and the Number of Individuals Born in Each State

State Group	Individuals	State Group	Individuals
Thirteen Original States		*States Admitted to*	
and the District		*the Union between*	
of Columbia		*1845 and 1863*	
Connecticut	15	California	5
Delaware	6	Florida	1
District of Columbia	2	Iowa	2
Georgia	8	Kansas	3
Maryland	16	Minnesota	2
Massachusetts	53	Nevada	0
New Hampshire	9	Oregon	1
New Jersey	14	Texas	4
New York	42	West Virginia	1
North Carolina	7	Wisconsin	3
Pennsylvania	32	Total	22
Rhode Island	7		
South Carolina	10	*States Admitted to*	
Virginia	34	*the Union between*	
Total	255	*1864 and 1959*	
		Alaska	0
States Admitted to the		Arizona	1
Union between		Colorado	0
1791 and 1844		Hawaii	0
Alabama	2	Idaho	1
Arkansas	1	Montana	0
Illinois	3	Nebraska	0
Indiana	4	New Mexico	0
Kentucky	6	North Dakota	0
Louisiana	1	Oklahoma	1
Maine	3	South Dakota	0
Michigan	2	Utah	0
Mississippi	1	Washington	0
Missouri	7	Wyoming	0
Ohio	17	Total	3
Tennessee	5		
Vermont	5		
Total	57		

original states. A common method of grouping the fifty states into two
sections is to use the Mississippi River as the dividing line with twenty-six

states east of the Mississippi and twenty-four to the west of it. Even though the population center of the United States is now just across the Mississippi a few miles east of St. Louis, Missouri, only twenty-nine (8.6 percent) of these Americans were born west of the Mississippi, and thirteen of these twenty-nine were born in states bordering the Mississippi. Perhaps by the end of this century as the population center moves further west, more persons born west of the Mississippi will be honored on U.S. stamps.

Table 31
Numerical Summary of the Birthplaces of the Foreigners Listed in Table 24

Country	Number	Country	Number
Argentina	1	Hungary	1
Biblical Palestine	3	India	1
British Isles	14	Italy	11
England	12	Japan	1
Scotland	2	Netherlands	5
Canada	1	Norway	1
China	1	Philippines	1
Czechoslovakia	1	Poland	3
Finland	1	Spain	12
France	9	Sweden	1
Germany	2	Switzerland	1
Hawaii	1	Venezuela	1
		Total	73

Table 32
Numerical Summary of the Birthplaces of the Foreign-born Americans
Listed in Table 27

Country	Number	Country	Number
British Isles	32	Greece	1
England	15	Haiti	1
Ireland	9	Hungary	1
Scotland	7	Netherlands	1
Wales	1	Poland	3
British West Indies	1	Portugal	1
Canada	6	Sweden	1
France	1	Switzerland	2
Germany	3	Total	54

Table 33
Numerical Summary of the Birthplaces of the Native-born Americans
  Listed in Table 28

State	Number	State	Number
Alabama	2	Minnesota	2
Arizona	1	Mississippi	1
Arkansas	1	Missouri	7
California	5	New Hampshire	9
Connecticut	16	New Jersey	14
Delaware	6	New York	42
District of Columbia	2	North Carolina	7
Florida	1	Ohio	17
Georgia	8	Oklahoma	1
Idaho	1	Oregon	1
Illinois	3	Pennsylvania	32
Indiana	4	Rhode Island	7
Iowa	2	South Carolina	10
Kansas	3	Tennessee	5
Kentucky	6	Texas	4
Louisiana	1	Vermont	5
Maine	3	Virginia	34
Maryland	16	West Virginia	1
Massachusetts	53	Wisconsin	3
Michigan	2	Total	337

NOTE

1. An exception to this is Kamehameha I, who was born in Hawaii around 1758 and died there in 1819. During Kamehameha's lifetime, Hawaii was an independent country; therefore, he is viewed as a foreigner in this study.

9 Minorities

The 391 Americans honored on stamps can be divided into three categories based on racial ascendency. The three categories are white Americans, black Americans, and American Indians. Table 34 gives the approximate percentage of the American population that constitutes each racial group as well as the number and percentage of each that have been honored on U.S. stamps. The percentage of the American population comprising each group has varied in the different historical periods, but the percentages listed below give an idea of the proportional representation of each group.

The eleven blacks and the eight Indians are identified and listed in Tables 35 and 36 and accompanied by the Scott Numbers of the stamps on which they were honored. They are listed chronologically by birth date to give a historical perspective to the periods in American history in which they lived.

Three of the eleven blacks were eighteenth-century figures; three were active during the nineteenth century; the productive years of four blacks began in the nineteenth century and ended in the twentieth; and one black was exclusively of the twentieth century.

Benjamin Banneker, a mathematician and astronomer, was born in Maryland in 1731, just four months before George Washington was born in Virginia. His scientific interests were not limited to astronomy and mathematics, but also included entomology and other sciences. At the age of twenty-two he constructed the first wooden striking clock of its kind made

BLACK HISTORY

CENTENNIAL OF BOOKER T. WASHINGTON

UNITED STATES OF AMERICA

25TH ANNIVERSARY OF THE 13AMENDMENT TO THE CONSTITUTION

POSTAGE 3 CENTS

Contributors To The Cause...

Salem Poor ✦ Gallant Soldier

U.S. 10c

HENRY O. TANNER

W.C. HANDY
father of the Blues

6c

UNITED STATES

Martin Luther King Jr.

Black Heritage USA 15c

1863-1963 UNITED STATES 5 CENTS

EMANCIPATION PROCLAMATION

Paul Laurence
Dunbar

American poet

10 cents U.S. postage

USA

15c

Benjamin Banneker

Black Heritage USA 15c

MR. GEORGE WASHINGTON CARVER

UNITED STATES POSTAGE

3c

UNITED STATES 6c

"BATTLE OF BUNKER'S HILL"

John Trumbull
AMERICAN ARTIST

FREDERICK DOUGLASS

25c
U.S. POSTAGE

LINCOLN

4c
UNITED STATES

Harriet Tubman

Black Heritage USA 13c

in America. Banneker published a series of almanacs containing the results of his astronomical observations and calculations; editions were issued regularly from 1791 to 1802. In 1791, Washington appointed him a member of the commission to make up the blueprints for the new capital, the District of Columbia. He died in 1806, outliving George Washington by seven years.

Peter Salem and Salem Poor fought bravely in the Battle of Bunker Hill and other Revolutionary battles, such as Lexington and Concord, Valley Forge, and White Plains. Peter Salem was praised for shooting down the British major, John Pitcairn, at Bunker Hill in 1775. Salem Poor displayed such exceptional bravery and courage in the Battle of Bunker Hill that he was cited for his extraordinary battlefield valor.

Frederick Douglass was born into slavery in Maryland in 1817. In 1838, he escaped to the North where he was hired by the Massachusetts Anti-Slavery Society as an agent and began traveling and speaking against slavery. His autobiography, *Narrative of the Life of Frederick Douglass, an American Slave*, was published in 1845. After the Civil War he lived in Washington, D.C. He served as assistant secretary to the Santo Domingo Commission from 1877 to 1881 and was minister to Haiti from 1889 to 1891. He died in 1895 in Washington, D.C.

Another black active in the abolitionist movement of the 1840s and 1850s was Harriet Tubman, the only black woman to be honored on a stamp. Tubman was born in Maryland around 1820 and escaped to the North with the aid of the Underground Railroad in 1849. She became the most famous and successful conductor on the Underground Railroad, helping more than 300 slaves escape to the North. She also made speeches for the abolitionist cause. Tubman, who died in 1913, was often referred to as the "Moses of her People."

Booker T. Washington and George Washington Carver made Tuskegee Institute one of the world's most outstanding black educational institutions. Both Washington and Carver were born slaves and died as very famous men. Washington was born in Virginia in 1856 and began working and studying at nine years of age. From 1872 to 1875, he studied at Hampton Normal and Agricultural Institute. He taught for a few years and in 1881 became the first principal of Tuskegee Institute. He won a national reputation and became the most prominent black in the United States. His autobiography, *Up from Slavery*, published in 1901, is considered the last of the great slave narratives. Under his direction Tuskegee became one of the most prominent schools for blacks. Washington is the first black to be honored on a U.S. stamp; he was one of the five educators included in the Famous Americans Issues of 1940. He is also the only black to be honored on two U.S. stamps.

Carver was born in Missouri around 1864 and went to high school in Minneapolis. He received his bachelor's degree in 1894 and his master's degree in 1896 from Iowa State College of Agricultural and Mechanic Arts.

Table 34

Percentage of Whites and Minorities in the American Population and the Racial Ascendency of the Americans Honored on Stamps

Group	Percentage of Population	Individuals Honored on U.S. Stamps	
		Number	%
White Americans	81.14	372	95.14
Black Americans	12.00	11	2.81
Spanish-surnamed Americans	5.40	0	—
American Indians	0.40	8	2.05
Japanese-Americans	0.30	0	—
Chinese-Americans	0.22	0	—
Others	0.54	0	—
Total	100.00	391	100.00

Table 35

American Blacks Honored on U.S. Postage Stamps
  Arranged Chronologically by Birthdates

Name	Birth and Death Dates	Scott Numbers
Banneker, Benjamin	1731-1806	1804
Salem, Peter	1750?-1816	1361
Poor, Salem	fl. 1775-78	1560
Douglass, Frederick	1817-95	1290
Tubman, Harriet	1820?-1913	1744
Washington, Booker Taliaferro	1856-1915	873, 1074
Tanner, Henry Ossawa	1859-1937	1486
Carver, George Washington	1864-1943	953
Dunbar, Paul Laurence	1872-1906	1554
Handy, William Christopher	1873-1958	1372
King, Martin Luther, Jr.	1929-68	1771

Upon receipt of his master's degree he accepted an appointment by Booker T. Washington to the faculty of Tuskegee Institute where he remained until his death in 1943. At Tuskegee he was director of agricultural research, experimenting with such crops as peanuts, sweet potatoes, and soybeans from which he produced hundreds of by-products. He also urged farmers in the South to plant peanuts and sweet potatoes, crops that would replenish the soil depleted by growing cotton year after year. Carver was the foremost black scientist of his generation.

Three of the blacks whose careers spanned the nineteenth and twentieth

Table 36
American Indians Honored on U.S. Postage Stamps
Arranged Chronologically by Birthdates

Name	Birth and Death Dates	Scott Numbers
Powhatan	1550?-1618	328
Pocahontas	1595?-1617	328, 330
Shadoo, chief of the Kiawahs	fl. 1663-82	683
Sequoyah	1770?-1843	1851
Sacajawea	1787?-1812?	1063
Joseph, chief of the Nez Percé	1840?-1904	1364
Rogers, Will	1879-1935	975, 1801
Hayes, Ira Hamilton	1923-55	929

centuries were in the arts: Tanner, a painter; Dunbar, a poet; and Handy, a musician. Henry Ossawa Tanner was born in Pittsburgh and studied art for several years under Thomas Eakins at the Pennsylvania Academy of Fine Arts. Like other American painters of the nineteenth century, he wanted to study abroad, and in 1891, shortly before his twenty-second birthday, he went to Paris. By the mid-1890s, he had settled permanently in Paris and only occasionally visited the United States. By the end of the century he was famous internationally for his paintings, especially those with biblical themes and landscapes. His success as a painter gave inspiration to other black artists during the 1920s. Tanner died in Paris in 1937.

The poet, Paul Laurence Dunbar, was born in Dayton, Ohio in 1872 and educated in the public schools of Dayton. He also wrote novels, but they were never as popular as his verse. *Lyrics of Lowly Life, Lyrics of the Hearthside*, and *Poems of Cabin and Field* are some of his volumes of poetry. He was a personal friend of Booker T. Washington and wrote the school song for Tuskegee Institute. Dunbar produced most of his works during the last ten years of his life and undoubtedly would have become an even greater writer had he not died in 1906, just four months before his thirty-fourth birthday.

W. C. (William Christopher) Handy is called the "Father of the Blues" and was the writer of the first published blues. He was born in Alabama in 1873 but lived many years in Memphis where he developed the musical form later to be called "blues." Some of his songs are "St. Louis Blues," "Beale Street Blues," and "Memphis Blues." In his later years he owned a music publishing company in New York City, and, although blind and in poor health, he continued to manage the company until his death in 1958.

The much revered civil rights leader, Martin Luther King, Jr., is the only black in this group born in the twentieth century. King was born in Atlanta in 1929, studied at Morehouse and Crozier Theological Seminary, and later received his Ph.D. from Boston University. He became active in the civil rights movement in 1955 and soon moved to the foreground of the equal rights struggle. King's life and thought were influenced by Henry Thoreau's social ideas and the teachings of Mahatma Gandhi, and he followed Gandhi's strategy of nonviolence in his fight against poverty and injustice. In 1964 he became the youngest man ever to be awarded the Nobel Peace Prize. King's life ended suddenly and tragically; he was assassinated on April 4, 1968.

The eight American Indians honored on U.S. stamps reflect American history from the founding of Jamestown in 1607 to the end of World War II in 1945. Three of the Indians represent the seventeenth century, three are from the nineteenth century, and two are twentieth-century figures. No Indian active in the eighteenth century, such as Joseph Brant or Pontiac, has been honored on a stamp. Two Indians have been honored on two stamps each: Pocahontas and Will Rogers. Six of the Indians are men, and two, Pocahontas and Sacajawea, are women.

Powhatan, chieftain of a confederacy of several Algonquin tribes, opposed the presence of the English settlers who founded Jamestown in 1607 and who had begun taking over the best lands bordering the James River. There was much fighting between the Indians and the settlers, and in 1608 Captain John Smith was captured by Powhatan. According to Smith's own account, he was saved from execution by Powhatan's daughter, Pocahontas. John Rolfe, one of the English settlers, married Pocahontas in 1614, and their marriage helped promote peace between the settlers and the Indians. Rolfe and Pocahontas traveled to England in 1616 where Pocahontas fell ill and died in 1617. Her father, Powhatan, died a year later in 1618.

Shadoo was chief of the Kiawahs (a tribe now long extinct) in the 1660s and the 1670s. The Kiawahs lived in the area of Charleston, South Carolina, and befriended the English explorers and settlers who arrived in Carolina. William Hilton sailed from Barbados in 1663 to explore the Carolina coast in preparation for a permanent English settlement. Shadoo was among the Indians who traveled back to Barbados with Hilton and then later returned to Carolina. In 1666 Robert Sandford's ship arrived in Carolina, and Shadoo invited him and the crew to his town for entertainment and food. Letters written by Joseph West, William Sayle, and other colonists, who arrived there in 1670, attest to the friendly gestures and commendable help given them by the Kiawahs when they settled at Albemarle Point on the Ashley River and founded Charles Town.

Sequoyah, born in Tennessee about 1770 of an English father and a part-Cherokee mother, was a silversmith, hunter, and trader, as well as a scholar. He began working on an alphabet for the Cherokee language in 1809 and by 1821 had developed a syllabary of eighty-six characters adapted from the English, Greek, and Hebrew alphabets. At first, the Indian chief-

AMERICAN INDIANS

Heiltsuk, Bella Bella
Indian Art USA 15c

Acoma: School of American Research
Pueblo Art USA 13c

HAIDA CEREMONIAL CANOE

USA 19c
Sequoyah

WILL ROGERS

Performing Arts USA 15c

USA 13c

Chief Joseph National Portrait Gallery
United States Postage 6c

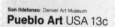

San Ildefonso: Denver Art Museum
Pueblo Art USA 13c

Tlingit
Indian Art USA 15c

tains gave much resistance to the written language, but it was accepted and within a few years thousands of Cherokees were able to read and write in their own language. Sequoyah died in 1843 while on an excursion to locate other Cherokees who were thought to have crossed the Mississippi at the time of the Revolution. In 1890 the Sequoia National Park was established in California and named after Sequoyah. His name is also perpetuated in the name of the largest and oldest living things on earth, the sequoias, or redwood trees, some of which are more than 4,000 years old.

Sacajawea, a Shoshone Indian, was only fourteen years old when she was captured and sold to a French-Canadian trapper, Toussaint Charbonneau, in 1800. He married her in 1804, the same year in which the Lewis and Clark expedition arrived to spend the winter with the Mandan Indians in North Dakota. Lewis and Clark engaged Charbonneau and Sacajawea to travel with them as guides and interpreters. They traveled with Lewis and Clark to the west coast and then returned to North Dakota. According to contemporary sources, she died in 1812, but her death date is in doubt because an old Shoshone Indian woman turned up in Wyoming in 1875 claiming to be Sacajawea; she lived until 1884.

Joseph, chief of the Nez Percé, was born in Oregon around 1840. His father died in 1871, and Joseph became the leader of one of the groups of Nez Percé that refused to leave the land ceded to the federal government by a fraudulent treaty in 1863. An ultimatum was issued in 1877 for the Indians to leave the land peaceably or be removed by force. Joseph decided that it would be best to leave and avoid bloodshed. Soon after his decision, due to no fault of Joseph, some of the Nez Percé killed several whites and fighting broke out between the soldiers and the Indians. Joseph tried to lead his people to Canada, but was captured on October 5, 1877. Thereafter, he dedicated his life to the welfare of his tribe until his death in 1904.

Will Rogers always claimed to be one-quarter Indian, and for this reason he is considered an Indian in this study. Rogers, humorist, entertainer, and actor, was born in Oklahoma in 1879. In his youth he worked as a cowboy. In 1902, he traveled abroad, and, upon his return to the United States in 1904, he became a performer in Wild West and vaudeville shows in New York. He later appeared in the Ziegfeld Follies and was making movies as early as 1918. He became widely known for his humorous and satirical comments on the political and social scene and was called a "cowboy philosopher." Rogers was killed with Wiley Post (Scott Numbers C95 and C96) in an airplane crash in Alaska in 1935.

Ira Hamilton Hayes, a Pima Indian, was born in Arizona in 1923. In 1942, Hayes enlisted in the Marine Corps and was sent to Hawaii in 1944 and to Iwo Jima in 1945. Hayes is one of the six marines who raised the American flag on Mount Suribachi on February 23, 1945. The photograph of the marines taken by Joe Rosenthal was later used as a model for the Marine Corps War Memorial in Arlington National Cemetery. Of the six marines who raised the flag on Mount Suribachi, only three survived the fighting on Iwo Jima, one of whom was Hayes. Hayes returned to Arizona and died just ten years later in 1955.

The nineteen blacks and Indians discussed above are the only individuals that this author could determine who represent the various minorities that comprise approximately 19 percent of the American population.

Table 37 arranges in chronological order the twenty-one stamps on which the nineteen blacks and Indians have been honored for a total of twenty-two times. The chronological arrangement points out that no representative of a minority group was honored on a stamp during the first sixty years of U.S. postage stamp history. During the next fifty years, 1907 to 1956, only three stamps honored blacks, but Indians were honored seven times. In the fourteen years from 1967 to 1980, three Indians and nine blacks were honored. These nine blacks comprise 82 percent of all blacks ever honored on U.S. postage stamps.

The information in Table 37 indicates that throughout the 134-year

Table 37
Stamps on Which Blacks and Indians Have Been Honored, Arranged Chronologically by Date of Issuance

Year	Name	Black or Indian	Scott Number
1907	Powhatan	Indian	328
1907	Pocahontas	Indian	328
1907	Pocahontas	Indian	330
1930	Shadoo	Indian	683
1940	Washington, Booker Taliaferro	Black	873
1945	Hayes, Ira Hamilton	Indian	929
1948	Carver, George Washington	Black	953
1948	Rogers, Will	Indian	975
1954	Sacajawea	Indian	1063
1956	Washington, Booker Taliaferro	Black	1074
1967	Douglass, Frederick	Black	1290
1968	Salem, Peter	Black	1361
1968	Joseph	Indian	1364
1969	Handy, William Christopher	Black	1372
1973	Tanner, Henry Ossawa	Black	1486
1975	Dunbar, Paul Laurence	Black	1554
1975	Poor, Salem	Black	1560
1978	Tubman, Harriet	Black	1744
1979	King, Martin Luther, Jr.	Black	1771
1979	Rogers, Will	Indian	1801
1980	Banneker, Benjamin	Black	1804
1980	Sequoyah	Indian	1851

history of U.S. postage stamps blacks and Indians have been honored only twenty-two times and account for a mere 2.52 percent of the 873 persons on U.S. stamps. A glance at Table 22 in Chapter 7 shows that, during the first 114 years (1847-1960) of U.S. postage stamp history, 555 persons were honored, and, according to the data presented in Table 37, only ten of these were blacks and Indians, who account for only 1.8 percent of the 555 persons. However, during the twenty years from 1961 to 1980, 318 persons were honored on stamps and twelve (3.77 percent) of these were blacks and Indians. Thus the percentage of blacks and Indians can be seen to have more than doubled in recent years, but the percentage of persons in these groups honored on stamps is still much lower than their proportion of the American population.

SUMMARY

There have been eleven blacks and eight Indians honored on U.S. postage stamps. The first time that identified Indians appeared on a stamp occurred in 1907 when Pocahontas and her father, Powhatan, were depicted on a stamp commemorating the tercentenary of the founding of Jamestown, Virginia. It was not until 1940 that the first black was honored on a stamp: Booker T. Washington was depicted on a stamp in a series of American educators in the Famous Americans Issues.

The eleven blacks represent periods in American history ranging from the Revolutionary War to the 1960s. The lives of the eight Indians span a period of some 400 years, that is, from the 1500s to the middle of the twentieth century.

Blacks and Indians are the only minorities represented on U.S. stamps; no Spanish-surnamed American, Japanese-American, Chinese-American, or any other minority person has been so honored. Although the number of stamps honoring minority persons has gone up in the past few years, the percentage of persons representing these groups is quite low. Perhaps in the next decade or two the number of minority persons honored on U.S. stamps will increase dramatically.

10 Historical and Professional Perspectives

The individuals honored on stamps represent many historical eras and are from a variety of fields of endeavor. In order to place the 464 individuals in a historical and professional perspective, biographical data concerning them were studied with a twofold purpose: (1) to classify all the individuals according to the century when they were professionally active or productive or when they accomplished the feat for which they were honored on a stamp, and (2) to categorize them in broad professional groups giving an overview of the types of professions or endeavors represented by the individuals on U.S. stamps.

The classification of persons into a specific century, such as 1700 to 1799 and 1800 to 1899, is not always possible because many were active during the last years of one century and the early years of the next. Thomas Jefferson is one such individual who was just as active in the last years of the eighteenth century as he was during the first decade of the nineteenth century when he was President of the United States. In order to accommodate such cases, intermediate periods of 1750 to 1850 and 1850 to 1950 were created and used to show that some individuals were active both before and after the turn of the century. Table 38 lists the eleven time periods in which all 464 individuals were active or productive. From this table, it can be seen that the largest group is that of the eighteenth century, the period of the Revolutionary War and the founding of our nation, during which 136

AMERICAN HISTORY

Rise of the Spirit of Independence

Drafting the Articles of Confederation

York Town, Pennsylvania 1777 13¢

Bunker Hill 1775 by Trumbull

US Bicentennial 10c

French Alliance 1778

US Bicentennial 13c

individuals, or almost 30 percent, were active professionally. The number of individuals listed during the nineteenth century is almost equal to that of the eighteenth. If one considers the small groups that were active in the intermediary periods, 1750-1850 and 1850-1950, it is quite clear that approximately one-third of the individuals lived and were active during the 1700s and another one-third during the 1800s. In other words, two-thirds of all individuals who have been honored by stamps lived between 1700 and 1899.

The next tabulation (Table 39) lists the seventeen general professional categories into which all the 464 individuals were placed. Some categories are quite encompassing in order to furnish a succinct overview of the field such as Aerospace covering four pilots and one astronaut. Art is used in a broad sense and includes architects, lithographers, sculptors, painters, and the subjects of paintings when these are not notable for anything other than being the subject of a painting, for example, Elizabeth Clarke Copley, the daughter of the painter, John Singleton Copley. Literature encompasses writers of all kinds, poets, novelists, playwrights, journalists, and philosophers. Science comprises engineering, as well as the pure and applied sciences. Many individuals might be classed easily in more than one category, but in all cases the field of endeavor was selected in which the person was the most outstanding or better known. The largest group is Government and Politics in which 171 of the individuals, or almost 37 percent, were engaged. Military is the second largest group, including several patriots of the Revolutionary War. In a recent study of all the persons who have appeared on the covers of *Time* magazine, it was determined that more than one-half (55.6 percent) were statesmen, politicians, and military personnel.[1] With this in mind, it is not surprising to discover that more than one-half (51.29 percent) of the individuals honored on stamps are also noted for their endeavors in government, politics, and the armed forces.

A further examination of Table 39 points out that the four categories often considered as components of what may be referred to as the "arts" (Art, Entertainment, Literature, and Music) are made up of 107 individuals, or almost one-fourth (23.06 percent) of the 464 honorees. This indeed proves that the "arts" are well represented on U.S. stamps. The high percentage of persons in the "arts" seems even more astonishing when one combines the four categories that may be regarded as the "sciences" (Aerospace, Inventions, Medicine, and Science) and discovers that this group is made up of only 39 individuals, or just 8.41 percent of all individuals.

In rank order, the top six categories are Government and Politics, Military, Art, Literature, Colonization, and Exploration. These six categories alone account for 381 of the individuals and comprise 84.1 percent of all those identified on U.S. stamps!

The general professional categories are arranged alphabetically under the

Table 38
Time Periods in Which the 464 Individuals Were Active

Period	Number of Individuals	Percentage of Individuals
First century	3	0.65
1000-1099	1	0.22
1300-1399	1	0.22
1400-1499	14	3.02
1500-1599	11	2.37
1600-1699	18	3.88
1700-1799	136	29.31
1750-1850	25	5.38
1800-1899	130	28.02
1850-1950	31	6.68
1900-1980	94	20.25
Total	464	100.00

Table 39
General Professional Categories of the 464 Individuals

Fields of Endeavor	Number of Individuals	Percentage of Individuals
Aerospace	5	1.08
Art	57	12.28
Biblical personages	3	0.65
Business	3	0.65
Colonization	26	5.60
Education	6	1.29
Entertainment	3	0.65
Exploration	23	4.96
Government and politics	171	36.84
Inventions	16	3.45
Literature	37	7.97
Medicine	8	1.72
Military	67	14.44
Music	10	2.16
Science	10	2.16
Social reform	16	3.45
Sports	3	0.65
Total	464	100.00

various time periods in Table 40. In Table 41 the time periods are listed chronologically under each of the general professional categories. In perusing Table 40, one can determine the fields of endeavor represented in any specific period. Table 41 may be examined to discern the span of time in which individuals honored on stamps were active and productive in any professional area.

The information given in these two tables indicates that the professional categories of the various time periods accurately reflect the history of the United States. Leif Erikson discovered the North American continent sometime around the year 1000. Christopher Columbus reached the islands of the Caribbean in 1492, and colonization began a few years later in the sixteenth century. From the sixteenth century until late in the nineteenth century, exploration and colonization played an important role in the history of the United States. This is exemplified by looking at the numbers of individuals involved in exploration and colonization in Table 41 for the years 1400 to the present. All parts of the United States were colonized by the end of the nineteenth century; the table shows no one listed under the heading Colonization since that time.

No one who lived prior to the 1700s was categorized in Government and Politics or in Military; but data in Table 41 indicate that the largest numbers were in the eighteenth century. This can be explained easily by the fact that many of those who signed the Declaration of Independence and our Constitution have been depicted on stamps. Also, many Revolutionary heroes and patriots have been portrayed on our stamps. Politicians and statesmen from the eighteenth and nineteenth centuries appear in almost equal numbers.

One fifteenth-century inventor, Johann Gutenberg, was portrayed on a stamp; all of the other inventors, except Guglielmo Marconi, are Americans who began inventing all sorts of things at the end of the eighteenth century. This is quite consistent with the introduction of mechanical inventions during the period 1760-1830, often referred to as the Industrial Revolution. The "industrial revolution" in the United States can be said to have started with Eli Whitney's invention of the cotton gin in 1793 and with Robert Fulton's inventions to saw marble, twist hemp rope, and spin flax patented in the 1790s. Americans have been inventing great things since then, and this is reflected in the number of individuals listed under Inventions in the time periods covered from 1800 to 1980.

A glance at the professional groups under each time period in Table 40 discloses that the number of groups increased greatly for the nineteenth century. There are no persons honored on stamps who were active in the areas of Business, Education, Medicine, Music, Social Reform, or Sports prior to the 1800s; there is nobody in Aerospace or Entertainment before the twentieth century. These fields of endeavor signify the progress and maturation of the country through the social, economic, cultural, and scientific advances taking place after the War of 1812 ended in 1815 when the

Table 40
General Professional Categories Grouped by Time Periods

Time Periods and Fields of Endeavor	Number of Individuals	Time Periods and Fields of Endeavor	Number of Individuals
First century		1800-1899 (*continued*)	
Biblical personages	3	Education	5
1000-1099		Exploration	5
Exploration	1	Government and politics	35
1300-1399		Inventions	5
Literature	1	Literature	17
1400-1499		Medicine	4
Art	6	Military	16
Exploration	7	Music	4
Inventions	1	Science	3
1500-1599		Social reform	9
Art	4	Sports	2
Colonization	3	1850-1950	
Exploration	2	Art	5
Literature	1	Business	1
Science	1	Education	1
1600-1699		Exploration	1
Art	2	Government and politics	4
Colonization	11	Inventions	4
Exploration	4	Literature	6
Literature	1	Medicine	1
1700-1799		Music	2
Art	7	Science	3
Colonization	5	Social reform	2
Exploration	2	Sports	1
Government and politics	84	1900-1980	
Literature	1	Aerospace	5
Military	36	Art	7
Science	1	Business	2
1750-1850		Entertainment	3
Art	7	Exploration	1
Colonization	1	Government and politics	33
Government and politics	15	Inventions	4
Inventions	2	Literature	10
1800-1899		Medicine	3
Art	19	Military	15
Colonization	6	Music	4
		Science	2
		Social reform	5
		Total	464

Table 41
Time Periods of the 464 Individuals Grouped by General Professional Categories

Field of Endeavor and Time Period	Number of Individuals	Field of Endeavor and Time Period	Number of Individuals
Aerospace		Government and Politics (*continued*)	
1900-1980	5	1800-1899	35
Art		1850-1950	4
1400-1499	6	1900-1980	33
1500-1599	4	Inventions	
1600-1699	2	1400-1499	1
1700-1799	7	1750-1850	2
1750-1850	7	1800-1899	5
1800-1899	19	1850-1950	4
1850-1950	5	1900-1980	4
1900-1980	7	Literature	
Biblical personages		1300-1399	1
First century	3	1500-1599	1
Business		1600-1699	1
1850-1950	1	1700-1799	1
1900-1980	2	1800-1899	17
Colonization		1850-1950	6
1500-1599	3	1900-1980	10
1600-1699	11	Medicine	
1700-1799	5	1800-1899	4
1750-1850	1	1850-1950	1
1800-1899	6	1900-1980	3
Education		Military	
1800-1899	5	1700-1799	36
1850-1950	1	1800-1899	16
Entertainment		1900-1980	15
1900-1980	3	Music	
Exploration		1800-1899	4
1000-1099	1	1850-1950	2
1400-1499	7	1900-1980	4
1500-1599	2	Science	
1600-1699	4	1500-1599	1
1700-1799	2	1700-1799	1
1800-1899	5	1800-1899	3
1850-1950	1	1850-1950	3
1900-1980	1	1900-1980	2
Government and politics		Social reform	
1700-1799	84	1800-1899	9
1750-1850	15	1850-1950	2

Table 41—*Continued*

Field of Endeavor and Time Period	Number of Individuals
Social Reform (*continued*)	
1900-1980	5
Sports	
1800-1899	2
1850-1950	1
Total	464

United States was completely independent politically. Thereafter, Americans became able, for the first time, to concentrate on the task of building and developing the American republic.

Table 41 represents earlier centuries, but it shows how the number of individuals in the areas of Art, Inventions, Literature, and Science increased significantly after 1800. On the other hand, the number of individuals of the eighteenth century in the Military category is more than double those of the following two centuries. Undoubtedly, this is due to the many military leaders, heroes, heroines, and patriots of the Revolutionary War who have been honored on stamps. Noteworthy also is the fact that the numbers of individuals in the Military category for the nineteenth and twentieth centuries are almost exactly the same.

SUMMARY

The classification of each of the 464 individuals into a general professional area and the categorization of each individual into a time period corresponding to the years in which each was professionally active or productive demonstrates how the individuals honored on U.S. stamps reflect the history and development of the United States. One example is that almost three-fourths of those involved in the exploration and colonization of our country were active before 1800, the time when most of the country was explored and colonized. The largest group of individuals falls into the category of Government and Politics, and the second largest category is for the Military. The categories pertaining to the "arts" contain almost one-fourth of the 464 individuals whereas those of the "sciences" account only for slightly more than one-twelfth of all individuals. The development of the country and the advances made since 1800 are quite evident when noting that the maximum number of professional categories in any time period before 1800 is seven, but thirteen different categories are needed to classify those of the nineteenth and twentieth centuries.

NOTE

1. Lehnus, Donald J., *Who's on* TIME? *A Study of* TIME*'s Covers from March 3, 1923 to January 3, 1977* (New York: Oceana Publications, 1980), p. 19.

UNITED STATES PRESIDENTS

11 The Professions
and the Individuals

Many of the 464 individuals honored on U.S. stamps were engaged in several fields of interest or endeavor during their lifetimes. For the purpose of this study, however, only the major political positions held and the most significant occupations or professions in which each was engaged were considered. All individuals who were active in more than one profession or who held several prominent positions are listed under each profession in which they were engaged and made some noteworthy contribution, as well as under each prominent position held during their lives. For this reason, many of the individuals appear more than once in Tables 42 and 43, and the total number of names in these tables is 707, surpassing the number of different individuals who have been honored on the stamps.

The information provided in the preceding chapter indicated that almost 37 percent of the individuals were active principally in government and politics, and the other 63 percent were engaged in a variety of other endeavors. For this reason, it is useful and convenient to provide two different lists indicating the professions of the individuals. The first group (Table 42) includes both Americans and foreigners who were politicians or statesmen or who were active in other aspects of government or politics. The Americans are listed by positions held in the following order: Presidents, First Ladies, Vice-Presidents, Supreme Court Justices, Secretaries of Departments, Senators, Congressmen, Governors, Mayors, Presidential

Table 42
Politicians and Statesmen

AMERICAN
Presidents

Adams, John	Harrison, William H.	Pierce, Franklin
Adams, John Quincy	Hayes, Rutherford B.	Polk, James K.
Arthur, Chester Alan	Hoover, Herbert	Roosevelt, Franklin D.
Buchanan, James	Jackson, Andrew	Roosevelt, Theodore
Cleveland, Grover	Jefferson, Thomas	Taft, William H.
Coolidge, Calvin	Johnson, Andrew	Taylor, Zachary
Eisenhower, Dwight D.	Johnson, Lyndon B.	Truman, Harry S
Fillmore, Millard	Kennedy, John F.	Tyler, John
Garfield, James Abram	Lincoln, Abraham	Van Buren, Martin
Grant, Ulysses S.	McKinley, William	Washington, George
Harding, Warren G.	Madison, James	Wilson, Woodrow
Harrison, Benjamin (1833-1901)	Monroe, James	

First Ladies

Madison, Dolley	Roosevelt, Eleanor	Washington, Martha

Vice-Presidents

Adams, John	Gerry, Elbridge	Truman, Harry S
Arthur, Chester Alan	Jefferson, Thomas	Tyler, John
Clinton, George	Johnson, Andrew	Van Buren, Martin
Coolidge, Calvin	Johnson, Lyndon B.	
Fillmore, Millard	Roosevelt, Theodore	

Supreme Court Justices

Blair, John	Jay, John	Stone, Harlan Fiske
Chase, Samuel	Marshall, John	Taft, William H.
Holmes, Oliver Wendell	Paterson, William	Wilson, James
Hughes, Charles Evans	Rutledge, John	

Secretaries of Departments
(The term after the name indicates the Department)

Adams, John Quincy (State)	Lincoln, Benjamin (War)
Blair, Montgomery (Post Office)	McHenry, James (War)
Clay, Henry (State)	Madison, James (State)
Davis, Jefferson (War)	Marshall, George C. (State; Defense)
Dulles, John Foster (State)	Marshall, John (State)
Gallatin, Albert (Treasury)	Mellon, Andrew W. (Treasury)
Grant, Ulysses S. (War)	Monroe, James (State; War)
Hamilton, Alexander (Treasury)	Perkins, Frances (Labor)
Hoover, Herbert (Commerce)	Seward, William H. (State)
Hughes, Charles Evans (State)	Sherman, William T. (War)
Hull, Cordell (State)	Stanton, Edwin M. (Justice; War)
Jay, John (Foreign Affairs)	Stone, Harlan Fiske (Justice)
Jefferson, Thomas (State)	Taft, William H. (War)
Kennedy, Robert F. (Justice)	Van Buren, Martin (State)
Knox, Henry (War)	Webster, Daniel (State)

Senators

Adams, John Quincy
Baldwin, Abraham
Bassett, Richard
Blount, William
Buchanan, James
Butler, Pierce
Carroll, Charles
Clay, Henry
Davis, Jefferson
Dayton, Jonathan
Douglas, Stephen A.
Dulles, John Foster
Few, William
Fremont, John C.
Gallatin, Albert
George, Walter F.
Gilman, Nicholas

Harding, Warren G.
Harrison, Benjamin
(1833-1901)
Harrison, William H.
Houston, Sam
Hull, Cordell
Jackson, Andrew
Johnson, Andrew
Johnson, Lyndon B.
Johnson, William S.
Kennedy, John F.
Kennedy, Robert F.
King, Rufus
Langdon, John
Lee, Richard Henry
McMahon, James O'Brien
Monroe, James

Morris, Gouverneur
Morris, Robert
Norris, George W.
Paterson, William
Pierce, Franklin
Pinckney, Charles
Read, George
Seward, William H.
Sherman, Roger
Taft, Robert A.
Truman, Harry S
Tyler, John
Van Buren, Martin
Walton, George
Webster, Daniel

Congressmen (Including members of the Continental Congress)

Adams, John
Adams, John Quincy
Adams, Samuel
Baldwin, Abraham
Bartlett, Josiah
Bedford, Gunning
Blount, William
Buchanan, James
Butler, Pierce
Carroll, Charles
Carroll, Daniel
Chase, Samuel
Clark, Abraham
Clay, Henry
Clinton, George
Clymer, George
Crockett, Davy
Cutler, Manasseh
Davis, Jefferson
Dayton, Jonathan
Dickinson, John
Douglas, Stephen A.
Ellery, William
Few, William
Fillmore, Millard
FitzSimons, Thomas
Floyd, William
Franklin, Benjamin
Gallatin, Albert
Garfield, James A.

Gerry, Elbridge
Gilman, Nicholas
Gorham, Nathaniel
Greeley, Horace
Hamilton, Alexander
Hancock, John
Harrison, Benjamin
(1726-1791)
Harrison, William
Henry
Hayes, Rutherford B.
Henry, Patrick
Hewes, Joseph
Heyward, Thomas
Hooper, William
Hopkins, Stephen
Hopkinson, Francis
Houston, Sam
Hull, Cordell
Huntington, Samuel
Ingersoll, Jared
Jackson, Andrew
Jay, John
Jefferson, Thomas
Jenifer, Daniel of
St. Thomas
Johnson, Andrew
Johnson, Lyndon B.
Johnson, William S.
Kennedy, John F.

King, Rufus
LaGuardia, Fiorello H.
Langdon, John
Lee, Richard Henry
Lewis, Francis
Lincoln, Abraham
Livingston, Philip
Livingston, Robert R.
Livingston, William
Lynch, Thomas
McHenry, James
McKean, Thomas
McKinley, William
Madison, James
Mann, Horace
Marshall, John
Middleton, Arthur
Mifflin, Thomas
Monroe, James
Morgan, Daniel
Morris, Gouverneur
Morris, Lewis
Morris, Robert
Nelson, Thomas
Norris, George W.
Otis, Samuel A.
Paca, William
Paine, Robert Treat
Pierce, Franklin
Pinckney, Charles

99

Table 42—*Continued*

AMERICAN (*continued*)

Congressmen (continued)

Polk, James Knox	Sevier, John	Whipple, William
Pulitzer, Joseph	Sherman, Roger	Williams, William
Rayburn, Sam	Spaight, Richard D.	Williamson, Hugh
Read, George	Stockton, Richard	Willing, Thomas
Ross, George	Sullivan, John	Wilson, James
Rush, Benjamin	Tyler, John	Witherspoon, John
Rutledge, Edward	Walton, George	Wolcott, Oliver
Rutledge, John	Wayne, Anthony	Wythe, George
St. Clair, Arthur	Webster, Daniel	

Governors (including colonial, territorial, and state governors)
(The term following the name indicates the place governed.)

Adams, Samuel (Massachusetts)
Bartlett, Josiah (New Hampshire)
Bassett, Richard (Delaware)
Blount, William (Territory South of the River Ohio)
Carteret, Philip (New Jersey)
Cleveland, Grover (New York)
Clinton, George (New York)
Coolidge, Calvin (Massachusetts)
Dickinson, John (Maryland; Pennsylvania)
Franklin, Benjamin (Pennsylvania)
Fremont, John C. (Arizona)
Gerry, Elbridge (Massachusetts)
Goethals, George W. (Canal Zone)
Hancock, John (Massachusetts)
Harrison, Benjamin (Virginia) (1726-1791)
Harrison, William H. (Indiana)
Hayes, Rutherford B. (Ohio)
Henry, Patrick (Virginia)
Hopkins, Stephen (Rhode Island)
Houston, Sam (Tennessee)
Huntington, Samuel (Connecticut)
Jackson, Andrew (Florida)
Jay, John (New York)
Jefferson, Thomas (Virginia)
Jenifer, Daniel (Maryland)
Johnson, Andrew (Tennessee)
Langdon, John (New Hampshire)
Livingston, William (New Jersey)

McKean, Thomas (Delaware; Pennsylvania)
McKinley, William (Ohio)
Mifflin, Thomas (Pennsylvania)
Monroe, James (Virginia)
Nelson, Thomas (Virginia)
Oglethorpe, James (Georgia)
Paca, William (Maryland)
Paterson, William (New Jersey)
Penn, William (Pennsylvania)
Pinckney, Charles (South Carolina)
Polk, James K. (Tennessee)
Read, George (Delaware)
Roosevelt, Franklin (New York)
Roosevelt, Theodore (New York)
Rutledge, Edward (South Carolina)
Rutledge, John (South Carolina)
St. Clair, Arthur (Northwest Terr.)
Sargent, Winthrop (Mississippi)
Sevier, John (Tennessee)
Seward, William H. (New York)
Smith, Alfred E. (New York)
Smith, John (Virginia)
Spaight, Richard D. (North Carolina)
Stevenson, Adlai E. (Illinois)
Stuyvesant, Peter (New Netherland)
Sullivan, John (Massachusetts)
Taft, William H. (Philippines)
Tyler, John (Virginia)
Van Buren, Martin (New York)
Walton, George (Georgia)

Governors (continued)

West, Joseph (South Carolina)
Williams, Roger (Rhode Island)

Wilson, Woodrow (New Jersey)
Wolcott, Oliver (Connecticut)

Mayors

Cleveland, Grover
　(Buffalo, New York)

LaGuardia, Fiorello H.
　(New York City)

Presidential Candidates Never Attaining the Presidency

Clay, Henry
Clinton, George
Douglas, Stephen A.
Fremont, John C.
Greeley, Horace

Hughes, Charles E.
Jay, John
King, Rufus
Pinckney, Charles
　Cotesworth

Scott, Winfield
Smith, Alfred E.
Stevenson, Adlai E.
Webster, Daniel

Miscellaneous

Austin, Stephen F.
Brearley, David
Broom, Jacob
Jackson, William

Lee, Jason
Mason, George
Mazzei, Philip
Paine, Thomas

Pinckney, Charles
　Cotesworth
Thomson, Charles

FOREIGN

Argentina
San Martín, José de

China
Sun, Yat-sen

Czechoslovakia
Masaryk, Tomas G.

Finland
Mannerheim, Carl G. E.

France
Barbé-Marbois, François
Cadillac, Antoine
Louis XVI, King

Germany
Reuter, Ernst

Great Britain
Charles II, King
Churchill, Winston

Hawaii
Kamehameha I, King

Hungary
Kossuth, Lajos

India
Gandhi, Mahatma

Italy
Garibaldi, Giuseppe

Philippines
Magsaysay, Ramón

Poland
Paderewski, Ignacy Jan

Spain
Ferdinand the Catholic, King
Gálvez, Bernardo de
Isabella the Catholic, Queen
Noriega, Antonio

Sweden
Hammarskjold, Dag

Venezuela
Bolívar, Simón

Candidates Never Attaining the Presidency, and Miscellaneous. Foreign political leaders and royalty are arranged by country. The second group (Table 43) lists in alphabetical order all other professions, occupations, and activities for which the individuals were honored on stamps. The individuals are subarranged alphabetically by name in both Tables 42 and 43.

Table 43
Professions, Occupations, and Other Activities

ACTORS AND ENTERTAINERS
Cohan, George M.   Fields, W. C.   Rogers, Will

ARCHITECTS
Bulfinch, Charles   Jefferson, Thomas   Richardson, Henry Hobson
Davis, Alexander Jackson   Latrobe, Benjamin Henry   Strickland, William
Furness, Frank Heyling   Renwick, James   Wright, Frank Lloyd

ARTISTS
Cartoonist
Disney, Walt

Graphic artists
Currier, Nathaniel   Ives, James Merrit   Prang, Louis
Hokusai

Painters
Albers, Josef   Goya, Francisco de   Raphael
Audubon, John James   Harnett, William M.   Remington, Frederic
Benton, Thomas Hart   Homer, Winslow   Russell, Charles M.
Cassatt, Mary   Liotard, Jean Etienne   Sandham, Henry
Chardin, Jean   Lotto, Lorenzo   Sloan, John
Copley, John Singleton   Master of the St. Lucy   Stuart, Gilbert Charles
David, Gerard   Legend   Tanner, Henry Ossawa
Eakins, Thomas   Memling, Hans   Terborch, Gerard
Eyck, Jan van   Michelangelo Buonarroti   Trumbull, John
Gainsborough, Thomas   Moses, "Grandma" Anna Mary West, Benjamin
Ghirlandaio, Domenico   Peale, Charles Willson   Whistler, James A. M.
Giorgione   Peto, John Frederick   Yohn, Frederick C.

Sculptors
Della Robbia, Andrea   French, Daniel C.   St. Gaudens, Augustus

Silversmith
Revere, Paul

ASTRONAUT
Armstrong, Neil Alden

AVIATION PIONEERS
Chanute, Octave   Lindbergh, Charles A.   Wright, Orville
Curtiss, Glenn H.   Post, Wiley   Wright, Wilbur
Earhart, Amelia   Scott, Blanche Stuart

BUSINESSPERSONS AND INDUSTRIALISTS
Carnegie, Andrew   Ford, Henry   Mellon, Andrew William
Eastman, George   Giannini, Amadeo Peter

EDUCATORS
Bell, Alexander G.   Hopkins, Mark   Sullivan, Anne M.
Carver, George Washington   Mann, Horace   Washington, Booker T.
Dewey, John   Sequoyah   Willard, Frances Elizabeth
Eliot, Charles William

ENGINEERS

Chanute, Octave
Ericsson, John
Fulton, Robert
Goethals, George Washington
Marconi, Guglielmo
(See also INVENTORS)

EXPLORERS

Balboa, Vasco Núñez de
Byrd, Richard E.
Charbonneau, Toussaint
Clark, William
Columbus, Christopher
Cook, James
Coronado, Francisco
Erikson, Lief
Fremont, John C.
Hudson, Henry
Joliet, Louis
Lewis, Meriwether
Marquette, Jacques
Nicolet, Jean
Ortega, José Francisco de
Peary, Robert E.
Pérez, Juan
Pinzón, Martín Alonso
Pinzón, Vicente Yáñez
Sacajawea
Triana, Rodrigo de

FRONTIERSMEN, PIONEERS, AND COLONISTS

Appleseed, Johnny
Boone, Daniel
Clark, George Rogers
Comstock, Henry
Crockett, Davy
Dare, Ananias
Dare, Eleanor White
Dare, Virginia
Lee, Jason
McLoughlin, John
Marshall, James Wilson
Oglethorpe, James
Penn, William
Putnam, Rufus
Sargent, Winthrop
Smith, John
Stuyvesant, Peter
Williams, Roger

HEROES, HEROINES, AND PATRIOTS OF THE REVOLUTIONARY WAR

Ludington, Sybil
Mazzei, Philip
Pitcher, Molly
Poor, Salem
Revere, Paul
Ross, Betsy
Salem, Peter
Salomon, Haym

INDIAN LEADERS

Joseph, chief of the Nez Percé
Pocahontas
Powhatan
Sequoyah
Shadoo, chief of the Kiawahs

INVENTORS

Bell, Alexander Graham
Chanute, Octave
Curtiss, Glenn H.
De Forest, Lee
Eastman, George
Edison, Thomas A.
Ford, Henry
Franklin, Benjamin
Fulton, Robert
Gutenberg, Johann
Howe, Elias
McCormick, Cyrus Hall
Marconi, Guglielmo
Morse, Samuel F. B.
Whitney, Eli
Wright, Orville
Wright, Wilbur
(see also ENGINEERS)

JOURNALISTS AND NEWSPAPERMEN

Douglass, Frederick
Franklin, Benjamin
Greeley, Horace
Harris, Joel Chandler
Ochs, Adolph Simon
Pulitzer, Joseph
Pyle, Ernie
White, William Allen

JUDGE

Moore, John Bassett
(See also SUPREME COURT JUSTICES in Table 30)

LABOR LEADER

Gompers, Samuel

MEDICINE

Nurses

Barton, Clara
Maass, Clara

Physicians

Blackwell, Elizabeth
Long, Crawford W.
McDowell, Ephriam
Mayo, Charles Horace
Mayo, William James
Papanicolaou, George N.
Reed, Walter

Table 43—*Continued*

MILITARY—AMERICAN
Army

Allen, Ethan	Kearny, Stephen W.	Pulaski, Casimir
Bouquet, Henry	Knox, Henry	Rochambeau, Comte de
Cobb, David	Kosciuszko, Thaddeus	St. Clair, Arthur
Eisenhower, Dwight D.	.afayette, Marquis de	Salem, Peter
Fox, George L.	Laurens, John	Scott, Winfield
Francisco, Peter	Lee, Robert E.	Sheridan, Philip Henry
Fremont, John C.	Lincoln, Benjamin	Sherman, William T.
Gates, Horatio	MacArthur, Douglas	Steuben, Friedrich Wilhelm von
Goethals, George W.	Marshall, George C.	Stevens, Ebenezer
Goode, Alexander D.	Morgan, Daniel	Stewart, Walter
Grant, Ulysses S.	O'Neill, William Owen	Sullivan, John
Greene, Nathanael	Patton, George Smith	Taylor, Zachary
Grosvenor, Thomas	Pershing, John Joseph	Trumbull, Jonathan
Hale, Nathan	Phillips, William	Warren, Joseph
Herkimer, Nicholas	Poling, Clark V.	Washington, George
Jackson, Andrew	Poor, Salem	Washington, John P.
Jackson, Thomas J.	Prescott, William	Wayne, Anthony

Marines

Block, Harlon H.	Gagnon, Rene A.	Sousley, Franklin R.
Bradley, John H.	Hayes, Ira H.	Strank, Michael

Navy

Barry, John	Jones, John Paul	Porter, David Dixon
Decatur, Stephen	Macdonough, Thomas	Sampson, William Thomas
Dewey, George	Perry, Matthew C.	Schley, Winfield Scott
Farragut, David	Perry, Oliver Hazard	

MILITARY—FOREIGN

Burgoyne, John	Forbes, John	Grasse, François de
Cornwallis, Charles		

MOTION PICTURE PRODUCERS

Disney, Walt	Griffith, D. W.

MUSICIANS, COMPOSERS, AND SONGWRITERS

Cohan, George M.	Herbert, Victor	Paderewski, Ignacy Jan
Foster, Stephen C.	Key, Francis Scott	Rodgers, Jimmie
Gershwin, George	MacDowell, Edward A.	Sousa, John Philip
Handy, William C.	Nevin, Ethelbert W.	

PAINTING SUBJECTS
(Includes only those who are not notable except as the subject of a painting used on a stamp.)

Copley, Elizabeth Clarke	Douglas, Mrs. John	Whistler, Anna Mathilda

PHILANTHROPISTS

Carnegie, Andrew	Eastman, George	Ford, Henry

PHILOSOPHERS

Dewey, John	Paine, Thomas	Thoreau, Henry David

PRINTERS
Daye, Stephen   Franklin, Benjamin   Gutenberg, Johann

RAILROAD ENGINEER
Jones, "Casey" John Luther

RELIGION
Biblical personages
Jesus   Joseph, husband of Mary   Mary, mother of Jesus

Clergy
Fox, George L.   King, Martin Luther, Jr.   Washington, John P.
Goode, Alexander D.   Poling, Clark V.   Williams, Roger

SCIENTISTS
Audubon, John James   Carver, George Washington   Goddard, Robert H.
Banneker, Benjamin   Copernicus, Nicolaus   Powell, John Wesley
Burbank, Luther   Einstein, Albert   Wiley, Harvey W.
    (See also ENGINEERS and INVENTORS)

SOCIAL REFORMERS AND CIVIC LEADERS
Addams, Jane   Keller, Helen   Stanton, Elizabeth
Anthony, Susan B.   King, Martin Luther, Jr.   Stone, Lucy
Barton, Clara   Low, Juliette Gordon   Tubman, Harriet
Bissell, Emily   Michael, Moina   Wiley, Harvey W.
Catt, Carrie C.   Mott, Lucretia   Willard, Frances Elizabeth
Douglass, Frederick   Muir, John

SPORTSPERSONS
Basketball
Naismith, James A.

Rowing
Biglin, Bernard
Biglin, John

WRITERS
Nonfiction
Carlyle, Thomas   Keller, Helen   Parkman, Francis
Douglass, Frederick   Muir, John   Thoreau, Henry David
Franklin, Benjamin   Paine, Thomas   Webster, Noah

Novelists and Story Writers
Alcott, Louisa May   Harris, Joel Chandler   Twain, Mark
Cather, Willa   Irving, Washington   Wharton, Edith
Cooper, James F.   Steinbeck, John

Playwrights
Cohan, George M.   O'Neill, Eugene   Shakespeare, William

Poets
Dante Alighieri   Jeffers, Robinson   Poe, Edgar Allan
Dickinson, Emily   Lanier, Sidney   Riley, James Whitcomb
Donne, John   Longfellow, Henry W.   Sandburg, Carl
Dunbar, Paul Laurence   Lowell, James Russell   Whitman, Walt
Emerson, Ralph Waldo   Masters, Edgar Lee   Whittier, John Greenleaf
Frost, Robert

AMERICAN POLITICIANS AND STATESMEN

All former presidents no longer alive have been depicted on one or more stamps, but only three first ladies have been so honored. Thirteen of the forty-two vice-presidents have been depicted; of these thirteen, there are eleven who also attained the presidency. The two vice-presidents depicted on stamps who never attained the presidency are George Clinton and Elbridge Gerry; they appear on stamps reproducing John Trumbull's painting, *The Declaration of Independence* (Scott Numbers 120, 1691, and 1692.)

There have been one hundred one different individuals appointed as Supreme Court justices, of which nine are currently serving on the bench. Eleven of the former ninety-two justices have been honored on stamps. Of these eleven former justices, six were also Chief Justices, namely, Charles Hughes, John Jay, John Marshall, Edward Rutledge, Harlan Stone, and William Howard Taft. Rutledge was appointed Chief Justice by President George Washington in 1795 and presided over the August term, but was not confirmed by the Senate.

Members of the Presidents' Cabinets hold important and influential positions; thirty (6.47 percent) of the 464 individuals on stamps have held a total of thirty-three different cabinet posts. Fourteen were Secretaries of State, including John Jay who was appointed as Secretary for Foreign Affairs. Nine were Secretaries of the War Department from the time of its creation in 1789 to 1947, when it became the Department of Defense. The only Secretary of Defense to be on a stamp was George C. Marshall. Three Secretaries of the Treasury and three Attorneys General of the Department of Justice have also been depicted. The remaining three were Secretary of Commerce, Postmaster General, and Secretary of Labor. Frances Perkins, the Secretary of Labor appointed by Franklin D. Roosevelt, was the only female cabinet member to be depicted on a stamp.

The 161 members of Congress (Senators and Representatives) account for the largest group of persons in American government and politics; forty-eight are Senators and 113 are Congressmen. Although this is a large group in comparison with all the others listed in Table 42, it is relatively small when one considers that approximately 11,000 different individuals have been members of Congress. These 161 members of Congress are presumably the most notable and memorable of the past 200 years.

The second largest group, that of governors, includes sixty-two individuals who held sixty-four governorships. Nine were governors of New York, including Peter Stuyvesant who was the director general of New Netherland from 1647 to 1664. Virginia has had seven governors honored on stamps; Massachusetts and Pennsylvania have had five each; New Jersey, South Carolina, and Tennessee four each; Delaware and Maryland three each; and Connecticut, Georgia, New Hampshire, Ohio, and Rhode Island have each had two governors so honored. Six states have had one governor each, namely, Arizona, Florida, Illinois, Indiana, Mississippi, and North Carolina. Two were governors of territories that comprised areas that now are made up of several states: one of these is the Northwest Territory which encompassed what is now Illinois, Indiana, Michigan, Ohio, Wisconsin, and part of Minnesota; the other is the Territory South of the River Ohio which included Kentucky, Tennessee, and the northern portions of Alabama and Mississippi. The other two were governors of the Canal Zone and the Philippines. It is worth noting that Arizona is the only state west of the Mississippi with a governor honored on a stamp.

As far as could be determined from biographical data available, Grover Cleveland and Fiorello La Guardia are the only mayors of cities to be on stamps. Of course, Grover Cleveland was portrayed because he was President of the United States, the only president to serve two nonconsecutive terms, from 1885 to 1889 and 1893 to 1897. He was also mayor of Buffalo, New York, in 1881 and 1882. LaGuardia, who was also a Congressman, is best known for his service as Mayor of New York City from 1934 to 1945.

Numerous persons have been presidential candidates since John Jay and John Adams ran against George Washington in 1789, but only eleven who never attained the presidency have been sufficiently prominent in other areas to deserve the honor of being on U.S. postage stamps.

There are ten persons listed under Miscellaneous because they never held any of the high ranking positions listed in Table 42 but were prominent in other political activities. Stephen Austin played an important role in the colonization of Texas. David Brearley, Jacob Broom, and Charles Cotesworth Pinckney (cousin of Charles Pinckney) were delegates to the Constitutional Convention in 1787 and signed the United States Constitution. George Mason was also a delegate to the Constitutional Convention but refused to sign. William Jackson was the secretary of the Constitutional Convention and signed the Constitution to attest the signatures of the delegates, but he has not been generally counted among the signers because he was not an official delegate from any state. Charles Thomson was the secretary of the Continental Congress and also signed the Declaration of Independence, but, like William Jackson, he was not a delegate and, therefore, is not usually counted among the fifty-six signers of the Declaration. Jason Lee was responsible to a great degree for the promotion of territorial status for Oregon and the establishment of its territorial government. Philip Mazzei, an Italian immigrant to Virginia and very close friend of Thomas Jefferson, became a patriot of the American Revolution and went back to Europe in 1785 never to return to America. Thomas Paine wrote several pamphlets advocating independence from England; his writings heartened patriots of the American Revolution and raised the spirits of the soldiers of the Continental Army.

FOREIGN POLITICIANS AND STATESMEN

The twenty-two foreign political leaders, representing sixteen different countries, come from periods ranging from the end of the fifteenth century to the middle of the twentieth.

José de San Martín and Simón Bolívar fought for and secured independence from Spain for several South American countries in the first quarter
of the nineteenth century. San Martín fought principally in Argentina and
Chile, and Bolívar in Venezuela, Colombia, Ecuador, Peru, and Bolivia.

Sun Yat-sen, the only Chinese to be depicted on American stamps, helped
bring about the fall of the Manchu dynasty in 1911 and became the first
president of the new Chinese Republic.

After the collapse of Austria-Hungary, Tomas G. Masaryk was elected
the first president of Czechoslovakia in 1918 and was reelected four times,
but had to resign in 1935 due to poor health.

Carl Gustaf Mannerheim was an important figure both politically and
militarily in Finland's fight for independence from Russia during the first
half of the twentieth century. He served as president of Finland from 1944
to 1946.

Three French statesmen have been on the stamps, and all were associated
closely with the history of the United States. Antoine Cadillac was the
founder of a French colony in 1701 on the present site of Detroit and later
served as governor of Louisiana from 1713 to 1716. The only treaty of
alliance ever made in U.S. history was the one approved by Louis XVI of
France and Benjamin Franklin in February 1778 and ratified by the Continental Congress three months later on May 4, 1778. A few years later
François Barbé-Marbois, minister of the treasury under Napoleon, skill-
fully negotiated the sale of Louisiana to the United States. The United
States had hoped to buy just part of Louisiana for ten million dollars, but
France needed as much money as possible, and thus, for fifteen million
dollars the United States acquired the entire area of Louisiana.

A German politician who has symbolized the resistance to Communist
aggression is Ernst Reuter, the mayor of West Berlin from 1948 to 1953. He
often referred to West Berlin as "an island of democracy in a red sea."

Only one English king has been on a stamp; Charles II appeared on the
stamp commemorating the 300th anniversary of the granting of the Carolina Charter to eight English noblemen in 1663. Another Englishman,
Winston Churchill, one of the greatest public figures of the twentieth century, was the prime minister of Great Britain during World War II and from
1951 to 1955. Churchill was made an honorary citizen of the United States
in 1963, the only person on whom the U.S. Congress has conferred such an
honor. (Marquis de Lafayette has often been considered an honorary
American citizen, but this was because two of the thirteen original states,
Maryland and Virginia, had given him local citizenship prior to the ratification of the U.S. Constitution in 1788. When the Constitution was adopted,
all persons who were citizens of any of the original thirteen states auto-
matically became citizens of the United States.)

Kamehameha I began to gain control of the Hawaiian Islands in 1782,
and by 1810 he controlled all the islands, united them into a kingdom, and

started a royal dynasty that lasted until 1893. He organized an effective government, welcomed foreign trade, and allowed traders to settle in the islands.

Lajos Kossuth was a leader in the nineteenth-century movement to free Hungary from Austrian domination. In 1848, he was appointed provisional governor of Hungary, but, in the following year when Hungarian forces were defeated, he resigned, fled into exile, and never returned.

Another person who dedicated himself to the securing of independence for his country was Mahatma Gandhi. After many years of struggling, he was assassinated in 1948, just two years before India's new constitution was to go into effect.

An Italian patriot and revolutionist, Giuseppe Garibaldi, played a central role in the movement for the unification of Italy until Victor Emmanuel assumed the throne of a united Italy in 1861. Considered as one of the greatest guerilla generals of all time, Garibaldi was even offered a command by President Lincoln during the Civil War. Garibaldi is still admired as a true idealist and an honest politician.

Ramon Magsaysay, a Filipino statesman, was the third president of the Republic of the Philippines, serving from 1953 until his death in 1957. Magsaysay worked endlessly to improve social and economic conditions of the poor.

Ignacy Jan Paderewski was a concert pianist with a strong desire for the political independence of his native Poland who gave much of his income for the Polish cause. In 1919 he became prime minister of Poland, but had to resign the same year. After the downfall of Poland in 1939, he became the president of the Polish National Council in Paris. He died in New York in 1941 and was buried at Arlington National Cemetery.

The Christian reconquest of Moslem Spain was completed in 1492, and that same year Queen Isabella and King Ferdinand gave Columbus ships to search for a western route to the Orient. Bernardo de Gálvez was a Spanish colonial administrator governing several places of the Gulf Coast area from Louisiana to Florida during the years 1777 to 1785. Antonio Noriega, the High Treasurer under King Carlos IV of Spain in 1801, was the subject of a Goya painting that was used in the series of stamps issued for the centenary of the Universal Postal Union (Scott Number 1537).

Since its beginning in 1945, the United Nations has had four secretaries-general, one of whom was honored on a stamp: Dag Hammarskjold, a Swedish political economist, who held that position from 1953 to 1961.

THE MAJOR PROFESSIONAL AND OCCUPATIONAL GROUPS

An examination of Table 43 shows that there are ten specific professions that include ten or more persons. These ten are in rank order:

Military—American—Army	51
Artists—Painters	35
Explorers	21
Frontiersmen, Pioneers, and Colonists	18
Inventors	17
Social Reformers and Civic Leaders	17
Writers—Poets	16
Military—American—Navy	11
Musicians, Composers, and Songwriters	11
Educators	10

The following sections discuss the persons who are listed in Table 43 in each of the above ten categories. The arrangement of the sections is the rank order given above.

MILITARY—AMERICAN—ARMY

It is not unexpected that the largest group in Table 43 is military in view of the data presented in the preceding chapter. But it may be somewhat surprising that the number of Army personnel is so disproportionate to those that represent the Marines and the Navy. All major wars in which the United States has been involved from the Revolution to World War II are represented on stamps by the men who participated in them. Fifty-one persons are listed under Army, and of these there are thirty-one (almost 61 percent) who fought in the Revolutionary War. The Civil War and World War II are symbolized by more persons than any other wars since the Revolution; eight World War II figures and five from the Civil War have been depicted on U.S. stamps.

The following information arranges chronologically all the Army personnel since the Revolution who have been honored on stamps and places them in their historic perspective. Two are better known for activities other than their feats in any particular war. George Goethals was chief engineer on the Panama Canal Commission and governor of the Canal Zone in the early years of the twentieth century. John C. Fremont explored the American West from the 1830s to the 1850s.

The other eighteen are best known for their accomplishments during specific wars. Andrew Jackson became popular for his defense of New Orleans in the War of 1812. Stephen Kearny and Winfield Scott were engaged in the Mexican War of the 1840s. Five military persons were key figures in the Civil War: Ulysses S. Grant, Thomas J. "Stonewall" Jackson, Robert E. Lee, Philip H. Sheridan, and William T. Sherman. William Owen "Buckey" O'Neill and John J. Pershing served in the Spanish-American War. Pershing was also in command of the World War I American Expeditionary Force in Europe. Douglas MacArthur, George C. Marshall, and George S. Patton fought in both World War I and World War II. Dwight D. Eisenhower became famous for his military strategy and actions in World War II.

The other four Army personnel are chaplains who were aboard the troop transport *Dorchester* when it was torpedoed off Greenland on February 3, 1943; they sacrificed their lives by giving up their lifejackets to others. These four chaplains, George L. Fox, Alexander D. Goode, Clark V. Poling, and John P. Washington, were posthumously awarded the Distinguished Service Cross in 1944.

ARTISTS—PAINTERS

The second largest group is that of painters; thirty-five painters have been honored on forty-three stamps. Twenty-one (60 percent) of the painters are Americans. These forty-three stamps honoring the thirty-five painters can be classed into three types: (1) stamps in which the principal design is a portrayal of a painter, (2) those issued with the purpose of honoring a painter with the principal design a work by the artist and not his portrait, and (3) stamps issued for reasons other than honoring a painter, but a work by the painter used as the principal design, and the painter's name included in the stamp design.

Eight painters have been portrayed on stamps, namely, John James Audubon (Scott Number 874), Michelangelo Buonarroti (Scott Number 1530), Charles Willson Peale (Scott Number 1064), Frederic Remington (Scott Number 888), Gilbert Charles Stuart (Scott Number 884), Henry Ossawa Tanner (Scott Number 1486), Benjamin West (Scott Number 1553), and James A. M. Whistler (Scott Number 885). All but one of these eight stamps were issued especially to honor the painter whose portrait was used. The one exception is the stamp portraying Michelangelo taken from a painting by Raphael and issued to commemorate the centenary of the Universal Postal Union. Michelangelo is also the only non-American member of this group.

Eleven stamps have been issued with the express purpose of honoring a painter in which the principal design was a reproduction of a work (or part of a work) by the artist instead of a portrait of the artist. These eleven are: John James Aubudon (Scott Number 1241), Mary Cassatt (Scott Number 1322), John Singleton Copley (Scott Number 1273), Thomas Eakins (Scott Number 1335), William M. Harnett (Scott Number 1386), Winslow Homer (Scott Number 1207), "Grandma" Moses (Scott Number 1370), Frederic Remington (Scott Number 1187), Charles Marion Russell (Scott Number 1243), John Sloan (Scott Number 1433), and John Trumbull (Scott Number 1361). All eleven of these painters are Americans, and this group contains the only two women painters ever honored on U.S. stamps: "Grandma" Moses and Mary Cassatt.

Twenty-four stamps have used the works of twenty-two artists as the principal design of stamps to honor persons or events other than the painters themselves where the artists' names appear in the stamp design. Examples of these are: John Singleton Copley's painting, *Nativity*, which was used as the design on a Christmas stamp (Scott Number 1701); Charles

Willson Peale's portrait of George Washington (Scott Number 1704); and Thomas Hart Benton's mural, *Independence and the Opening of the West*, used as the design for the stamp commemorating the sesquicentennial of Missouri's admission to the Union (Scott Number 1426).

Only two painters have had more than one stamp expressly issued to honor them: John James Audubon and Frederic Remington.

Although there are fourteen painters who are not Americans, not one foreign painter has had a U.S. stamp issued especially to honor him.

EXPLORERS

The twenty-one explorers are made up of the two discoverers of America, Leif Erikson and Christopher Columbus, and those who later explored the areas of what today is the United States, other parts of the Western Hemisphere, and the North and South Poles. Spain was the earliest major European power to explore and colonize the Western Hemisphere, so it is only natural that seven of the explorers are Spanish, including those who made the voyage with Columbus and those who came later to explore the New World. The seven Spanish explorers are: Vasco Núñez de Balboa, Francisco Coronado, José Francisco de Ortega, Juan Pérez, the Pinzón brothers, and Rodrigo de Triana.

Three are seventeenth-century French explorers, Louis Joliet, Jacques Marquette, and Jean Nicolet. Nicolet was the first white man to reach the area around Lake Michigan and what is now Wisconsin in 1634. Joliet and Marquette traveled together in 1673 down the Wisconsin and Mississippi rivers as far south as the mouth of the Arkansas River. James Cook and Henry Hudson were English. Hudson discovered the Hudson River and New York Bay and sailed as far north as Albany in 1609; the following year he reached Hudson Bay in Canada. Cook explored much of the South Pacific and arrived in Hawaii in 1778.

Sacajawea and her husband, Toussaint Charbonneau, accompanied Lewis and Clark on their expedition to the American West in the years 1804-1806. John C. Fremont explored much of the West from 1838 to the mid-1850s. Richard Byrd and Robert Peary were both polar explorers; Peary reached the North Pole in 1908, and Byrd explored both the North and South poles during the 1920s and 1930s.

FRONTIERSMEN, PIONEERS, AND COLONISTS

Settlers began arriving in the New World soon after its discovery, and others who were born here later continued to move west and to settle new land. Seventeen of these settlers and colonists who lived from the middle of the sixteenth century to the nineteenth century have been honored on U.S. stamps. Eleanor and Ananias Dare were the parents of the first child born in America of English settlers; Virginia was born in 1587. John Smith arrived at Jamestown, Virginia, in 1607 and later became president of that colony. Roger Williams founded Providence, Rhode Island, in 1636, and in 1647 Peter Stuyvesant arrived in New Amsterdam as the director general of New Netherland. William Penn was granted land in 1681 from Charles II and founded the colony of Pennsylvania. King George II of England gave a charter to James Oglethorpe in 1732, and the land was named for the king. Oglethorpe landed in Georgia the following year and founded the city of Savannah.

During the last quarter of the eighteenth century, George Rogers Clark, Daniel Boone, Rufus Putnam, and Winthrop Sargent settled in various places in the far west, such as Ohio, Kentucky, Tennessee, Illinois, and Mississippi. In the early years of the nineteenth century, Johnny Appleseed moved into the Ohio River Valley and began planting apple trees, and Davy Crockett was active on the frontier in western Tennessee.

As the country expanded westward, new territories were being settled and becoming part of the United States. John McLoughlin and Jason Lee went to Oregon and later saw it become a territory in 1848. That same year in California, James Wilson Marshall discovered gold during an excavation that started the famous gold rush of 1849. Ten years later, in 1859, Henry Comstock discovered the famous Comstock lode of silver and gold at Virginia City, Nevada.

INVENTORS

Seventeen inventors have been honored on stamps for their valuable contributions to the development of the country and to the improvement in the lives of its citizens. Guglielmo Marconi and Johann Gutenberg have been the only non-American inventors honored on U.S. stamps. An analysis of the types of inventions of these famous persons shows that seven were concerned with communications in one form or another: Alexander Bell, Lee De Forest, George Eastman, Thomas Edison, Johann Gutenberg, Guglielmo Marconi, and Samuel Morse. Six were involved with transportation, namely, Octave Chanute, Glenn Curtiss, Henry Ford, Robert Fulton, and Orville and Wilbur Wright. The other four were inventors of labor-saving devices: Elias Howe invented the sewing machine; Benjamin Franklin experimented with electricity and invented such things as bifocal eyeglasses, an improved heating stove, and the lightning rod; Cyrus McCormick invented a reaping machine; and Eli Whitney revolutionized cotton growing with his cotton gin.

SOCIAL REFORMERS AND CIVIC LEADERS

In the categories of First Ladies (Table 42), Nurses, and Painting Subjects (Table 43), all who are listed are women, but these categories are very small, totaling only eight women. Aside from these three categories, the one that contains the highest percentage of women is that of social reformers and civic leaders, with seventeen persons, thirteen (76.47 percent) of whom are women. Six of these women were active in the woman's rights movement, namely, Susan B. Anthony, Carrie Catt, Lucretia Mott, Elizabeth Stanton, Lucy Stone, and Frances Willard. Stanton and Mott organized the first woman's rights convention in the United States in 1848. Anthony, Stone, and Willard soon joined the movement and throughout their lives they advocated woman's rights and suffrage for women. Carrie Catt organized several associations at the end of the nineteenth century which advocated voting rights for women; she is the only one who lived to see the ratification of the Nineteenth Amendment to the Constitution granting nationwide suffrage to women. Anthony, Mott, Stone, and Willard were also active in the movements against slavery and alcohol; Willard was the president of the Woman's Christian Temperance Union from 1879 to 1898.

The other seven women in the category of social reformers dedicated themselves to the betterment of life and health for the underprivileged, the handicapped, and the sick, as well as the improvement of life for the American populace in general. The first of these is Harriet Tubman, who became the most famous and successful of the conductors of the Underground Railroad, whose purpose was to help slaves from the South escape to the North. Clara Barton secured medicine and supplies for wounded Civil War soldiers and later organized the American Red Cross in 1881. Jane Addams dedicated herself to the betterment of the urban poor and to help attain this goal established the famed Hull House in Chicago in 1889. Emily Bissell organized the first campaign using the sale of Christmas seals to raise money to combat and eliminate tuberculosis. She designed the first seals and began selling them in Wilmington, Delaware, and in Philadelphia in 1907. In Savannah in 1912, Juliette Gordon Low first organized a troop of Girl Guides which later became the national organization, Girl Scouts of the USA. Moina Michael, known as the "Poppy Lady," was inspired by John McCrae's poem, "In Flanders Fields," and in 1918 originated the Flanders Field Memorial Poppy to honor those who died in World War I. She presented her idea for a Poppy Day to the American Legion, which sponsored it in 1920; the British Legion adopted her idea in 1921. Michael also originated the annual memorial to soldiers and sailors who died at sea by making a seven-foot anchor of poppies and setting it adrift at Savannah; after 1930 the anchors were launched by naval authorities at Annapolis. Helen Keller lectured and wrote on behalf of the blind and deaf. Her efforts during the early decades of the twentieth century to improve their treatment were influential in removing the handicapped from asylums.

The four men are Frederick Douglass, Martin Luther King, Jr., John Muir, and Harvey Wiley. Douglass and King did much to improve the lives of American blacks; Douglass was active in the antislavery movement of the nineteenth century and in 1847 founded the abolitionist newspaper, the *North Star*; King was the principal leader during the 1950s and 1960s struggle to secure equal rights for blacks in all aspects of American life. During the later years of the nineteenth century, John Muir began campaigning for the setting aside of forest reserves and the establishment of national parks as reserves for the wonders of nature. Harvey Wiley was instrumental in securing Congressional passage of the Food and Drug Act of 1906.

WRITERS—POETS

Among the thirty-six persons listed as Writers, sixteen were poets. Although poetry is the oldest literary form, today it is perhaps not as widely popular as the novel or the short story. Nonetheless, twice as many poets have been honored on stamps as have novelists and story writers. Only two of the poets, Dante Alighieri and John Donne, were not American. Dante was an Italian poet who in the early years of the fourteenth century wrote the *Divine Comedy*, which is considered a masterpiece of world literature. Donne, an English poet, wrote in the early part of the seventeenth century and is considered the greatest of the metaphysical poets.

Ten of the Americans, Emily Dickinson, Paul Laurence Dunbar, Ralph Waldo Emerson, Sidney Lanier, Henry Wadsworth Longfellow, James Russell Lowell, Edgar Allan Poe, James Riley, Walt Whitman, and John Greenleaf Whittier, are of the nineteenth century. The other four, Robert Frost, Robinson Jeffers, Edgar Lee Masters, and Carl Sandburg, are of the twentieth century. Emily Dickinson is the only woman poet to have been honored on a stamp.

MILITARY—AMERICAN—NAVY

The group of eleven persons in the category of the Navy is considerably less than the fifty-one listed under Army. However, most of those in the Army category were involved in the Revolutionary War; during the Revolution the Continental Navy was small and played a minor role compared to that of the Continental Army. Only two Navy persons depicted on stamps, John Barry and John Paul Jones, were in the Revolutionary War. Stephen Decatur, Thomas Macdonough, and Oliver Perry were victorious over the British fleet in the War of 1812. Matthew Perry was significant in obtaining trading rights with Japan in 1854.

David Glasgow Farragut, the first admiral of the U.S. Navy, was adopted at the age of nine by the father of David Dixon Porter. Farragut and Porter were naval officers during the Civil War, and Porter commanded a mortar fleet under Farragut at New Orleans and on the Mississippi. The rank of rear admiral was created for Farragut in 1862 and conferred on him for his highly significant role in the Civil War. He became a full admiral in 1866, and upon his death in 1870 his foster brother, David Dixon Porter, became the second admiral of the U.S. Navy. Farragut and Porter are considered the two most outstanding naval commanders of the Union forces in the Civil War. George Dewey, William Sampson, and Winfield Schley were important in the Spanish-American War.

Although the Navy played a major role during World War II, not one person representing the Navy in the twentieth century has been honored on a stamp. A look at the list of Army personnel shows that several Army officers were active in the twentieth century and have been honored on stamps, for example, Dwight D. Eisenhower, George Marshall, George Patton, and John Pershing.

MUSICIANS, COMPOSERS, AND SONGWRITERS

Eleven men in the field of music have been on U.S. stamps. Nine can be classified as composers: George M. Cohan, Stephen Foster, George Gershwin, W. C. Handy, Victor Herbert, Edward McDowell, Ethelbert Nevin, Ignacy Paderewski, and John Philip Sousa. Cohan is best known for his songs and musical plays; Stephen Foster is famous for his popular songs, such as "Swanee River" and "Camptown Races." Gershwin wrote music for orchestra as well as musical comedies. Handy is known for his blues music; he was also a musician, and his chosen instrument was the cornet. Herbert was also a conductor and a cellist. McDowell, Nevin, and Paderewski were pianists as well as composers. Paderewski was the only musician who was not an American, but this Polish pianist lived and performed for many years in the United States. Sousa was just as famous as a bandleader as he was a composer.

Francis Scott Key was a lawyer and a poet and is classified here because his verse written in 1814 later became the lyrics for our national anthem, "The Star-spangled Banner." The only person to be honored on a stamp as a singer is Jimmie Rodgers, who stands foremost in country music as the person who broadened its appeal and made it a commercial success.

EDUCATORS

Ten persons who are outstanding in the field of education have been honored on stamps. Alexander Bell and Anne Sullivan were teachers of the handicapped: Bell was interested in teaching speech to the deaf, and Sullivan was the teacher of Helen Keller, who was afflicted with an illness at the age of nineteen months that left her blind, deaf, and mute. Booker T. Washington and George Washington Carver did much to improve the education of American blacks. Sequoyah devised a syllabary for the Cherokee language permitting thousands of American Indians to learn to read and write in their own language.

The other five persons made important contributions to the development of better educational systems and methods. Horace Mann revolutionized public education and advocated free public-supported common education that would be nonsectarian and taught by professionals. He served as the first secretary of the Massachusetts Board of Education from 1837 to 1848, during which time the first normal schools in the United States were established. A contemporary of Mann was Mark Hopkins, professor of moral philosophy and rhetoric at Williams College from 1830 to 1887, and its president from 1836 to 1872. Hopkins was considered more effective as a teacher than as a scholar or creative thinker. Charles William Eliot, a professor of mathematics and chemistry, was the president of Harvard from 1869 to 1909. He gradually introduced the "elective system" of undergraduate courses into the undergraduate college, eliminating the traditional system in which all students followed a prescribed course of study. After teaching in various schools for several years, Frances Willard accepted the presidency of Evanston College for Ladies in 1871. Two years later she became dean of women at Northwestern University when the two schools merged. She resigned in 1874 to join the growing national crusade against liquor. John Dewey was head of the University of Chicago's department of philosophy, psychology and pedagogy from 1894 to 1904. In 1904 he went to Columbia University, and during the next four decades he propelled Columbia's Teachers College into the forefront of American education.

OTHER PROFESSIONAL
AND OCCUPATIONAL GROUPS

The following sections contain brief sketches on the individuals in the other professions which were represented by nine or less persons. The following sections are arranged alphabetically as in Table 43.

ACTORS AND ENTERTAINERS

The only three actors who have been on stamps were contemporaries of each other; they are George M. Cohan, Will Rogers, and W. C. Fields who were born in 1878, 1879, and 1880, respectively. They also all died within a period of eleven years. Cohan appeared in many Broadway shows and was also a playwright. Fields and Rogers started out as vaudeville actors, were both in the Ziegfeld Follies after 1915, and made movies in Hollywood during the early 1930s.

ARCHITECTS

The nine architects were all Americans. Charles Bulfinch, Benjamin Latrobe, and Thomas Jefferson designed buildings in the latter part of the eighteenth century and the early years of the nineteenth. Jefferson designed his famous home, Monticello, as well as the buildings of the University of Virginia. Latrobe was engaged in 1815 to rebuild the U.S. Capitol after its destruction by the British in 1814, and Bulfinch suceeded him as architect of the U.S. Capitol in 1817, so the work of both is evident in the Capitol. Alexander Davis, Frank Furness, James Renwick, Henry Hobson Richardson, and William Strickland were all active in the nineteenth century. Frank Lloyd Wright was the only twentieth-century architect.

ARTISTS

In addition to the painters, nine other artists have been on stamps. One was a cartoonist, Walt Disney, the creator of Donald Duck, Mickey Mouse, and many other well-known animated cartoon characters.

Four of the persons in the category of artists were graphic artists. Hokusai was a Japanese wood engraver whose nineteenth-century drawings and color prints influenced art in other countries. Nathaniel Currier and James Ives were lithographers whose New York lithograph firm produced many fine prints that were very popular in the nineteenth century. Louis Prang, a contemporary of Currier and Ives, had his lithograph firm in Boston.

There were three sculptors, one of whom was an Italian and the other two were Americans. Andrea Della Robbia was a Florentine sculptor of the fifteenth and sixteenth centuries who was famous for his work in terra-cotta. Daniel Chester French and Augustus St. Gaudens were both active in the last quarter of the nineteenth century and the early years of the twentieth. French is well known for the seated marble figure of Abraham Lincoln in the Lincoln Memorial in Washington, D.C. St. Gaudens is famous for his equestrian statues of Sherman and Logan, as well as statues of Lincoln, Farragut, and others.

Paul Revere, the famous Revolutionary patriot, was also a distinguished and popular silversmith. His silverware was among the finest in the colonial and post-Revolutionary periods and is highly prized today.

ASTRONAUT

Neil Armstrong is the only astronaut included in the study because of the stamp honoring the landing of the "first man on the moon" (Scott Number C76). His name is not on the stamp, and his face is not visible because he is depicted wearing a spacesuit; but as history testifies, the first man on the moon was Neil Alden Armstrong, thus rendering the figure on the stamp an identifiable person.

AVIATION PIONEERS

Eight persons are included as pioneers in the field of aviation. Orville and Wilbur Wright made use of the results of Octave Chanute's experiments with gliders for their first airplane, *Flyer I*, later renamed the *Kitty Hawk*. Glenn Curtiss designed and built airplanes and also had a flying school to train aviators. One of his students was Blanche Stuart Scott, who claimed to be the only woman student personally taught by Curtiss. She soloed in 1910 —quite an accomplishment for a woman in that era, and especially since it was just seven years after the Wright brothers' historic flight at Kitty Hawk! In 1928, as a passenger, Amelia Earhart was the first woman to cross the Atlantic Ocean in an airplane. Four years later she made her own solo

SPACE EXPLORATION

US 10c

APOLLO SOYUZ 1975

MARINER 10 ★ VENUS/MERCURY

US 10c

APOLLO SOYUZ SPACE TEST PROJECT

UNITED STATES 1975

10c

Viking missions to Mars

Expanding human knowledge USA15c

US 8c

UNITED STATES IN SPACE

4c U.S. MAY IN SPACE

PROJECT MERCURY

In the beginning God...

APOLLO 8

SIX CENTS · UNITED STATES

PIONEER ★ JUPITER

US 10c

10c AIR MAIL

UNITED STATES

FIRST MAN ON THE MOON

US 10c

Skylab

US 5c

US 5c

crossing. Charles Lindbergh made history in 1927 and became the idol of millions with the first nonstop flight from New York to Paris, covering a distance of 3,600 miles in just thirty-three and a half hours. Wiley Post was the first solo flyer to circle the globe, a feat he accomplished in 1933 in less than eight days. He and his close friend, Will Rogers, were killed when their plane crashed in Alaska in 1935.

BUSINESSPERSONS AND INDUSTRIALISTS

The group of five businesspersons and industrialists includes two who were also classed as inventors, George Eastman and Henry Ford. The Eastman Kodak Company held a virtual monopoly on the market due to Eastman's policy of constant improvement and frequent price reductions. Ford introduced standardization and mass production and the revolutionary innovation of the conveyor belt assembly line. Andrew Carnegie became a millionaire from the iron and steel business. Amadeo Giannini was a California banker whose banking organization later became the largest bank in the United States, the Bank of America. Andrew Mellon acquired his millions through banking, the steel industry, and other enterprises. Mellon also served as Secretary of the Treasury from 1921 to 1932.

ENGINEERS

Five men are listed as engineers, including Robert Fulton and John Ericsson who were interested in ships. Fulton invented the submarine, but is best known for his steamboat, *Clermont*, and its record round trip in 1807 between New York City and Albany in just sixty-two hours. Ericsson's interest in ship design resulted in the famous warship, *Monitor*, which caused a revolution in naval warfare during the Civil War. Octave Chanute was a civil engineer who built railroads and railroad bridges and later began a study of aerodynamics which led to improved glider designs during the 1880s and 1890s. Marconi was an electrical engineer who made wireless telegraphy a reality in 1895. George Washington Goethals is known for his work on the Panama Canal which was completed in 1913 and opened to the world the following year.

HEROES, HEROINES, AND PATRIOTS OF
THE REVOLUTIONARY WAR

Three women and five men who were not military figures are recorded in history as patriots of the Revolutionary War. Sybil Ludington and Paul Revere are famous for their rides into the countryside to warn the colonists of the approaching British troops. Revere made his ride from Boston to Lexington on April 18, 1775. Just two years later on April 26, 1777, Ludington rode through parts of New York and Connecticut warning that the British were burning Danbury and advising the colonists to arm themselves to fight the British. Haym Salomon, whose financial genius served the cause of independence, also raised money and secured loans to carry on the war, and from his own pocket he gave money to pay the salaries of government officials and army officers. Betsy Ross made the first American flag, "the Stars and Stripes," in 1776. Peter Salem and Salem Poor were two blacks who fought for American independence in several Revolutionary War battles, including the Battle of Bunker Hill. Molly Pitcher became a heroine during the Battle of Monmouth when she manned her husband's cannon when he was overcome by heat. Philip Mazzei, an Italian immigrant and close friend of Thomas Jefferson, was a colonial agent sent to Europe to obtain a loan for the Commonwealth of Virginia. While in Europe, he maintained an official and politically important correspondence with Jefferson.

INDIAN LEADERS

Five Indian leaders have been honored on U.S. stamps. Shadoo, chief of the Kiawahs, befriended the English who arrived in South Carolina in 1669. Powhatan was an important chieftain at the time Jamestown was founded in 1607, and in 1614 his daughter, Pocahontas, married the English settler, John Rolfe. Joseph, chief of the Nez Percé tribe, fought to keep western lands for the Indians, but was defeated and captured in 1877. Sequoyah was a scholar who is also listed as an educator for developing a syllabary for his own Cherokee language. His name is perpetuated in the name of the coniferous tree, Sequoia.

JOURNALISTS AND NEWSPAPERMEN

The careers of the eight journalists and newspapermen range from the early eighteenth century to the middle of the twentieth century. Benjamin Franklin published the *Pennsylvania Gazette* from 1730 to 1748. Frederick Douglass founded the *North Star*, an abolitionist newspaper, in 1847 and edited it until 1860. Horace Greeley founded the *New York Tribune* in 1841 which came to exemplify the highest standards of journalism. Joel Chandler Harris was a journalist for the *Atlanta Constitution* from 1876 to 1900. Joseph Pulitzer, who established the Pulitzer Prizes, was owner of the *St. Louis Post-Dispatch*. In 1883 he purchased the *New York World*, and in 1887 he founded the *New York Evening World* which was to become known for its excellent reporting, political independence, and fearlessness in exposing corruption. A winner of the Pulitzer Prize for his editorial writing in 1923 was William Allen White, editor of the *Emporia Daily and Weekly Gazette*. The *Gazette*, whose editorials were widely reprinted, was one of the most notable small papers of the United States. Adolph Ochs published the *New York Times* from 1896 to 1935, during which time it became one of the world's most trusted and reliable sources of news. Another winner of the Pulitzer Prize was Ernie Pyle, one of the most famous war correspondents of World War II. He went where the fighting was the fiercest, and in 1945 he was killed by enemy fire on an island in the South Pacific.

JUDGE

Besides the Supreme Court justices who are listed in Table 42, the only other person who held an important judgeship was John Bassett Moore. He was a judge of the Permanent Court of International Justice (popularly known as the World Court) from 1921 to 1928.

LABOR LEADER

The only labor leader to be honored on a stamp was Samuel Gompers, who was the most important and influential person in the labor movement of the nineteenth century. He was chairman of the committee on the constitution for the Federation of Organized Trades and Labor Unions, as well as the first president of the American Federation of Labor.

MEDICINE

The two nurses portrayed on stamps are Clara Barton and Clara Maass. Barton founded the American Red Cross in 1881 and served as its president until 1904. Maass was a nurse from New Jersey who went to Cuba during the Spanish-American War and later volunteered for experiments conducted by Walter Reed and William Gorgas to find the cause of yellow fever. In 1901, she was bitten by the *Stegomyia fasciata* mosquito (later known as the *Aedes Aegypti*), developed yellow fever, and died ten days later on August 24.

Of the seven doctors, only one is a woman, Elizabeth Blackwell. Considered the first woman doctor of medicine in modern times, she graduated from the Geneva Medical School of Western New York in 1849. In 1809, Ephriam McDowell performed the first recorded operation of ovarian surgery in the United States when he removed a twenty-pound ovarian tumor. McDowell also performed a bladder operation on James K. Polk. Crawford Long is reportedly the first surgeon to use ether as an anesthetic, having employed it several times during the early 1840s. The Mayo brothers, Charles and William, were cofounders of the Mayo Clinic in 1889, and in 1915 they established the Mayo Foundation for Medical Education and Research. Charles specialized in surgery of the thyroid, and William in surgery of the abdomen. Walter Reed went to Cuba to research the cause of yellow fever in 1900 and a year later had proven that it was caused by a mosquito; by 1902, the mosquito was destroyed and there were no reported cases in Cuba. George Papanicolaou began developing tests for the early detection of cancer in the 1920s, and by the 1950s the test known as the "Pap test" was common procedure.

MILITARY—AMERICAN—MARINES

Six marines, Harlon Block, John Bradley, Rene Gagnon, Ira Hayes, Franklin Sousley, and Michael Strank, were immortalized in the famous Marine Corps War Memorial in Arlington National Cemetery. The statue by Felix W. De Weldon, dedicated in 1954 to commemorate the World War II battle on the island of Iwo Jima, portrays these six marines raising the American flag on Mt. Suribachi. The statue is based on Joe Rosenthal's famous photograph of that scene.

MILITARY—FOREIGN

Three of the four military men honored on stamps were British, and the other one was French. John Forbes commanded the expedition that captured Fort Duquesne from the French in 1758. Two were British army officers who fought against the Americans in the Revolution: John Burgoyne was forced to surrender at Saratoga in 1777, and Charles Cornwallis was beseiged at Yorktown by French and American troops in 1781. The French military person was François de Grasse, commander of the French fleet in the West Indies, who volunteered to help George Washington. De Grasse's fleet went to Chesapeake Bay, preventing the English fleet from aiding Cornwallis at Yorktown, so that Cornwallis capitulated to Washington in 1781.

MOTION PICTURE PRODUCERS

D. W. Griffith is considered as the most important person to establish the basic techniques of cinematic art. Between 1908 and 1931, he produced or directed almost 500 films. His first great film, *The Birth of a Nation* was released in 1915. Walt Disney, the world's best-known producer of animated motion picture cartoons, made several short movies and in 1938 released the classic, *Snow White and the Seven Dwarfs*. This film was followed by *Fantasia*, *Pinocchio*, *Dumbo*, *Bambi*, *Cinderella*, and many others.

PAINTING SUBJECTS

Elizabeth Clarke Copley, Mrs. John Douglas, and Anna Mathilda Whistler were subjects of paintings used on stamps and cannot be categorized in a profession. Elizabeth Copley's portrait was taken from a painting of the Copley family, and her likeness was singled out for use on the stamp to honor her father, John Singleton Copley. Mrs. John Douglas was the subject of a painting by Thomas Gainsborough used on a stamp to commemorate the centenary of the Universal Postal Union. Anna Mathilda McNeill Whistler is the figure in her son's painting entitled *Arrangement in Grey and Black No. 1: The Artist's Mother*, more commonly known as

Whistler's Mother. This painting by James A. M. Whistler was adapted for a stamp to commemorate Mother's Day in 1934.

PHILANTHROPISTS

Carnegie, Eastman, and Ford, the three listed as philanthropists, are also included in the area of Businesspersons and Industrialists. Carnegie gave huge sums of money for public education, public libraries, and international peace. Between 1886 and 1919, Carnegie donated more than forty million dollars for the construction of public libraries in the United States. The major beneficiaries of Eastman's millions were the four schools: Massachusetts Institute of Technology, Hampton Institute, Tuskegee Institute, and the University of Rochester. Henry Ford and his son, Edsel, together established the Ford Foundation, one of the major philanthropic institutions in the world.

PHILOSOPHERS

The three philosophers are Americans. Thomas Paine immigrated to America in 1774, after having been encouraged to do so by Benjamin Franklin. Two years later he wrote *Common Sense* which called for independence in powerful and stirring language. Other works by Paine are *The Rights of Man* and *The Age of Reason*. Henry David Thoreau wrote in the middle years of the nineteenth century, but his writings were not really appreciated until the twentieth. *Walden, or Life in the Woods* is his most popular work. His famous essay, "On the Duty of Civil Disobedience" was an impressive writing important to Mahatma Gandhi and Martin Luther King, Jr., among others. John Dewey is generally considered one of the greatest philosophers that America has produced. He was an adherent of the pragmatism formulated by C. S. Peirce and William James.

PRINTERS

Johann Gutenberg invented the first printing press to use movable type in Germany around 1450. Stephen Daye, the first printer in the English colonies in America, printed the *Bay Psalm Book* in 1640 in Cambridge, Massachusetts. This was the first book printed in English in the New World. Benjamin Franklin began working as a printer's apprentice at the age of twelve in Boston and worked as a printer in Philadelphia and London from 1723 to 1728. He owned and published the *Philadelphia Gazette* from 1730 to 1748.

RAILROAD ENGINEER

"Casey" Jones was immortalized in a ballad written about his heroic deed of saving the life of the firemen on the train, the Cannonball Express, which Jones was operating when it collided with a freight train. Jones was killed in the collision and became a hero of railroad men and of segments of the labor movement in the early years of the twentieth century.

RELIGION

The first ten amendments to the U.S. Constitution were adopted in 1791 and are often called the American Bill of Rights. The first part of the First Amendment reads: "Congress shall make no laws respecting an establishment of religion, or prohibiting the free exercise thereof." Christmas is the only legal federal public holiday in the United States that is of a religious nature. Therefore, the only stamps with a purely religious theme are the Christmas stamps. The first Christmas stamp came out in 1962, but it was not until 1966 that the Baby Jesus and his mother, Mary, were depicted on a stamp. Since that time, the Baby Jesus and Mary have appeared, always together, on ten stamps. Joseph, the husband of Mary, was also included on three of those ten stamps. No other biblical personage or venerated religious figure has ever been portrayed on a stamp.

The six clergyman depicted on stamps were honored for other than religious reasons. The four chaplains, George Fox, Alexander Goode, Clark Poling, and John Washington, sacrificed their lives when their ship sank in World War II. Roger Williams, a clergyman, was honored on a stamp as the founder of Rhode Island. Martin Luther King Jr., also a minister, was acclaimed for his leadership in the struggle for equal rights for American blacks from the middle of the 1950s until his assassination in 1968.

SCIENTISTS

The lives of the nine scientists cover a period of more than 400 years. Nicolaus Copernicus, a Polish astronomer and mathematician, developed the theory in the early years of the sixteenth century that the sun is the center of the universe, and not the earth, as was previously believed. Another astronomer and mathematician was Benjamin Banneker, who was also a surveyor and helped lay out the District of Columbia and the city of Washington in the 1790s. John James Audubon was a naturalist who devoted his life to ornithology and zoology, publishing several books on American birds between 1827 and 1839. Audubon was also a painter whose books were well illustrated with his drawings and paintings of birds. John Powell, a geologist, made the first of many exploratory journeys to the Rocky Mountain region in 1867. Powell was also the first to establish a definitive scheme for the classification of Indian languages, and in 1881 he became the director of the U.S. Geological Survey. The famed horticulturist, Luther Burbank, was more interested in producing improved varieties of cultivated plants than in scientific experimentation. Through hybridization and grafting, Burbank developed new and improved varieties of fruits, vegetables, and flowers during the last quarter of the nineteenth century and

CHRISTMAS

the early years of the twentieth. George Washington Carver, an agronomist and agricultural chemist, was director of agricultural research at Tuskegee Institute from 1896 to 1943. His experiments with the peanut and the sweet potato produced many valuable by-products from these plants, and at the same time he improved agricultural production in the South by showing that these two plants would replenish nutrients in the soil where previously only cotton had been grown. Harvey Wiley was a chemist and food analyst who was the chief chemist for the U.S. Department of Agriculture from 1883 to 1912. Robert Goddard was a physicist who pioneered in the field of rockets and rocket fuels. His experiments started in the early years of the twentieth century, and during the 1930s he conducted rocket research in New Mexico. Albert Einstein, another twentieth-century physicist, developed the general theory of relativity, the first theory since Newton's time to tackle the problem of gravitation. Einstein made many important contributions to physics, including his mass-energy equivalence formula ($E = mc^2$), which was important in the development of the atomic bomb.

SPORTSPERSONS

Only three persons in sports have been honored on stamps. Originating the game of basketball in 1891, James Naismith is considered the inventor of what is probably the only major modern game that owes its origin to a single person. The Biglin brothers, Bernard and John, were popular figures as the foremost oarsmen during the 1870s when professional rowing was a major national sport. However, the stamp on which they were depicted was issued to honor Thomas Eakins, whose painting of the Biglin brothers was chosen for the stamp design.

WRITERS—NONFICTION

Besides the sixteen poets discussed earlier, there are nine nonfiction writers, eight novelists and story writers, and three playwrights who have been honored on stamps. The nonfiction writers include six who were included in other categories: Frederick Douglass, Benjamin Franklin, Helen Keller, John Muir, Thomas Paine, and Henry Thoreau. The autobiography of Douglass, published in 1845, was entitled *Narrative of the Life of Frederick Douglass, an American Slave*. Franklin is known for *Poor Richard's Almanack* and the witty maxims and moral precepts that influenced the thought of that era, such as: "There are three faithful friends: an old wife, an old dog, and ready money"; "She that paints her face, thinks of her tail"; and "There's a time to wink as well as to see." Keller published the story of her life in several books, and in the early years of the twentieth century she began to write on blindness, a subject that until then had been taboo in women's magazines because of the relationship in many cases to venereal disease. Paine wrote, among other things, a series of pamphlets entitled, *The Crisis*, that bolstered the morale of the Continental

SPORTS

Army. The first appeared in 1776 and began with the memorable line, "These are times that try men's souls." Thoreau wrote several journals of his life that included his observations of natural phenomena and his experiences living close to nature. His *Journals* were published in fourteen volumes in 1907. Thomas Carlyle was a Scottish essayist and historian whose words, "Labor is life" were quoted on the 1956 stamp commemorating Labor Day. John Muir's writings were about the wonders of nature, whose titles are self-explanatory, *The Mountains of California*, *Our National Parks*, *Travels in Alaska*, to name a few. Francis Parkman was a historian who wrote many books on the history of North America. In 1846, he set out on the old Oregon Trail westward and in 1849 published *The California and Oregon Trail*. Noah Webster was a zealous nationalist who instituted spelling reforms that brought about the differences between American and British spelling. His great work, *American Dictionary of the English Language*, was published in 1828 and contained some 70,000 words. *Webster's Third New International Dictionary*, containing more than 460,000 entries, is the eighth in the series that began with Noah Webster's dictionary of 1828.

WRITERS—NOVELISTS AND STORY WRITERS

The eight American novelists and story writers represent two centuries of American fiction. James Cooper and Washington Irving were contemporaries and wrote in the first half of the nineteenth century. Cooper's best works, *The Deerslayer* and *The Last of the Mohicans*, deal with American frontier life, the settlers, and the Indians of the late eighteenth and early nineteenth centuries. Irving's tales, often called the first modern short stories, include *The Legend of Sleepy Hollow* and *Rip Van Winkle*. Louisa May Alcott wrote such classics in juvenile fiction as *Little Men* and *Little Women*, which made her famous in the field of juvenile literature and one of the most celebrated female authors of her day. During her last years she became interested in the woman's rights movement. Mark Twain was regarded as a popular novelist in his own day and later was ranked as a classic American novelist for his creation of the characters, Tom Sawyer and Huckleberry Finn. The fame of Joel Chandler Harris rests on his creation of Uncle Remus, who first appeared in *The Tar-Baby Story* of 1879. Even though Edith Wharton and Willa Cather were contemporaries who won Pulitzer Prizes, their works, like their backgrounds, were quite different. Wharton was from a distinguished and aristocratic New York family, and her early works reflected this background. Her two major works are *Ethan Frome* and *The Age of Innocence*, the latter winning her a Pulitzer Prize in 1921. Cather grew up in a frontier town in Nebraska, and her best novels, *O Pioneers!* and *My Antonia*, reflect the frontier life of her childhood. She received a Pulitzer Prize for her novel, *One of Ours*, just two years after Wharton. John Steinbeck, the only writer of this group born in the twentieth century, wrote realistic novels with sociological concern. One of his most famous novels, *The Grapes of Wrath*, won him a Pulitzer Prize in 1940. He was also awarded the Nobel Prize for Literature in 1962.

WRITERS—PLAYWRIGHTS

The three dramatists, William Shakespeare, George M. Cohan, and Eugene O'Neill, have one basic characteristic in common—they wrote plays in English. Shakespeare is the greatest literary genius of all times, and the universal themes of his plays written between 1589 and 1613 have caused them to be performed more than those of any other dramatist. Cohan was the author of many musical comedies and some plays, mostly written between 1905 and 1925. Like Cohan, his contemporary, O'Neill also came from an acting family. O'Neill is recognized as America's greatest playwright and as the first American to write serious and tragic drama. In 1933, George M. Cohan starred in O'Neill's only comedy, *Ah, Wilderness!* O'Neill won a Pulitzer Prize in 1928 and was awarded the Nobel Prize in Literature in 1936.

SUMMARY

Tables 44 and 45 are numerical summaries of the persons listed in Tables 42 and 43. These summary tables afford an overall view of the number of persons in each category and simplify numerical comparisons between any two or more groups listed in Tables 42 and 43.

All former presidents have been depicted on at least one stamp, except the three who are still living: Richard M. Nixon, Gerald Ford, and Jimmy Carter.

Martha Washington, honored on three stamps, is the only First Lady who has been on more than one stamp. Eleanor Roosevelt was depicted on a stamp just eleven months after she died, but Dolley Madison was not depicted on a stamp until she had been dead for 130 years.

Only two vice-presidents who never attained the presidency have been on stamps; George Clinton and Elbridge Gerry were not portrayed because of this position, but rather because they were signers of the Declaration of Independence.

Six of the eleven Supreme Court Justices honored on stamps were appointed in the last decade of the eighteenth century; two also were on the bench in the first decade of the nineteenth century. Only one Justice, John Marshall, was exclusively of the nineteenth century, serving from 1801 to 1835. Four twentieth-century Justices have been depicted on stamps, but not a single Justice who was on the bench from 1836 to 1901 has ever been honored on a stamp.

Secretaries of the Departments of State and War (or Defense) are the Secretaries most frequently portrayed on stamps. Fourteen, or almost one-

Table 44
Numerical Summary of the Politicians and Statesmen Listed in Table 42

American Politicians and Statesmen	Number	Foreign Politicians and Statesmen	Number
Presidents	35	Argentina	1
First Ladies	3	China	1
Vice-Presidents	13	Czechoslovakia	1
Supreme Court Justices	11	Finland	1
Secretaries of Departments	30	France	3
Senators	48	Germany	1
Congressmen	113	Great Britain	2
Governors	62	Hawaii	1
Mayors	2	Hungary	1
Presidential candidates never		India	1
attaining the presidency	13	Italy	1
Miscellaneous	10	Philippines	1
Total	340	Poland	1
		Spain	4
		Sweden	1
		Venezuela	1
		Total	22
Grand total		362 persons	

half, of the thirty secretaries honored on stamps were Secretaries of State, and nine, or almost one-third, were Secretaries of War (or Defense).

The 161 Senators and Congressmen who have been on stamps account for 48.5 percent of all American politicians and statesmen listed in Table 44. It is the largest group, understandably, when one considers that approximately 11,000 different individuals have been elected to Congress since the beginning of the United States. This group comprises less than 1.5 percent of those who have ever been members of Congress.

Sixty-two governors who held sixty-four governorships of twenty-three political units (colonies, territories, and states) have been honored on stamps. Although this is the second largest number of persons in Table 44, it is still relatively small when one considers that approximately 2,600 individuals have been colonial, territorial, and state governors. Of the twenty-four states west of the Mississippi River, only Arizona has had a governor honored on a stamp, whereas nineteen of the other twenty-six states have had a governor so honored. The states east of the Mississippi River which have never had the honor of having a governor on a stamp are: Alabama, Kentucky, Maine, Michigan, Vermont, West Virginia, and Wisconsin.

Fiorello LaGuardia was the mayor of New York City and is the only person portrayed on a stamp because of his mayorality. Grover Cleveland was the mayor of Buffalo, New York, but was depicted on a stamp because of his presidency.

The thirteen presidential candidates who never attained the presidency were persons prominent in other positions and professions and were honored on stamps for reasons other than having been unsuccessful presidential candidates. All but one held political positions such as Supreme Court justice, governor, senator, or congressman. The one exception is Winfield Scott, an army officer who was the foremost U.S. military figure between the Revolution and the Civil War and the most capable military leader of his time. Scott lost the presidential election to Franklin Pierce in 1852.

The ten persons listed in the miscellaneous category were involved in politics or governmental affairs of one kind or another, but were never appointed or elected to any of the positions listed in Table 44.

The largest group of persons in professional areas other than politics is the Military; seventy-two, or 21 percent of all persons listed in Table 45, are Military. Of the four military subcategories, the largest is the Army, and thirty-one (almost 61 percent of the fifty-one persons listed under the Army) fought in the Revolution. There are eleven persons who made outstanding contributions while in the Navy. Two were in the Revolutionary War; there were three each in the War of 1812 and the Spanish-American War; and two in the Civil War. Matthew Perry made his contribution by opening up Japan for trade with western powers in 1854. The six marines were the subjects of the famous photograph of the U.S. Marines raising the American flag on Mount Suribachi on Iwo Jima in World War II and the Marine Corps War Memorial in Arlington National Cemetery. All four foreign military men were eighteenth-century figures.

Table 45
Numerical Summary of the Professions, Occupations, and Other Activities
   Listed in Table 43

Actors and Entertainers		3
Architects		9
Artists		44
Cartoonist	1	
Graphic Artists	4	
Painters	35	
Sculptors	3	
Silversmith	1	

Table 45—*Continued*

Astronaut		1
Aviation Pioneers		8
Business persons and Industrialists		5
Educators		10
Engineers		5
Explorers		21
Frontiersmen, Pioneers, and Colonists		18
Heroes, Heroines, and Patriots of the Revolutionary War		8
Indian Leaders		5
Inventors		17
Journalists and Newspapermen		8
Judge		1
Labor Leader		1
Medicine		9
Nurses	2	
Physicians	7	
Military—American		68
Army	51	
Marines	6	
Navy	11	
Military—Foreign		4
Motion Picture Producers		2
Musicians, Composers, and Songwriters		11
Painting-Subjects		3
Philanthropists		3
Philosophers		3
Printers		3
Railroad Engineer		1
Religion		9
Biblical Personages	3	
Clergy	6	
Scientists		9
Social Reformers and Civic Leaders		17
Sportspersons		3
Basketball	1	
Rowing	2	
Writers		36
Nonfiction	9	
Novelists and Story Writers	8	
Playwrights	3	
Poets	16	
Total		345

Thirty-five painters have been honored on stamps, but only seventeen had stamps especially issued to honor them. The others only had their works reproduced and their names included in the designs of stamps issued to honor or commemorate other persons or events. Twenty-two of the painters are Americans; the other fourteen are Europeans, including six Italians, five Dutch, and one each from England, Spain, and Switzerland. The other nine artists include a cartoonist, four graphic artists, four sculptors, and a silversmith.

The earliest of the twenty-one explorers honored on stamps was Leif Erikson, who reached the North American continent around the year 1000. The other explorers represent every century from the fifteenth to the twentieth. The eight Spanish explorers are from the fifteenth and sixteenth centuries; the three representing French interests explored in the seventeenth century; one of the two English explorers was active in the early years of the seventeenth century, and the other explored in the latter part of the eighteenth century. Four Americans and one French-Canadian explored the American West during the 1880s, and two Americans traveled to the polar regions in the twentieth century.

Individuals representing the different periods in the settling and colonizing of the United States have been honored on stamps, beginning with the English settlers who arrived in the New World at the end of the sixteenth century. Others from England and the Netherlands came during the seventeenth and eighteenth centuries. During the eighteenth century, pioneers and colonists moved westward away from the Atlantic coast, and in the nineteenth century others ventured to the Far West and the Pacific coast.

The history of the early years of the American republic is well reflected in U.S. stamps, as shown by the large number of stamps honoring explorers, settlers, Indian leaders, and those who participated in the Revolutionary War. There are thirty-six persons who fought in the Revolutionary War listed in the Military category; nineteen explorers ranging from Leif Erikson to John Fremont of the nineteenth century; eighteen settlers, pioneers, and colonists; eight heroes, heroines, and patriots of the Revolutionary War; and five Indian leaders. These groups contain eighty-six individuals active from the year 1000 to the 1850s, representing 25 percent of all persons listed in Table 45.

The seventeen inventors are responsible for inventing or improving and refining such apparatuses and devices as the printing press, telephone, telegraph, photographic equipment, radio, phonograph, motion pictures, incandescent electric lamp, sewing machine, cotton gin, bifocal eyeglasses, a grain-reaping machine, ships, airplanes, and automobiles. All the inventors, except Gutenberg and Marconi, were Americans.

More than three-fourths of the social reformers and civic leaders are women. Six women were very active in the woman's rights movement. The other seven women gave their time to help others, improve society, and make the country better for everyone, especially the poor, the sick, the handicapped, and minorities. Of the four men in this group, two struggled to make life better for American blacks; one was a conservationist; and the other one improved American lives through a law to ensure pure food and drugs for consumers.

The writers were categorized into four groups: nonfiction writers, novelists and story writers, poets, and playwrights. Although poetry is not as popular as other literary forms, more poets have been honored on stamps than any of the other categories of writers. Sixteen, or almost one-half of the writers, are poets. The nine nonfiction writers include two historians, a lexicographer, two writers on nature, a philosopher, an abolitionist, a writer on blindness, and one who wrote aphorisms and other witty pieces. Three of the novelists and story writers are women, and five are men. The three playwrights are men. All but four of the thirty-six writers are Americans; these four are Carlyle, Dante, Donne, and Shakespeare. Dante was an Italian poet of the thirteenth and fourteenth centuries; Donne and Shakespeare were English contemporaries who lived at the end of the sixteenth century and the first years of the seventeenth century. Carlyle was a nineteenth-century Scottish essayist and historian. The Americans range from the eighteenth century to the twentieth. Franklin, Paine, and Webster wrote during the eighteenth century. Although Webster wrote and published in the 1700s, his great work, an American English dictionary, was published in 1828. Nineteen (or almost 60 percent) of the American writers are from the nineteenth century, and ten (31.25 percent) produced their literary works in the twentieth century.

All but two of the eleven persons in the field of music were composers as well as musicians. Francis Scott Key and Jimmie Rodgers were the two who were not composers. Key was a lawyer and poet who wrote the poem that later became the words of the American national anthem. Jimmie Rodgers was the only one in this group who gained his fame as a singer, making country music part of the nation's heritage.

The ten educators are Americans. Bell, Carver, Dewey, and Sullivan were active both in the nineteenth and twentieth centuries. The other six made their major contributions to the field of education in the nineteenth century.

Only three actors have been honored on U.S. stamps, and these three were contemporaries. No actress has yet been so honored.

Frank Lloyd Wright is the only twentieth-century architect among the nine architects honored on stamps. The others were all active in the eighteenth and nineteenth centuries.

The group of eight aviation pioneers consists of four pilots and four persons who designed and experimented with aircraft. Scott and Earhart were women pilots, and Lindbergh and Post were record-making pilots in their day. Chanute, Curtiss, and the Wright brothers laid the foundation for modern aviation.

Of the five persons listed as businesspersons and industrialists, Carnegie, Eastman, and Ford are also known for their philanthropy. Mellon did, however, give his large art collection to the federal government along with sufficient funds to construct and endow the National Gallery of Art. Giannini founded the Bank of America, the largest bank in the United States, and the largest private bank in the world.

Four of the five engineers are Americans, all of whom were involved in transportation. Fulton and Ericsson designed ships; Chanute built railroads and railroad bridges and experimented with aerodynamics; Goethals worked on canals and later directed the construction of the Panama Canal. Marconi, an Italian, was an electrical engineer.

Three of the Indian leaders, Powhatan, Pocahontas, and Shadoo, befriended the English settlers who arrived in the seventeenth century. Joseph, chief of the Nez Percé, and Sequoyah were concerned with improving the lives of the Indians during the nineteenth century.

The earliest of the famous American newspapermen honored on stamps is Benjamin Franklin. The nineteenth-century newspapermen are Douglass, Greeley, Harris, and Pulitzer. Those of the twentieth century are White, Ochs, and Pyle.

Two nurses and seven physicians represent the field of medicine. The two nurses were women, and just one of the physicians was a woman.

Griffith and Disney are the only producers of motion pictures to be honored on stamps. Griffith was a pioneer in cinematic art, and Disney was a pioneer in the production of animated motion picture cartoons.

The three persons classified as painting subjects made no important contribution in another field, and their claim to fame is the fact that they were the subjects of paintings used on stamps to honor other persons or events.

The three men listed because of their philosophical works were also included in other areas. Paine was also considered as a patriot of the Revolution, Dewey as an educator, and Thoreau as a nonfiction writer.

Two of the three individuals considered as printers are known only for this reason: Gutenberg invented the printing press with movable type, and Daye was the first printer in the English colonies in America. Franklin was a person with many interests and talents, and one of these was printing.

The only persons to be honored on U.S. stamps solely for religious reasons are the Baby Jesus; his mother, Mary; and Mary's husband, Joseph. They are depicted only on Christmas stamps.

The nine scientists honored on stamps include Audubon, a zoologist; Powell, a geologist; Burbank, a horticulturist; two physicists, Goddard and Einstein; two who were astronomers and mathematicians, Banneker and Copernicus; and two chemists: Carver was an agronomist and agricultural chemist, and Wiley, a food analyst.

Only one person has been honored on a stamp because of a sport, James Naismith. America's most popular ball games in rank order are baseball, football, and basketball; but, Naismith, the originator of basketball, is the only person honored on a stamp in relation to a sport. No individual in football or baseball has ever been so honored.

There are four major categories that have only one person listed in them. These are the astronaut, Neil Armstrong; the judge, John Bassett Moore; the labor leader, Samuel Gompers; and Casey Jones, the railroad engineer.

From the above information concerning the persons honored on stamps, it can be seen that a wide array of individuals from many professions, occupations, and activities during all eras of American history are well represented. Although persons in politics and the military predominate, there is an abundance of persons exemplifying other professions and fields of endeavor to prove that U.S. stamps give credit to those who made valuable social, economic, cultural, and scientific contributions to the progress and growth of the American republic.

12 Persons Honored While Alive or Less Than Ten Years after Death

Stamps are often used as a means to honor our national heroes, prominent persons, and others who have made valuable contributions to society and humankind in general. Postmasters General have expressed this same view with such statements as:

The postage stamps of a nation are a picture gallery of its glories. They depict in miniature its famous men and women, the great events of its history, its organizations, its industries, its natural wonders. —Arthur E. Summerfield[1]

Postage stamps are a pictorial history of all the arts, sciences, and human progress since earliest civilization. Stamps have been, and will continue to be, a bond of communication between peoples of the world. They provide a means of satisfying man's eternal quest for knowledge of his fellowmen by graphically portraying the culture, history, famous individuals and scenic wonders of the nations of the world.
—John A. Gronouski[2]

Our stamps remind us, and tell others, of our most cherished beliefs. They recall the men and women whose contributions carved our civilization from a wilderness and shielded our liberties from onslaughts of tyranny. Our stamps have helped to strengthen our resolve in time of war and they have reiterated our basic commitment to peace. — Lawrence F. O'Brien[3]

During the first nineteen years, 1847-1865, of U.S. postage stamp history, only four individuals were honored on stamps, namely, Benjamin Franklin, George Washington, Thomas Jefferson, and Andrew Jackson. All four were dead several years before they were so honored; Franklin had been dead for fifty-seven years, Washington for forty-eight, Jefferson was dead for thirty years, and Jackson for eighteen years. Although there was no law prohibiting the portrayal of living persons on stamps during those early years, only persons long deceased were honored on U.S. stamps. It was not until 1866 that such a law was passed; an appropriations bill passed by the Thirty-Ninth Congress dated April 7, 1866, includes the following item:

For plates, engraving, printing, and paper for national currency notes, two hundred and fifty thousand dollars: Provided, that no portrait or likeness of any living persons hereafter engraved, shall be placed upon any of the bonds, securities, notes, fractional or postal currency of the United States.[4]

The above statement is the source for the current law in the *United States Code* which reads:

No portrait shall be placed upon any of the bonds, securities, notes, fractional or postal currency of the United States, while the original of such portrait is living.[5]

There is no federal law stating that a living person cannot be "honored" on a stamp, only that no one can be portrayed while alive. Also, there is no law indicating the length of time that must elapse after a person's death before portrayal on a U.S. postage stamp. There are, however, standards which serve as guidelines for the selection of individuals who are to be portrayed. On March 26, 1957, a Citizens' Stamp Advisory Committee was established; it was made up of people outside the U.S. Postal Service. The purpose of the Committee was to advise on matters relating to the subject matter, design, production, and issuance of postage stamps with the most appropriate and appealing themes.[6] The standards or criteria for the selection of individuals to be portrayed on stamps have changed over the years. The following paragraphs point out the major differences that have evolved in the selection of individuals since the Citizens' Stamp Advisory Committee was established in 1957.

Because federal law prohibits the portrayal of any living person on a U.S. postage stamp, the various editions of the standards for the selection of subjects for stamps always include the statement: "No living person shall be honored by portrayal on any United States postage stamp." One of the seven criteria adopted by the Citizens' Stamp Advisory Committee on August 30, 1957, and published in the 1958 edition of the standards for commemorative stamps, was the following: "No American citizen may be honored by a United States commemorative postage stamp until at least 25 years after death."[7] The reason for such an untenable statement is not known. It seems very strange indeed that the Committee would approve a criterion making it impossible for American citizens to be on stamps until twenty-five years after death, while at the same time allowing aliens with resident status in this country and foreigners living outside our borders to be honored on stamps at any time after death. This is precisely what did happen because the following year two stamps were issued to honor Ernst Reuter, mayor of West Berlin. Reuter died on September 29, 1953, and exactly six years later on September 29, 1959, Reuter was depicted on two stamps in the Champion of Liberty series (Scott Numbers 1136 and 1137). Another set of two stamps in the same series was issued on October 26, 1960 honoring Carl Gustaf Emil Mannerheim, former president of Finland, who had only been dead since 1951 (Scott Numbers 1165 and 1166).

The definite referral to commemorative stamps in the above criterion implies that Americans who have been dead for less than twenty-five years may be honored on regular issues or memorial stamps. The definitions of "regular stamps" (regular issues) and "memorial stamps" published in the 1958 edition of the standards for stamp selection are:

1. Regular stamps, ranging in denomination from 1/2 cent to $5 are kept in constant supply. Portraits of former Presidents, other prominent persons, and national shrines are traditionally the subjects.
2. Memorial stamps are infrequently issued to honor an American official who dies in office.[8]

Because the criterion adopted in 1957 refers exclusively to U.S. commemorative stamps, it allows for American citizens who have been dead for less than twenty-five years to be honored on either "regular stamps" or "memorial stamps," but not on "commemoratives." By any dictionary definition a "commemorative stamp" honoring an individual is also a "memorial stamp."

In 1960, three stamps (Scott Numbers 1161, 1170, and 1172) were issued portraying three American statesmen; two had been Senators and the other one was a former Secretary of State; all three had been dead for less than eight years. A stamp was issued on October 10, 1960 portraying Senator Robert Alphonse Taft, who had died slightly more than seven years earlier. Just three weeks after the Taft stamp came out, another one was issued on November 5 depicting Walter Franklin George, who had died three years earlier. A month later on December 6, a stamp bearing the likeness of the former Secretary of State, John Foster Dulles, was issued; Dulles had died on May 24, 1959. At the time of death, Taft was a Senator and George was President Eisenhower's special ambassador to the North Atlantic Treaty Organization, but Dulles had resigned his office thirty-nine days before his death and therefore did not die in office. Although it may seem to be a purely academic question, one might ask if the stamps portraying these three individuals are "regular issues" or "memorial stamps," or were the criteria adopted in 1957 simply not observed. Later editions of the standards for stamp selection published in 1973 and 1977 redefined "memorial stamps." The new definition is: "Memorial stamps are presently issued only for the purpose of honoring recently deceased American presidents."[9]

None of the members of the Citizens' Stamp Advisory Committee who adopted the criteria in 1957 were members of the committee when other editions of the criteria were published in 1964 and 1966. The criteria in these editions do not include any statement concerning the length of time after death that must elapse before an American citizen or anyone else may be portrayed on a postage stamp.[10] The 1973 edition of the standards for the selection of stamp subjects, however, does include definite statements concerning the length of time after death that must elapse before an individual may be portrayed on a U.S. stamp. The first two criteria listed in this edition are:

1. Living persons. No living person shall be honored by portrayal on any United States postage stamp.
2. Significant Anniversaries. All postage stamps, including commemoratives, honoring individuals will be issued preferably on significant anniversaries of their births, and not before ten years after their deaths. The exceptions are memorial stamps and regular issues honoring recently deceased presidents.[11]

Between the publication of the 1957 standards in January 1958 and the standards that came out in February 1973, there were twenty-three stamps issued portraying eighteen individuals who had been dead for less than ten years. The length of time between death and the issuance of a stamp ranges from 101 days to nine years and nine months. After the 1973 standards were published, two stamps were issued portraying two individuals who had been dead for less than a year, but they were the former Presidents, Harry S Truman and Lyndon B. Johnson (Scott Numbers 1499 and 1503). They died less than a month apart; Truman died in December 1972, and a stamp bearing his likeness came out in May 1973; Johnson died in January 1973 and was portrayed on a stamp in August of that year. Because the 1973 standards made an exception for recently deceased presidents, the issuance of these two stamps fell into the guidelines set by the new standards.

The current standards were published in October 1977; they are similar to those of 1973, although the wording is slightly changed. The first two criteria for stamp selection in the 1977 edition read:

1. Living Persons. No living person shall be honored by portrayal on any United States postage stamp. A person may be portrayed on a postage stamp ten years after his or her death.

2. Significant Anniversaries. All postage stamps, including commemoratives, honoring individuals will be issued preferably on significant anniversaries of their births. The exceptions are memorial stamps and regular issues honoring recently deceased presidents. A former president may be honored with a stamp on his first birthdate following his death.[12]

The criteria listed in the 1973 and 1977 editions of *Stamp Selection: Who and Why* concerning the length of time that must elapse after death before anyone may be portrayed on a postage stamp have been fully heeded. Table 46 lists all the stamps issued since 1973 which depict individuals who have died since 1962. The data in the table point out that all but two of them were dead for more than ten years before their portrayal on a stamp. The two exceptions are former Presidents, Truman and Johnson, and the criteria indicate that stamps may be issued on their first birthdates following death. The stamps honoring these two presidents were issued in 1973 on their respective birthdays, May 8 and August 27.

Neither the criteria for stamp selection nor federal law indicate that a living person may not be honored on a postage stamp; the only indication is that no one may be "honored by portrayal" until after death. This implies that stamps may be emitted to honor living persons by including their names in the design of the stamps. There are eight individuals who have been honored on stamps while alive; they are listed at the beginning of Table 47. The first of these was Charles A. Lindbergh who was honored on an air mail stamp giving tribute to him for his nonstop flight from New York to Paris in May 1927. This stamp (Scott Number C10) came out just three weeks after his historic flight; the legend on the stamp includes the words "United States Postage—Lindbergh—Air Mail." In 1929, a stamp was issued to commemorate the fiftieth anniversary of the invention of the first incandescent electric lamp by Thomas Alva Edison and the inscription reads: "Edison's First Lamp—Electric Light's Golden Jubilee." Four years later in 1933, a stamp was issued for use on letters mailed through the Little America post office in the territory of the South Pole. This stamp (Scott Number 733) honors Richard Evelyn Byrd and his expeditionary crew who discovered new lands and mapped unknown parts of Antarctica; the inscription contains the words "Byrd Antarctic Expedition II." Three astronauts, Neil A. Armstrong, Edwin E. Aldrin, and Michael Collins, piloted the spacecraft *Apollo XI* to the moon in 1969. On July 20, they landed on the surface of the moon in the lunar landing module *Eagle*, and Armstrong was the first one to descend the ladder and touch the moon's surface. Less than two months later, a stamp (Scott Number C76) came out commemorating this event. Armstrong's name does not appear on the stamp, nor is his face visible, but the design includes a drawing of a man in a spacesuit setting foot on the moon's surface; the inscription reads: "First Man on the Moon." Because Armstrong was the first man on the moon, the figure in the draw-

Table 46

Individuals Deceased Since 1962 and Portrayed on Stamps Issued from 1973 to 1980 —Arranged by Scott Number

Scott Number	Name	Death Date	Date of Issuance of Stamp	Time Lapse between Death and Issuance
1485	Jeffers, Robinson	January 20, 1962	August 13, 1973	11 years, 205 days
1499	Truman, Harry S	December 26, 1972	May 8, 1973	0 years, 133 days
1503	Johnson, Lyndon B.	January 22, 1973	August 27, 1973	0 years, 217 days
1526	Frost, Robert	January 29, 1963	March 26, 1974	11 years, 56 days
1731	Sandburg, Carl	July 22, 1967	January 6, 1978	10 years, 168 days
1754	Papanicolaou, George N.	February 19, 1962	May 13, 1978	16 years, 83 days
1770	Kennedy, Robert Francis	June 6, 1968	January 12, 1979	10 years, 220 days
1771	King, Martin Luther, Jr.	April 4, 1968	January 13, 1979	10 years, 284 days
1773	Steinbeck, John	December 20, 1968	February 27, 1979	10 years, 69 days
1821	Perkins, Frances	May 14, 1965	April 10, 1980	14 years, 332 days
1824	Keller, Helen	June 1, 1968	June 27, 1980	12 years, 26 days
C99	Scott, Blanche Stuart	January 12, 1970	December 30, 1980	10 years, 353 days

ing must therefore represent Armstrong. Another person in this group of individuals honored on stamps while alive is Thomas Hart Benton; part of his mural *Independence and the Opening of the West* was used as the design of the stamp commemorating the sesquicentennial of Missouri's admission to the Union (Scott Number 1426). Benton's name appears on the stamp and according to the criteria set forth in Chapter 3, this qualifies Benton to be considered as an individual honored on a stamp. The remaining three persons honored while alive are the three marines, John Bradley, Rene Gagnon, and Ira Hayes who were on the stamp depicting the six marines raising the flag on Mount Suribachi on Iwo Jima during World War II (Scott Number 929); the other three marines, Harlon Block, Franklin Sousley, and Michael Strank, did not survive the battle of Iwo Jima.

The first person ever to be honored on U.S. stamp shortly after death was Abraham Lincoln. He was also the fifth individual to be honored on U.S. stamps; the four who preceded him were Benjamin Franklin, George Washington, Thomas Jefferson, and Andrew Jackson. Lincoln was shot on April 14, 1865 and died the following morning; a fifteen-cent stamp (Scott Number 77) was issued in his honor a little over a year later.[13] The next person to be portrayed on a stamp soon after dying was Edwin M. Stanton (Scott Number 149); he died in 1869 and less than fifteen months later a stamp came out in his honor. President James Garfield was shot on July 2, 1881, died on September 19, and on April 10, 1882 a stamp bearing his likeness was issued (Scott Number 205).

A perusal of the data listed in Table 47 shows that from 1882 until 1973 there were nineteen stamps honoring seventeen different individuals who had died less than a year before the issuance of a stamp in their honor. The first of these was Franklin D. Roosevelt, who died on April 12, 1945; a stamp bearing his name and the legend "Towards United Nations, April 25, 1945" went on sale in San Francisco on April 25, 1945 (Scott Number 928). This stamp had been planned before Roosevelt's death and its purpose was to observe the meeting of delegates from more than fifty countries to draft a charter for the United Nations, as well as a tribute to Roosevelt for his efforts to create an international organization to promote and maintain peace among nations. The stamp was intended as a tribute to Roosevelt while alive, but his sudden death prevented this, and instead, it paid homage to him after death. A series of four stamps portraying Roosevelt was issued between July 1945 and January 1946; no other recently deceased president has ever been honored in this way.

The shortest time that elapsed between the death of a person and the appearance of a stamp portraying him was just twenty-nine days. This happened in 1923 when President Warren G. Harding died suddenly in San Francisco on August 2, and a stamp bearing his likeness came out on September 1. Besides Harding and Roosevelt, seven other presidents have been

Table 47

**Persons Honored on Stamps Less Than Ten Years after Death or While Alive
—Arranged by the Length of Time between Death and Issuance of the Stamp**

Name	Birth and Death Dates	Date of Issuance of Stamp	Time Lapse Between Death and Issuance	Honored or Depicted	Scott Number
Armstrong, Neil Alden	August 5, 1930-	September 9, 1969	0*	Honored	C76
Benton, Thomas Hart	April 15, 1889-January 19, 1975	May 8, 1971	0*	Honored	1426
Bradley, John Henry	July 10, 1923-	July 11, 1945	0*	Depicted	929
Byrd, Richard Evelyn	October 25, 1888-March 11, 1957	October 9, 1933	0*	Honored	733
Edison, Thomas Alva	February 11, 1847-October 9, 1931	June 5, 1929	0*	Honored	654
Gagnon, Rene Arthur	March 7, 1926-	July 11, 1945	0*	Depicted	929
Hayes, Ira Hamilton	January 12, 1923-January 24, 1955	July 11, 1945	0*	Depicted	929
Lindbergh, Charles Augustus	February 4, 1902-August 26, 1974	June 18, 1927	0*	Honored	C10
Roosevelt, Franklin Delano	January 30, 1882-April 12, 1945	April 25, 1945	0 years, 13 days	Honored	928
Harding, Warren G.	November 2, 1865-August 2, 1923	September 1, 1923	0 years, 29 days	Depicted	610
Roosevelt, Franklin Delano	January 30, 1882-April 12, 1945	June 27, 1945	0 years, 76 days	Depicted	932
Taft, William Howard	September 15, 1857-March 8, 1930	June 4, 1930	0 years, 88 days	Depicted	685
Stevenson, Adlai Ewing	February 5, 1900-July 14, 1965	October 23, 1965	0 years, 101 days	Depicted	1275
Roosevelt, Franklin Delano	January 30, 1882-April 12, 1945	July 26, 1945	0 years, 105 days	Depicted	930
Churchill, Winston	November 30, 1874-January 24, 1965	May 13, 1965	0 years, 109 days	Depicted	1264
Sousley, Franklin Runyon	September 19, 1925-March 21, 1945	July 11, 1945	0 years, 112 days	Depicted	929
Block, Harlon Henry	November 6, 1924-March 1, 1945	July 11, 1945	0 years, 132 days	Depicted	929
Strank, Michael	November 10, 1919-March 1, 1945	July 11, 1945	0 years, 132 days	Depicted	929
Truman, Harry S	May 8, 1884-December 26, 1972	May 8, 1973	0 years, 133 days	Depicted	1499
Roosevelt, Franklin Delano	January 30, 1882-April 12, 1945	August 24, 1945	0 years, 134 days	Depicted	931
Magsaysay, Ramon	August 31, 1907-March 17, 1957	August 31, 1957	0 years, 167 days	Depicted	1096
Kennedy, John Fitzgerald	May 29, 1917-November 22, 1963	May 29, 1964	0 years, 189 days	Depicted	1246
Eisenhower, Dwight David	October 14, 1890-March 28, 1969	October 14, 1969	0 years, 200 days	Depicted	1383
Garfield, James Abram	November 19, 1831-September 19, 1881	April 10, 1882	0 years, 203 days	Depicted	205
Johnson, Lyndon B.	August 27, 1908-January 22, 1973	August 27, 1973	0 years, 217 days	Depicted	1503
Roosevelt, Franklin Delano	January 30, 1882-April 12, 1945	January 30, 1946	0 years, 293 days	Depicted	933
Hoover, Herbert	August 10, 1874-October 20, 1964	August 10, 1965	0 years, 295 days	Depicted	1269
Rayburn, Sam	January 6, 1882-November 16, 1961	September 16, 1962	0 years, 304 days	Depicted	1202

Table 47—*Continued*

Name	Dates	Date	Age		Number
Roosevelt, Eleanor	October 11, 1884-November 7, 1962	October 11, 1963	0 years, 338 days	Depicted	1236
Hammarskjold, Dag	July 29, 1905-September 18, 1961	October 23, 1962	1 year, 35 days	Depicted	1203
Smith, Alfred Emanuel	December 30, 1873-October 4, 1944	November 26, 1945	1 year, 53 days	Depicted	937
Lincoln, Abraham	February 12, 1809-April 15, 1865	June 17, 1866	1 year, 63 days	Depicted	77
Stanton, Edwin McMasters	December 19, 1814-December 24, 1869	March 6, 1871	1 year, 72 days	Depicted	149
Eisenhower, Dwight David	October 14, 1890-March 28, 1969	August 6, 1970	1 year, 131 days	Depicted	1393
Catt, Carrie Chapman	January 9, 1859-March 9, 1947	July 19, 1948	1 year, 132 days	Depicted	959
Dulles, John Foster	February 25, 1888-May 24, 1959	December 6, 1960	1 year, 196 days	Depicted	1172
Harding, Warren G.	November 2, 1865-August 2, 1923	March 19, 1925	1 year, 229 days	Depicted	553
Harrison, Benjamin	August 20, 1833-March 13, 1901	November 18, 1902	1 year, 250 days	Depicted	308
Disney, Walt	December 5, 1901-December 15, 1966	September 12, 1968	1 year, 272 days	Depicted	1355
Wright, Orville	August 19, 1871-January 30, 1948	December 17, 1949	1 year, 321 days	Depicted	C45
Wilson, Woodrow	December 28, 1856-February 3, 1924	December 28, 1925	1 year, 329 days	Depicted	623
Sherman, William Tecumseh	February 8, 1820-February 14, 1891	March 21, 1893	2 years, 35 days	Depicted	225
Eisenhower, Dwight David	October 14, 1890-March 28, 1969	May 10, 1971	2 years, 43 days	Depicted	1394
Stone, Harlan Fiske	October 1, 1872-April 22, 1946	August 25, 1948	2 years, 122 days	Depicted	965
McKinley, William	January 29, 1843-September 14, 1901	April 21, 1904	2 years, 220 days	Depicted	326
George, Walter Franklin	January 29, 1878-August 4, 1957	November 5, 1960	3 years, 93 days	Depicted	1170
Fox, George L.	March 15, 1900-February 3, 1943	May 28, 1948	3 years, 115 days	Depicted	956
Goode, Alexander D.	May 10, 1911-February 3, 1943	May 28, 1948	3 years, 115 days	Depicted	956
Poling, Clark V.	August 7, 1910-February 3, 1943	May 28, 1948	3 years, 115 days	Depicted	956
Washington, John P.	July 16, 1908-February 3, 1943	May 28, 1948	3 years, 115 days	Depicted	956
Kennedy, John Fitzgerald	May 29, 1917-November 22, 1963	May 29, 1967	3 years, 188 days	Depicted	1287
Roosevelt, Theodore	October 27, 1858-January 6, 1919	October 27, 1922	3 years, 294 days	Depicted	557
Scott, Winfield	June 13, 1786-May 29, 1866	April 20, 1870	3 years, 326 days	Depicted	153
Lincoln, Abraham	February 12, 1809-April 15, 1865	September 9, 1869	4 years, 147 days	Depicted	122

Albers, Josef	March 19, 1888-March 25, 1976	September 12, 1980	Honored	4 years, 171 days	1833
Michael, Moina	1870-May 10, 1944	November 9, 1948	Depicted	4 years, 183 days	977
White, William Allen	February 10, 1868-January 29, 1944	July 31, 1948	Depicted	4 years, 184 days	960
Grant, Ulysses S.	April 27, 1822-July 23, 1885	June 2, 1890	Depicted	4 years, 314 days	223
Addams, Jane	September 6, 1860-May 21, 1935	April 26, 1940	Depicted	4 years, 341 days	878
Carver, George Washington	ca. 1864-January 5, 1943	January 5, 1948	Depicted	5 years, 0 days	953
Lincoln, Abraham	February 12, 1809-April 15, 1865	April 20, 1870	Depicted	5 years, 5 days	148
Coolidge, Calvin	July 4, 1872-January 5, 1933	November 17, 1938	Depicted	5 years, 316 days	834
Reuter, Ernst	January 29, 1889-September 29, 1953	September 29, 1959	Depicted	6 years, 0 days	1136-1137
MacArthur, Douglas	January 26, 1880-April 5, 1964	January 26, 1971	Depicted	6 years, 296 days	1424
Wright, Frank Lloyd	June 8, 1869-April 9, 1959	June 8, 1966	Depicted	7 years, 60 days	1280
Taft, Robert Alphonse	September 8, 1889-July 31, 1953	October 10, 1960	Depicted	7 years, 71 days	1161
Harding, Warren G.	November 2, 1865-August 2, 1923	December 1, 1930	Depicted	7 years, 121 days	684
Moses, "Grandma" Anna Mary	September 7, 1860-December 13, 1961	May 1, 1969	Honored	7 years, 139 days	1370
Patton, George Smith	November 11, 1885-December 21, 1945	November 11, 1953	Depicted	7 years, 325 days	1026
Fremont, John Charles	January 21, 1813-July 13, 1890	June 10, 1898	Depicted	7 years, 332 days	288
Marshall, George Catlett	December 31, 1880-October 16, 1959	October 24, 1967	Depicted	8 years, 8 days	1289
Sousa, John Philip	November 6, 1854-March 6, 1932	May 3, 1940	Depicted	8 years, 58 days	880
Hull, Cordell	October 2, 1871-July 23, 1955	October 6, 1963	Depicted	8 years, 74 days	1235
Garfield, James Abram	November 19, 1831-September 19, 1881	February 22, 1890	Depicted	8 years, 156 days	224
Taft, William Howard	September 15, 1857-March 8, 1930	December 8, 1938	Depicted	8 years, 275 days	831
French, Daniel Chester	April 20, 1850-October 7, 1931	September 16, 1940	Depicted	8 years, 345 days	887
Roosevelt, Theodore	October 27, 1858-January 6, 1919	August 13, 1928	Depicted	9 years, 220 days	648
Mannerheim, Carl Gustaf	June 4, 1867-January 27, 1951	October 26, 1960	Depicted	9 years, 273 days	1165-1166

*This is one of the eight individuals honored on a stamp while still alive.

portrayed on stamps within a few months of their demise, namely, William H. Taft, Harry S Truman, John F. Kennedy, Dwight D. Eisenhower, James A. Garfield, Lyndon B. Johnson, and Herbert Hoover.

Adlai E. Stevenson, former governor of Illinois and ambassador to the United Nations, died in 1965, and a stamp was issued in his honor three months after his death. Two individuals depicted on stamps shortly after their deaths were foreigners, Winston Churchill and Ramon Magsaysay. Churchill, one of the twentieth century's great leaders, was greatly respected and admired by the American people; as proof of this high esteem and admiration, a U.S. stamp portraying Churchill was issued less than four months after his death. Magsaysay, the third president of the Philippines, lost his life in an airplane crash in 1957 and was the subject of the first stamp issued in the Champion of Liberty series that came out less than six months after he was killed. Block, Sousley, and Strank, three of the six marines who raised the flag on Mount Suribachi on Iwo Jima on February 23, 1945, died in battle within a month of this famed flag-raising. In July of that same year, a stamp commemorating the battle of Iwo Jima was issued; it depicted the six marines raising the American flag on Mount Suribachi. Sam Rayburn, one of the most powerful Speakers of the House of Representatives, died in November 1961; the following September a stamp was issued portraying this Congressman. The only woman to be honored on a stamp in less than a year after death was Eleanor Roosevelt, former First Lady, who died in November 1962 and was portrayed on a stamp emitted the next October.

The other persons listed in Table 47 are those who were honored or depicted on stamps from one to ten years after death. The arrangement is by the length of time that elapsed between the death date and the date of issuance of the stamp honoring that person.

Table 48 lists in alphabetical order the sixty-four individuals who were on the seventy-two stamps in Table 47. This alphabetical listing of the individuals makes it conspicuous that almost everyone honored on two or more stamps shortly after death are former American presidents. The only exceptions are Mannerheim and Reuter; each was portrayed on two stamps in the Champion of Liberty series. The presidents honored on two or more stamps are Eisenhower, Garfield, Harding, Kennedy, Lincoln, Franklin Roosevelt, Theodore Roosevelt, and Taft. The presidents who were only honored on one stamp shortly after death are Coolidge, Grant, Harrison, Hoover, Johnson, McKinley, Truman, and Wilson. These sixteen presidents were honored on thirty (41.67 percent) of the seventy-two stamps listed in Tables 47 and 48. This definitely indicates that American presidents are the persons most frequently honored on stamps within a short period after their demise. Franklin D. Roosevelt stands out among the presidents because five stamps honoring him were issued within ten months of his death. No other president, or anyone else for that matter, has been honored by having so many stamps issued as a tribute in such a short time after death.

Abraham Lincoln was the first president and the first person to be honored on a stamp soon after death. Since that time in 1866, when a stamp was issued as a tribute to Lincoln, all but four presidents appeared on at least one stamp within six years after death. The four who were not honored for many years after dying are Chester A. Arthur, Grover Cleveland, Rutherford B. Hayes, and Andrew Johnson. Arthur died in 1886 and was not on a stamp until 1938, a period of fifty-two years. Cleveland passed away in 1908, and a stamp in his honor came out fifteen years later in 1923. Hayes had been dead for almost thirty years before a stamp honoring him was issued in 1922. Johnson is the only president ever to be impeached, and perhaps this is one of the reasons that sixty-three years elapsed between his death in 1875 and his appearance on a stamp in 1938!

Only five women are among those listed in Tables 47 and 48, namely, Jane Addams, Carrie Catt, Moina Michael, "Grandma" Moses, and Eleanor Roosevelt. "Grandma" Moses is the only one not depicted; one of her paintings was used as the stamp design.

Five foreigners have appeared on U.S. stamps within ten years of their deaths; they are Churchill, Hammarskjold, Magsaysay, Mannerheim, and Reuter. Churchill, an honorary American citizen, was depicted on a U.S. stamp within four months after dying. Magsaysay was killed in an airplane accident and appeared on a stamp less than six months later. Hammarskjold was also killed in an airplane crash, and just thirteen months elapsed before he was portrayed on a U.S. stamp. The fact that these three foreigners were portrayed on U.S. stamps so soon after death does indeed show great respect and pays them tribute afforded very few individuals, whether they be Americans or foreigners. Mannerheim and Reuter were honored with two stamps each in the "Champion of Liberty" series; those portraying Mannerheim were issued a little less than ten years after his death, and the two depicting Reuter came out exactly six years after he died.

The seventy-two stamps honoring persons while alive or less than ten years after death have been distributed according to the period in which they were issued and are presented in Table 49. Only twelve (16.67 percent) of the seventy-two stamps were issued during the first seven periods (1847-1920). More than one-half (54.16 percent) of the seventy-two stamps came out between 1941 and 1970, and during Period 10 (1941-50) almost 38 percent of the thirty-seven stamps honoring individuals honored those who had been dead less than ten years. Almost one-fourth (22.22 percent) of the seventy-two stamps came out between 1961 and 1970, but only six (8.33 percent) were issued from 1971 to 1980. Of these six stamps that came out in the last ten years (1971-80), only one has a date of issuance that would be inconsistent with the 1973 and 1977 standards. This is the stamp depicting Douglas MacArthur issued on January 26, 1971, just six years and ten months after his death. Three stamps portrayed the former presidents

Table 48
Alphabetical List of Persons Honored on Stamps Less Than Ten Years
   after Death or While Alive

Name	Scott Number	Time Lapse between Death and Issuance
Addams, Jane	878	4 yrs. 341 days
Albers, Josef	1833	4 yrs. 171 days
Armstrong, Neil Alden	C76	0*
Benton, Thomas Hart	1426	0*
Block, Harlon Henry	929	0 yrs. 132 days
Bradley, John Henry	929	0*
Byrd, Richard Evelyn	733	0*
Carver, George Washington	953	5 yrs. 0 days
Catt, Carrie C.	959	1 yr. 132 days
Churchill, Winston	1264	0 yrs. 109 days
Coolidge, Calvin	834	5 yrs. 316 days
Disney, Walt	1355	1 yr. 272 days
Dulles, John Foster	1172	1 yr. 196 days
Edison, Thomas Alva	654	0*
Eisenhower, Dwight D.	1383	0 yrs. 200 days
Eisenhower, Dwight D.	1393	1 yr. 131 days
Eisenhower, Dwight D.	1394	2 yrs. 43 days
Fox, George L.	956	3 yrs. 115 days
Fremont, John Charles	288	7 yrs. 332 days
French, Daniel Chester	887	8 yrs. 345 days
Gagnon, Rene Arthur	929	0*
Garfield, James Abram	205	0 yrs. 203 days
Garfield, James Abram	224	8 yrs. 156 days
George, Walter F.	1170	3 yrs. 93 days
Goode, Alexander D.	956	3 yrs. 115 days
Grant, Ulysses S.	223	4 yrs. 314 days
Hammarskjold, Dag	1203	1 yr. 35 days
Harding, Warren G.	610	0 yrs. 29 days
Harding, Warren G.	553	1 yr. 229 days
Harding, Warren G.	684	7 yrs. 121 days
Harrison, Benjamin	308	1 yr. 250 days
Hayes, Ira Hamilton	929	0*
Hoover, Herbert	1269	0 yrs. 295 days
Hull, Cordell	1235	8 yrs. 74 days
Johnson, Lyndon B.	1503	0 yrs. 217 days
Kennedy, John F.	1246	0 yrs. 189 days
Kennedy, John F.	1287	3 yrs. 188 days
Lincoln, Abraham	77	1 yr. 63 days
Lincoln, Abraham	122	4 yrs. 147 days
Lincoln, Abraham	148	5 yrs. 5 days
Lindbergh, Charles A.	C10	0*
MacArthur, Douglas	1424	6 yrs. 296 days

Table 48—*Continued*

Name	Scott Number	Time Lapse between Death and Issuance
McKinley, William	326	2 yrs. 220 days
Magsaysay, Ramon	1096	0 yrs. 167 days
Mannerheim, Carl Gustaf	1165-1166	9 yrs. 273 days
Marshall, George C.	1289	8 yrs. 8 days
Michael, Moina	977	4 yrs. 183 days
Moses, "Grandma"	1370	7 yrs. 139 days
Patton, George Smith	1026	7 yrs. 325 days
Poling, Clark V.	956	3 yrs. 115 days
Rayburn, Sam	1202	0 yrs. 304 days
Reuter, Ernst	1136-1137	6 yrs. 0 days
Roosevelt, Eleanor	1236	0 yrs. 338 days
Roosevelt, Franklin D.	928	0 yrs. 13 days
Roosevelt, Franklin D.	932	0 yrs. 76 days
Roosevelt, Franklin D.	930	0 yrs. 105 days
Roosevelt, Franklin D.	931	0 yrs. 134 days
Roosevelt, Franklin D.	933	0 yrs. 293 days
Roosevelt, Theodore	557	3 yrs. 294 days
Roosevelt, Theodore	648	9 yrs. 220 days
Scott, Winfield	153	3 yrs. 326 days
Sherman, William T.	225	2 yrs. 35 days
Smith, Alfred E.	937	1 yr. 53 days
Sousa, John Philip	880	8 yrs. 58 days
Sousley, Franklin Runyon	929	0 yrs. 112 days
Stanton, Edwin M.	149	1 yr. 72 days
Stevenson, Adlai E.	1275	0 yrs. 101 days
Stone, Harlan Fiske	965	2 yrs. 122 days
Strank, Michael	929	0 yrs. 132 days
Taft, Robert Alphonse	1161	7 yrs. 71 days
Taft, William Howard	685	0 yrs. 88 days
Taft, William Howard	831	8 yrs. 275 days
Truman, Harry S	1499	0 yrs. 133 days
Washington, John P.	956	3 yrs. 115 days
White, William Allen	960	4 yrs. 184 days
Wilson, Woodrow	623	1 yr. 329 days
Wright, Frank Lloyd	1280	7 yrs. 60 days
Wright, Orville	C45	1 yr. 321 days

*This is one of the eight individuals honored on a stamp while still alive.

Table 49

Comparison of Stamps Honoring Persons Less Than Ten Years after Death or While Alive with the Number of Person Stamps Issued during Each Period

Period	Number of Person Stamps	Number of Stamps Honoring Persons Less Than Ten Years After Death	Percentage
1. 1847-60	10	0	—
2. 1861-70	25	4	5.56
3. 1871-80	2	1	1.39
4. 1881-90	10	3	4.17
5. 1891-1900	27	2	2.78
6. 1901-10	36	2	2.78
7. 1911-20	18	0	—
8. 1921-30	34	9	12.50
9. 1931-40	109	6	8.33
10. 1941-50	37	14	19.44
11. 1951-60	77	9	12.50
12. 1961-70	82	16	22.22
13. 1971-80	118	6	8.33
Total	585	72	100.00

Eisenhower, Johnson, and Truman. The other two stamps honored painters; works of Josef Albers and Thomas Benton were used as the central design which included their names, but they were not portrayed.

If the current standards for the selection of persons to be portrayed on stamps are observed, then the next person to be depicted on a stamp shortly after death probably will be one of the following: Richard M. Nixon, Gerald Ford, Jimmy Carter, or Ronald Reagan. Undoubtedly each of these four will be portrayed on a stamp on his next birthday following his demise. Other persons may be honored while alive or shortly after death, but will not be depicted.

SUMMARY

Persons honored on U.S. stamps may be depicted or just have their names included in the stamp design. Most persons are honored on stamps long after they have died, but a few are honored very soon after dying, and occasionally some are honored while alive. Of the 464 individuals honored on U.S. stamps, eight (1.72 percent) were honored while alive; seventeen (3.66 percent) were honored within one year of death; thirty-nine (8.41 percent) appeared on stamps between one and ten years after death; and 400

(86.21 percent) had been dead for more than ten years before they were honored on a U.S. postage stamp.

Prior to the establishment of the Citizens' Stamp Advisory Committee in 1957, the basic criterion for the selection of persons to be honored on stamps was the federal law prohibiting the portrayal of living persons on U.S. stamps. The first set of seven criteria published in 1958 included one which stated that no American citizen could be honored on a U.S. commemorative stamp until at least twenty-five years after death. This standard or criterion was in effect for a very short time. Later editions of the standards published in 1964 and 1966 did not include any indication concerning the length of time that must elapse between death and the date of issuance of a stamp in that person's honor. The editions of 1973 and 1977 set forth the criterion that persons could not be portrayed until ten years after death, but an exception was made for recently deceased American presidents. Since the establishment of this criterion, no one, except, of course, a former president, has been portrayed before the tenth anniversary of the person's death.

The sixty-four individuals honored on stamps soon after their demise or while alive include sixteen presidents who comprise exactly one-fourth of all those in this category. These sixteen presidents appeared on thirty (41.67 percent) of the seventy-two stamps listed in Tables 47 and 48. Only four deceased presidents since Lincoln have not been honored on stamps shortly after death, namely, Chester Arthur, Grover Cleveland, Rutherford B. Hayes, and Andrew Johnson.

Five foreigners were in this group of persons honored on stamps before they had been dead for ten years. Two of these, Churchill and Magsaysay, were portrayed on stamps before they had been dead for six months. Hammarskjold was dead for just thirteen months when he appeared on a stamp. Reuter was dead for six years; and Mannerheim had been dead for almost ten years before being honored on two U.S. stamps.

No standard or federal law prevents a living person from being honored on a U.S. stamp, but both prohibit portrayal of anyone who is not deceased. In the future, the only persons who will be portrayed on stamps shortly after death will be former presidents; all others must wait for ten years. Some artists may see their works and names in stamp designs while alive, but they will not be portrayed. Perhaps a few others will see their names or their creative endeavors of one kind or another on U.S. stamps, but no one will live to see a U.S. stamp bearing his or her own likeness.

NOTES

1. U.S., Post Office Department, *A Guide for the Selection of United States Commemorative Postage Stamps* (Washington, D.C.: U.S. Government Printing Office, 1958), p. [3].

2. U.S., Post Office Department, *Standards Governing the Issuance of United States Commemorative Postage Stamps* (Washington, D.C.: U.S. Government Printing Office, 1964), p. [3].

3. U.S., Post Office Department, *Standards for United States Commemorative Postage Stamps* (Washington, D.C.: U.S. Government Printing Office, 1966), p. [3].

4. An Act Making Additional Appropriations . . . , April 7, 1866. *U.S., Statutes at Large*, vol. 14, chap. 28, sec. 12, p. 25.

5. *United States Code*, 1976 ed., Title 31—Money and Finance, sec. 413, p. 1307.

6. U.S., Post Office Department, *A Guide for the Selection of United States Commemorative Postage Stamps* (Washington, D.C.: U.S. Government Printing Office, 1958), p. 4.

7. Ibid., p. 10.

8. Ibid., p. 6.

9. U.S., Postal Service, *Stamp Selection: Who and Why* (Washington, D.C.: U.S. Government Printing Office, 1973), p. [6]; U.S., Postal Service, *Stamp Selection: Who and Why* (Washington, D.C.: U.S. Government Printing Office, 1977), p. [6].

10. U.S., Post Office Department, *Standards Governing the Issuance of United States Commemorative Postage Stamps* (Washington, D.C.: U.S. Government Printing Office, 1964), 15 pp.; U.S., Post Office Department, *Standards for United States Commemoraive Postage Stamps* (Washington, D.C.: U.S. Government Printing Office, 1966), 15 pp.

11. U.S., Postal Service, *Stamp Selection: Who and Why* (Washington, D.C.: U.S. Government Printing Office, 1973), p. [9].

12. U.S., Postal Service, *Stamp Selection: Who and Why* (Washington, D.C.: U.S. Government Printing Office, 1977), p. [9].

13. The exact date of the issuance of this stamp differs in various sources. The U.S. Postal Service's publication *United States Postage Stamps* gives the date as June 17, 1866; the *Scott Specialized Catalogue of United States Stamps* lists the date as May 1866; and the *Minkus New American Stamp Catalog* gives the date as April 15, 1866.

13 The Most Frequently Honored Individuals

There can be no doubt that it is an indication of high esteem and regard for anyone to be honored on a U.S. postage stamp. This is even more evident when one learns that throughout the history of U.S. postage stamps only 464 individuals have been so honored. Because so few individuals are honored on stamps, it is reasonable to assume that only the most highly revered individuals are honored on more than one stamp. The eminence and historical importance of any individual may be measured by the number of times one's likeness or name is included in the design of different postage stamps. Only 134 (28.88 percent) of the 464 individuals have been honored on two or more stamps; the other 330 (71.12 percent) have been on just one stamp.

Table 50 tabulates the number of "individuals" with the number of times each has been on a stamp and points out the number of "persons" on the stamps that these "individuals" represent. The difference between "person" and "individual" was explained in Chapter 7, where it was specified that the 873 persons are made up of only 464 different individuals because many individuals have been on two or more stamps. For example, Benjamin Franklin has been on thirty-eight stamps and accounts for thirty-eight of the 873 persons, although he is only one of the 464 individuals. A study of Table 50 shows that just six individuals (1.3 percent of the 464 individuals) comprise more than one-fifth (20.74 percent) of the 873 persons who have

FREQUENTLY HONORED INDIVIDUALS

Table 50
Individuals and the Number of Stamps on Which Each Was Honored

Individuals		Number of Stamps on Which Each Individual Was Honored	Persons	
Number	%		*Number*	%
330	71.12	1	330	37.80
81	17.45	2	162	18.56
23	4.95	3	69	7.90
10	2.15	4	40	4.58
5	1.07	5	25	2.86
4	0.86	6	24	2.75
2	0.43	7	14	1.60
1	0.22	8	8	0.92
2	0.43	10	20	2.29
1	0.22	11	11	1.26
1	0.22	18	18	2.06
1	0.22	19	19	2.18
1	0.22	21	21	2.41
1	0.22	38	38	4.35
1	0.22	74	74	8.48
Total				
464	100.00		873	100.00

ever been honored on U.S. postage stamps. These six individuals have appeared 181 times! The information given in Table 50 also points out that the thirty most frequently honored individuals constitute almost the same percentage (35.74 percent) of the 873 persons as do the 330 individuals honored on a single stamp, this latter group comprising 37.8 percent of all persons.

The names of the 134 individuals who appeared on two or more stamps are listed in rank order and subarranged alphabetically in Table 51. (Please refer to Appendix II for a complete alphabetical list of the 464 individuals and the Scott Numbers of the stamps on which each has appeared.) George Washington, the most frequently honored individual, has been on seventy-four stamps, almost twice as many as the second ranking individual, Benjamin Franklin. Washington and Franklin are also the two who were chosen to be on the first U.S. postage stamps issued in 1847. Since their first appearances in 1847, they have been portrayed on stamps in almost every ten-year period. Franklin was on almost double the number of stamps as the third-ranking individual, Abraham Lincoln.

Table 52 tabulates the number of stamps by period for the six most frequently portrayed individuals: George Washington, Benjamin Franklin,

Table 51
Individuals Honored on Two or More Stamps

Name	Number of Stamps	Name	Number of Stamps
Washington, George	74	Rutledge, Edward	3
Franklin, Benjamin	38	Steuben, Friedrich von	3
Lincoln, Abraham	21	Thomson, Charles	3
Jefferson, Thomas	19	Washington, Martha	3
Columbus, Christopher	18	Williams, William	3
Jackson, Andrew	11	Wilson, James	3
Jesus	10	Wilson, Woodrow	3
Mary, mother of Jesus	10	Witherspoon, John	3
Roosevelt, Theodore	8	Wolcott, Oliver	3
Isabella the Catholic	7	Wright, Orville	3
Roosevelt, Franklin D.	7	Wright, Wilbur	3
Ferdinand the Catholic	6	Adams, Samuel	2
Hamilton, Alexander	6	Anthony, Susan B.	2
Livingston, Robert R.	6	Balboa, Vasco N. de	2
Monroe, James	6	Bartlett, Josiah	2
Adams, John	5	Bell, Alexander Graham	2
Garfield, James A.	5	Bolívar, Simón	2
Grant, Ulysses S.	5	Boone, Daniel	2
Sherman, Roger	5	Buchanan, James	2
Webster, Daniel	5	Burgoyne, John	2
Dickinson, John	4	Carroll, Charles	2
Donne, John	4	Chanute, Octave	2
Harding, Warren G.	4	Chase, Samuel	2
Harrison, Benjamin (1833-1901)	4	Clark, Abraham	2
Lafayette, Marquis de	4	Cleveland, Grover	2
Lee, Robert E.	4	Clinton, George	2
Madison, James	4	Cook, James	2
Morris, Robert	4	Copley, John S.	2
Nelson, Thomas	4	Currier, Nathaniel	2
Read, George	4	Edison, Thomas A.	2
Audubon, John James	3	Einstein, Albert	2
Clay, Henry	3	Ellery, William	2
Clymer, George	3	Farragut, David	2
Eisenhower, Dwight D.	3	Floyd, William	2
Hancock, John	3	Fulton, Robert	2
Huntington, Samuel	3	Gandhi, Mahatma	2
Joseph, husband of Mary	3	Garibaldi, Giuseppe	2
Lewis, Francis	3	Gates, Horatio	2
McKean, Thomas	3	Gerry, Elbridge	2
McKinley, William	3	Harrison, Benjamin (1726-1791)	2
Marshall, John	3	Harrison, William H.	2
Perry, Oliver H.	3	Hayes, Rutherford B.	2

Table 51—*Continued*

Name	Number of Stamps	Name	Number of Stamps
Henry, Patrick	2	Peale, Charles Willson	2
Hewes, Joseph	2	Phillips, William	2
Heyward, Thomas	2	Pinzón, Martín Alonso	2
Hooper, William	2	Pinzón, Vicente Yáñez	2
Hopkins, Stephen	2	Pocahontas	2
Hopkinson, Francis	2	Post, Wiley	2
Houston, Sam	2	Prescott, William	2
Jackson, Stonewall	2	Raphael	2
Jones, John Paul	2	Remington, Frederic	2
Kennedy, John F.	2	Reuter, Ernst	2
Key, Francis Scott	2	Rogers, Will	2
Kossuth, Lajos	2	Rush, Benjamin	2
Lee, Richard H.	2	San Martín, José de	2
Livingston, Philip	2	Scott, Winfield	2
Lynch, Thomas	2	Sherman, William T.	2
Mannerheim, Carl Gustaf	2	Stockton, Richard	2
Marquette, Jacques	2	Sun, Yat-sen	2
Masaryk, Tomas G.	2	Taft, William H.	2
Memling, Hans	2	Taylor, Zachary	2
Middleton, Arthur	2	Trumbull, John	2
Morgan, Daniel	2	Walton, George	2
Morris, Lewis	2	Washington, Booker T.	2
Paca, William	2	Whipple, William	2
Paderewski, Ignacy Jan	2	Willing, Thomas	2
Paine, Robert Treat	2	Wythe, George	2

Abraham Lincoln, Thomas Jefferson, Christopher Columbus, and Andrew Jackson. Stamps honoring Washington have been issued in all but two periods (1871-80 and 1891-1900), and Franklin has been on at least one stamp in ten of the thirteen periods. Lincoln and Jefferson were on stamps that came out in nine of the thirteen periods. Lincoln first was portrayed on a stamp in 1866, a year after his assassination, and since then has been on a stamp in all but three of the subsequent periods. Lincoln is the only one of these six individuals who was alive during the early years of U.S. postage stamp history, thus explaining why he was not portrayed during Period 1 (1847-60). Portrayal of living persons on stamps was not prohibited by law until 1866, but even before the law was passed no living person had been portrayed on a U.S. postage stamp.[1] Columbus was only on stamps issued

Table 52
Number of Stamps Distributed by Period for the Six Most Frequently Honored Individuals

Period	George Washington	Benjamin Franklin	Abraham Lincoln	Thomas Jefferson	Christopher Columbus	Andrew Jackson
1. 1847-60	6	3	0	1	0	0
2. 1861-70	7	5	3	3	1	2
3. 1871-80	0	0	0	0	0	0
4. 1881-90	2	2	1	0	0	2
5. 1891-1900	0	0	0	2	16	0
6. 1901-10	13	2	2	2	0	1
7. 1911-20	3	13	0	0	0	0
8. 1921-30	6	1	1	1	0	0
9. 1931-40	20	2	2	1	0	3
10. 1941-50	2	1	2	0	0	0
11. 1951-60	6	3	8	3	1	0
12. 1961-70	2	0	1	1	0	3
13. 1971-80	7	6	1	5	0	0
Total	74	38	21	19	18	11

during three different periods, and sixteen of the eighteen stamps depicting Columbus were in the series commemorating the World's Columbian Exposition issued in 1893. The eleven stamps portraying Andrew Jackson were issued during five of the thirteen periods. Thus it can be seen that the four most frequently honored individuals, Washington, Franklin, Lincoln, and Jefferson, have also been portrayed on stamps during at least nine of the thirteen periods, proving that their eminence has not waned, but has remained steady.

Even though foreigners account for just 16.72 percent of the 873 persons honored on all U.S. stamps and only 15.73 percent of the 464 individuals, the data in Table 53 point out that the percentage of foreigners honored on two or more stamps increases while the percentage of Americans (native- and foreign-born) decreases! This implies that foreigners are more likely to be honored on two or more stamps than are Americans.

Table 53
Comparisons of the Numbers and Percentages of Americans and Foreigners Who Have Been Honored on U.S. Stamps

	Persons on All Stamps		Individuals on All Stamps		Persons Honored on Two or More Stamps		Individuals Honored on Two or More Stamps	
	No.	*%*	*No.*	*%*	*No.*	*%*	*No.*	*%*
Americans	727	83.28	391	84.27	440	81.03	106	79.10
Foreigners	146	16.72	73	15.73	103	18.97	28	20.90
Total	873	100.00	464	100.00	543	100.00	134	100.00

Twenty-eight (38.36 percent) of the seventy-three foreign individuals have been on two or more stamps, but only 106 (27.11 percent) of the 391 Americans have been so frequently honored. Of the 146 foreign persons honored on U.S. stamps there are 103 (70.55 percent) who appeared on two or more stamps, but the percentage of Americans is lower; in fact, just 440 (60.52 percent) of the 727 American persons were honored on two or more stamps. Thus, one may conclude that even though fewer foreigners than Americans are honored on U.S. stamps, a foreigner who is so honored is more likely to be on two or more stamps than is an American!

Table 54 lists in rank order the twenty-eight foreigners who have been on two or more U.S. stamps. Spain is the most represented country with five

Table 54
Foreigners Honored on Two or More Stamps

Name	Number of Stamps	Name	Number of Stamps
Columbus, Christopher	18	Garibaldi, Giuseppe	2
Jesus	10	Kossuth, Lajos	2
Mary, mother of Jesus	10	Mannerheim, Carl Gustaf	2
Isabella the Catholic	7	Marquette, Jacques	2
Ferdinand the Catholic	6	Masaryk, Tomas G.	2
Donne, John	4	Memling, Hans	2
Lafayette, Marquis de	4	Paderewski, Ignacy Jan	2
Joseph, husband of Mary	3	Phillips, William	2
Steuben, Friedrich von	3	Pinzón, Martín Alonso	2
Balboa, Vasco N. de	2	Pinzón, Vicente Yáñez	2
Bolívar, Simón	2	Raphael	2
Burgoyne, John	2	Reuter, Ernst	2
Cook, James	2	San Martín, José de	2
Gandhi, Mahatma	2	Sun, Yat-sen	2

persons (17.86 percent) followed by Great Britain with four persons (14.29 percent). The other nineteen persons represent thirteen different countries.

SUMMARY

Almost three-fourths of the individuals ever honored on U.S. stamps are represented on only one stamp. Only fifty-three (11.42 percent) of the 464 individuals have been on three or more stamps, and of these there are six individuals who account for more than 20 percent of the 873 persons. Washington and Franklin both appeared on the first U.S. postage stamps and were portrayed on more stamps than anyone else. Stamps honoring Washington, Franklin, Lincoln, and Jefferson have been issued in at least nine of the thirteen periods, showing that their prominence has not diminished over the years.

Foreigners only account for about 16 percent of the persons and individuals honored on all U.S. stamps, but an analysis of American and foreign persons honored on two or more stamps reveals that foreigners constitute about 20 percent of those appearing twice or more. From this it may be concluded that even though foreigners are honored less frequently than Americans, their chances of being on two or more stamps are greater than those of Americans!

NOTE

1. An Act Making Additional Appropriations . . ., April 7, 1866. U.S., *Statutes at Large*, vol. 14, chap. 28, sec. 12, p. 25.

14 Persons on Stamps Acclaimed by Others and Persons Acclaimed by Others But Never on U.S. Stamps

PERSONS ON STAMPS ACCLAIMED BY OTHERS

It cannot be denied that to be honored on a U.S. postage stamp is indeed a great tribute, but one may ask how else some of these 464 individuals have been honored. Many of the individuals honored on U.S. stamps have rendered valuable services to their countries or made great contributions to humankind and are acclaimed by figuring prominently in histories, encyclopedias, biographical dictionaries, general reference works, biographies, and other publications. Some have been awarded prizes and medals for outstanding feats and achievements; others are remembered and extolled for deeds, accomplishments, and other acts which have contributed to the advancement of civilization and the improvement of life for all.

One group of Americans considered to be among the most notable are those elected to the Hall of Fame for Great Americans. Eligibility for election to the Hall of Fame is based on an individual's historical significance in the arts, sciences, humanities, government, business, or labor. Another important factor is that the individual must be dead before becoming eligible to be considered and then must be voted upon by the more than one hundred members of the college of electors who represent all fifty states. The Hall of Fame for Great Americans began in 1900 with the election of twenty-nine notable Americans and ceased with the election of three individuals in 1976. From 1900 to 1976, a total of 102 persons were elected to the Hall of Fame; of these people, sixty-seven (65.69 percent) have also been honored on U.S. stamps. The names of these sixty-seven individuals are listed in Table 55. All persons elected for their contributions and achievements in the areas of politics and the military have been honored on at least one U.S. stamp. These sixty-seven individuals elected to the Hall of Fame, who also have appeared on U.S. stamps, account for just 17.14 percent of the 391 American individuals, but they have appeared on stamps 290 times and represent 39.89 percent of the 727 American persons who have been honored on U.S. stamps.

Another great honor for an individual is to have his or her achievements or contributions recognized by an award such as a Nobel Prize, a Pulitzer Prize, or the Presidential Medal of Freedom. Forty of these prizes and medals have been given to twenty-five individuals who have also been honored on U.S. stamps. The following paragraphs specify the names of these twenty-five individuals and the honors they have received.

Nobel Prizes are given for outstanding achievements in six different areas, namely, Chemistry, Economics, Literature, Peace, Physics, and Physiology and Medicine. These awards were established and funded by Alfred Nobel in his will and are considered to be a universal recognition of an individual's prominence and notable contribution to one of the six areas. Twelve individuals who have been honored on U.S. stamps have received Nobel Prizes since the first one was awarded in 1901. The first American to receive a Nobel Prize was Theodore Roosevelt, who was awarded the Nobel Peace Prize in 1906. Guglielmo Marconi and Albert Einstein received Nobel Prizes for their contributions in the field of physics. Winston Churchill, Eugene O'Neill, and John Steinbeck were awarded Prizes for their literary works. The Nobel Peace Prize has been awarded to Jane Addams, Dag Hammarskjold, Cordell Hull, Martin Luther King, Jr., George C. Marshall, Theodore Roosevelt, and Woodrow Wilson.

Joseph Pulitzer (Scott Number 946) established awards to be given annually in the areas of journalism, music, and letters (one each for a work of the following types: biography, drama, fiction, history, and poetry). The first award was made in 1917 and since that time twenty awards have been made to eleven individuals who have also been honored on U.S. stamps. These individuals and the areas of their achievements are the following: William Allen White received a Pulitzer Prize for his editorial writing and another one for his autobiography; Charles A. Lindbergh and John F. Kennedy won Prizes for their biographical writings; Eugene O'Neill was awarded four Prizes for drama; in the area of poetry Robert Frost won four Prizes; Carl Sandburg was awarded two Pulitzer Prizes for poetry and a third Prize for a historical work; another Pulitzer History Prize was given to John J. Pershing; Willa Cather, John Steinbeck, and Edith Wharton each won a Prize for a fictional work; Ernie Pyle was given a Pulitzer Prize in

Table 55

Individuals Elected to the Hall of Fame for Great Americans Who Also Have Been Honored on U.S. Postage Stamps

ARTISTS
Painters
Stuart, Gilbert Charles
Whistler, James A. M.
Sculptor
Saint Gaudens, Augustus

BUSINESSMAN AND PHILANTHROPIST
Carnegie, Andrew

EDUCATORS
Hopkins, Mark
Mann, Horace
Washington, Booker T.

FRONTIERSMAN
Boone, Daniel

INVENTORS
Bell, Alexander Graham
Edison, Thomas Alva
Fulton, Robert
Howe, Elias
Morse, Samuel F. B.
Whitney, Eli
Wright, Orville
Wright, Wilbur

JUDGES
Holmes, Oliver Wendell (1841-1935)
Marshall, John

MEDICINE
Reed, Walter

MILITARY
Farragut, David G.
Grant, Ulysses S.
Jackson, Stonewall
Jones, John Paul
Lee, Robert E.
Sherman, William T.

MUSICIANS AND COMPOSERS
Foster, Stephen Collins
MacDowell, Edward Alexander
Sousa, John Philip

POLITICIANS AND STATESMEN
Adams, John
Adams, John Quincy
Clay, Henry
Cleveland, Grover
Franklin, Benjamin
Hamilton, Alexander
Henry, Patrick
Jackson, Andrew
Jefferson, Thomas
Lincoln, Abraham
Madison, James
Monroe, James
Penn, William
Roosevelt, Franklin D.
Roosevelt, Theodore
Washington, George
Webster, Daniel
Wilson, Woodrow

RELIGION
Williams, Roger

SCIENTISTS
Audubon, John James
Burbank, Luther
Carver, George Washington

SOCIAL REFORMERS AND CIVIC LEADERS
Addams, Jane
Anthony, Susan B.
Barton, Clara
Willard, Frances E.

WRITERS
Non-Fiction
Paine, Thomas
Parkman, Francis
Thoreau, Henry David
Novelists and Story Writers
Cooper, James Fenimore
Irving, Washington
Twain, Mark
Poets
Emerson, Ralph Waldo

Table 55—*Continued*

WRITERS (*continued*)
  Poets (continued)
    Lanier, Sidney
    Longfellow, Henry W.
    Lowell, James Russell
    Poet, Edgar Allan
    Whitman, Walt
    Whittier, John Greenleaf

1944 for his outstanding service as a foreign correspondent during World War II.

The Presidential Medal of Freedom, the nation's highest civilian award, was established in 1963 and is given in recognition of meritorious service. Eight individuals also appearing on U.S. stamps have been awarded this medal. They are: Neil A. Armstrong, Walt Disney, Lyndon B. Johnson, Helen Keller, John F. Kennedy, Martin Luther King, Jr., Carl Sandburg, and John Steinbeck.

PERSONS ACCLAIMED BY OTHERS BUT NEVER ON U.S. STAMPS

HALL OF FAME FOR GREAT AMERICANS

The thirty-five individuals elected to the Hall of Fame for Great Americans who have never been honored on U.S. stamps are listed in Table 56. The following paragraphs contain brief biographical data on these thirty-five individuals.

Actors and Entertainers

Edwin Booth and Charlotte Cushman were two of the foremost actors of the nineteenth century. Both were widely acclaimed for their Shakespearian roles.

Businessmen and Philanthropists

Peter Cooper built the first American steam locomotive which was known as "Tom Thumb" (Scott Number 1006). He also introduced the Bessemer process into the American steel industry (Scott Number 1090). Cooper was the chief financial backer of the Atlantic cable (Scott Number 1112). In 1859, he founded Cooper Union in New York City, an institution devoted to free public education especially for adults.

George Peabody accumulated a vast fortune from several business enterprises, and gave most of it away during his lifetime. He founded and
endowed the Peabody Institutes in Baltimore, Maryland and in Peabody,
Massachusetts, the Peabody Museums at Harvard and Yale Universities,
and also created the Peabody Education Fund for institutions in the South.

Educators

Mary Lyon, Alice Freeman Palmer, and Emma Willard were pioneers in
the promotion of education for women in the nineteenth century. Sylvanus
Thayer, an army engineer, was also a nineteenth-century educator. Thayer
upgraded the quality of military education during his years as Superinten-
dent of the United States Military Academy at West Point (Scott Number
789) and became known as the "Father of Military Education."

Engineers and Inventors

James B. Eads invented a diving bell for salvaging sunken steamers and
their cargoes. His major achievement was the building of the Eads Bridge
across the Mississippi River at Saint Louis (Scott Number 293). George
Westinghouse invented air brakes for trains and automatic railroad signal
devices. In 1886, he organized the Westinghouse Electric Company.

Judges and Lawyers

Louis Brandeis and Joseph Story were Associate Justices of the U.S.
Supreme Court. Story served from 1811 to 1845, and Brandeis was on the
bench from 1916 to 1939. James Kent was chief judge of the New York
State Supreme Court from 1804 to 1823. Rufus Choate was an eminent jury
lawyer and also served as a U.S. Senator and Congressman during the 1830s
and 1840s.

Medicine

William Crawford Gorgas, a physician, helped rid Havana, Cuba of yellow fever mosquitoes after proving in 1901 that these mosquitoes were responsible for transmitting this disease. Walter Reed (Scott Number 877),
Clara Maass (Scott Number 1699), and William Gorgas worked together in
Cuba to discover the cause of yellow fever.

William T. G. Morton, a dentist, was the first to publicize and use ether
as an anaesthetic. Morton's claim to be the discoverer was disputed by
others, including Crawford W. Long (Scott Number 875). Even though
Morton was not the first to use ether, it was he who brought it into common
use.

Religion

Phillips Brooks was rector of Trinity Church (Scott Number 1839) in
Boston from 1869 to 1891, and author of the Christmas hymn, "O Little
Town of Bethlehem."

Table 56
Individuals Elected to the Hall of Fame for Great Americans Who Have Never Been Honored on U.S. Postage Stamps

ACTORS AND ENTERTAINERS
    Booth, Edwin
    Cushman, Charlotte S.

BUSINESSMEN AND
    PHILANTHROPISTS
    Cooper, Peter
    Peabody, George

EDUCATORS
    Lyon, Mary
    Palmer, Alice Freeman
    Thayer, Sylvanus
    Willard, Emma

ENGINEERS AND INVENTORS
    Eads, James Buchanan
    Westinghouse, George

JUDGES AND LAWYERS
    Brandeis, Louis
    Choate, Rufus
    Kent, James
    Story, Joseph

MEDICINE
    Gorgas, William Crawford
    Morton, William T. G.

RELIGION
    Brooks, Phillips
    Channing, William Ellery
    Edwards, Jonathan

SCIENTISTS
    Agassiz, Louis
    Gibbs, Josiah Willard
    Gray, Asa
    Henry, Joseph
    Maury, Matthew Fontaine
    Michelson, Albert Abraham
    Mitchell, Maria
    Newcomb, Simon

SOCIAL REFORMERS AND CIVIC
    LEADERS
    Beecher, Henry Ward
    Wald, Lillian D.

WRITERS
    Non-Fiction
      Bancroft, George
      Motley, John Lothrop
    Novelists and Story Writers
      Hawthorne, Nathaniel
      Stowe, Harriet Beecher
    Poets
      Bryant, William Cullen
      Holmes, Oliver Wendell
      (1809-1894)

William Ellery Channing, the "Apostle of Unitarianism," preached humanitarianism and tolerance in religion rather than a new creed. His writings influenced many American authors, including Ralph Waldo Emerson (Scott Number 861), Henry W. Longfellow (Scott Number 864), and other transcendentalists.

Jonathan Edwards was a theologian and a powerful Congregational preacher of the eighteenth century. His theological masterpiece, published in 1754, was entitled, *The Freedom of the Will*. This work sets forth metaphysical and ethical arguments for determinism.

Scientists

This group of eight scientists consists of three physicists, two astronomers, a botanist, a natural historian, and an oceanographer.

Josiah Willard Gibbs taught mathematical physics at Yale University from 1871 until his death in 1903, and his investigations established the basic theory of physical chemistry. He is considered the greatest American theoretical scientist up to his time.

Joseph Henry made major contributions to the development of the electromagnet and invented and operated the first electromagnetic telegraph. In 1846, he became the first secretary and director of the Smithsonian Institution (Scott Numbers 943 and 1838) and at the Smithsonian he developed a weather report system that eventually became the U.S. Weather Bureau.

The first American to be awarded the Nobel Physics Prize was Albert Abraham Michelson. He determined with a high degree of accuracy the speed at which light travels and performed experiments proving that absolute motion of the earth through the ether is not measurable. Michelson's experiments served as the starting point in the development of the theory of relativity by Albert Einstein (Scott Numbers 1285 and 1774).

Maria Mitchell and Simon Newcomb were nineteenth-century astronomers. Mitchell discovered a new comet in 1847 which gained her immediate recognition and, in 1848, she became the first woman to be elected to the American Academy of Arts and Sciences. In 1865, she was appointed as director of the observatory and professor of astronomy at Vassar College. Newcomb was director of the publication, *American Nautical Almanac*, from 1877 to 1897. From his computations of the orbits of six planets, Newcomb made tables of the planetary system which were adopted by most observatories of the world.

Louis Agassiz was professor of natural history at Harvard University from 1848 until his death in 1873. He traveled widely, observed, and wrote on such varied topics as fossil fish, glaciers, and the natural history of the Americas. Agassiz influenced a generation of American scientists by urging the study of science directly from nature.

Asa Gray was also a professor of natural history at Harvard during the years that Agassiz was there. Gray helped revise the taxonomic procedure of Linnaeus on the basis of a more natural classification. He popularized the study of botany, and his *Manual of Botany of the Northern United States* has been the primary work in the field since it was published in 1848. Gray was a founder of the National Academy of Sciences and also served as president of the American Academy of Arts and Sciences for a period of ten years.

Matthew F. Maury was a naval officer and oceanographer who published the first work on modern oceanography in 1855. His wind and current charts of the Atlantic Ocean reduced sailing time on many routes. Maury also prepared charts of the bottom of the Atlantic Ocean, encouraged the idea of an Atlantic cable (Scott Number 1112), and was consulted often when the project began.

Social Reformers and Civic Leaders

Henry Ward Beecher, brother of Harriet Beecher Stowe, was a clergyman with a very eloquent and convincing manner of speaking. He was a leader in the antislavery movement of the 1840s and 1850s, as well as a proponent of woman suffrage and an advocate of the theory of evolution.

Lillian D. Wald was a public health nurse who observed the wretched living conditions in New York City's Lower East Side in the 1890s. She worked to establish educational, recreational, and social programs in the underprivileged neighborhoods and organized the Henry Street Settlement House. She helped found the National Organization of Public Health Nursing and was its first president. Mainly due to Wald's suggestion, Congress established the U.S. Children's Bureau in 1908.

Writers

George Bancroft wrote a ten-volume history of the United States that was published between 1834 and 1874, establishing him as the nation's foremost historian. He was appointed Secretary of the Navy by President Polk in 1845 when the United States Naval Academy (Scott Number 794) was simultaneously established at Annapolis.

In 1856, John Lothrop Motley published *The Rise of the Dutch Republic*, the work for which he is best known. Although no longer considered historically valid, it was a popular and influential work at that time.

Nathaniel Hawthorne, one of the great masters of American fiction, left a legacy of writings that are among the best of American literature. His masterwork, *The Scarlet Letter*, is considered one of the few great American novels.

Harriet Beecher Stowe's most famous work, *Uncle Tom's Cabin*, was published in 1852. This antislavery novel ranks among the most influential ever written, and its effect was to force the nation's attention on the slavery issue and stir the conscience of Americans, thereby influencing the course of American history.

William Cullen Bryant was considered the nation's finest poet after publishing a small volume of verse in 1821 which contained his famed "Thanatopsis." From 1827 to 1878, he was editor and part-owner of the *New York Evening Post* which became one of the country's leading newspapers under his guidance.

Oliver Wendell Holmes, father of the famous supreme court Justice of the same name (Scott Number 1288), was a physician and educator, but is best known for his writings, particularly his poetry. His essay, "The Contagiousness of Puerperal Fever," in which he blamed the spread of the disease on unsanitary obstetricians, caused great controversy. His best-known poems are "Old Ironsides," "The Chambered Nautilus," and "The Deacon's Masterpiece, or, The Wonderful One-Hoss Shay."

NOBEL PEACE PRIZE

Since the first Nobel Peace Prize was awarded in 1901, sixteen Americans have been honored with this highly esteemed prize. Six of these Americans have also been on U.S. stamps. Of the remaining ten, three are still living, namely, Norman Borlaug, Henry Kissinger, and Linus Pauling. The other seven have been dead for ten years or more and have not been honored on U.S. stamps. The following paragraphs furnish basic information on the accomplishments for which these seven individuals were awarded the Nobel Peace Prize.

Emily G. Balch, an economist and social reformer, helped found the Women's International League for Peace and Freedom, and was its first secretary from 1919 to 1922. In 1931, Balch was appointed to a committee to study conditions in Haiti, and was the principal author of the committee's report which hastened the withdrawal of U.S. troops from that country in 1934.

Ralph J. Bunche was professor of political science at Howard University from 1928 to 1950. In 1948 and 1949, he was a member of the United Nations Palestine Commission and mediated a truce between the Jews and Arabs.

Nicholas M. Butler was a professor of philosophy and education at Columbia University from 1890 to 1902 and served as that institution's president from 1902 to 1945. He worked for peace and directed conferences on international arbitration; his series of articles entitled, "The Basis of Durable Peace," was published in the *New York Times* and won him international recognition. Butler shared the Peace Prize with Jane Addams (Scott Number 878) in 1931.

Charles G. Dawes, politician and financier, served as Vice President during Calvin Coolidge's second term, 1924-29. He was author of the Dawes Plan, a complex plan of industrial and economic reorganization designed to solve Germany's serious economic problems and to provide a schedule for Germany's payment of reparations after World War I.

Frank B. Kellogg was a U.S. Senator from 1917 to 1923 and Secretary of State during Calvin Coolidge's second term. Kellogg worked with the French foreign minister, Aristide Briand, to formulate the Kellogg-Briand Pact. The sixty-two nations that were signatories of this pact renounced war as an instrument of national policy and pledged themselves to settle all disputes by peaceful means.

John R. Mott was active in the Young Men's Christian Association (YMCA) and served from 1915 to 1931 as the YMCA's general secretary. Mott strived to bring about national ecumenical conferences in countries all over the world. The International Missionary Council was thus created, joining with other ecumenical groups to form the World Council of Churches in 1948. For his international church and missionary work Mott shared the Nobel Peace Prize with Emily G. Balch in 1946.

Elihu Root was a politician who served as Secretary of War under Presidents McKinley and Roosevelt from 1899 to 1904. From 1905 to 1909 he was Theodore Roosevelt's Secretary of State, and from 1909 to 1915 Root was a U.S. Senator. Under Roosevelt, he improved U.S. relations with Latin America and fostered civilian governments in Puerto Rico and the Philippines. He also concluded the Root-Takahira Agreement of 1908 with Japan. In this agreement, Japan and the United States agreed to maintain the status quo in the Pacific and uphold the Open Door Policy in China. Root was prominent in the dispute over North Atlantic fisheries in 1910, and his arbitration strengthened U.S.-Canadian relations.

NOBEL AND PULITZER PRIZES FOR LITERATURE

Many authors have been awarded Nobel and Pulitzer prizes for their writings, but only twelve of these authors have been honored on U.S. stamps. Most of the other authors have received just one of these prizes and are probably not sufficiently deserving or noteworthy to be honored on U.S. stamps. There are, however, eight authors who have received two or more of these prizes and have been dead for at least ten years, but have never been honored on U.S. stamps.

The following list gives the names of these eight individuals, their prizes, and the years when they were received. The birth and death dates of each are included with the name.

Benet, Stephen Vincent (1898-1943)
    Pulitzer Poetry Prizes, 1929 and 1944

Faulkner, William (1897-1962)
    Nobel Literature Prize, 1949
    Pulitzer Fiction Prizes, 1955 and 1963

Hemingway, Ernest (1899-1961)
    Nobel Literature Prize, 1954
    Pulitzer Fiction Prize, 1953

Lewis, Sinclair (1885-1951)
    Nobel Literature Prize, 1930
    Pulitzer Fiction Prize, 1926

Nevins, Allan (1890-1971)
    Pulitzer Biography Prizes, 1933 and 1937

Robinson, Edwin Arlington (1869-1935)
    Pulitzer Poetry Prizes, 1922, 1925, and 1928

Sherwood, Robert E. (1896-1955)
  Pulitzer Biography Prize, 1949
  Pulitzer Drama Prizes, 1939 and 1941

Tarkington, Booth (1869-1946)
  Pulitzer Fiction Prizes, 1919 and 1922

SUMMARY

The eighty-six Americans and the three foreigners who have been acclaimed by being elected to the Hall of Fame, awarded Nobel and Pulitzer Prizes and given the Presidential Medal of Freedom, as well as featured on U.S. stamps, account only for 19 percent of the 464 individuals honored on U.S. stamps. The other 376 individuals may not be any less eminent because many of them made outstanding contributions of different types and are historically significant in many areas of endeavor.

Sixty-seven, or two-thirds, of the Americans elected to the Hall of Fame have had U.S. stamps issued in their honor; these sixty-seven individuals have been featured on U.S. stamps exactly 290 times and account for 40 percent of the 727 American persons honored on U.S. stamps. There are twenty-five recipients of Nobel and Pulitzer Prizes and the Presidential Medal of Freedom who have been featured on U.S. stamps. Three of these twenty-five are also in the Hall of Fame; they are Jane Addams, Theodore Roosevelt, and Woodrow Wilson, and all three have also been awarded the Nobel Peace Prize. The eminence of these eighty-nine individuals cannot be disputed.

A comparison of the list of Americans honored on U.S. stamps with the individuals in the Hall of Fame and the recipients of the Nobel and Pulitzer Prizes points out fifty prominent Americans who have not been honored on U.S. stamps. These fifty Americans are composed of thirty-five who are in the Hall of Fame, seven recipients of the Nobel Peace Prize who have been dead for ten years, and eight authors who have won two or more Nobel or Pulitzer literary prizes and who died prior to 1972. Some of these individuals perhaps may not be sufficiently meritorious to have stamps issued in their honor, but others are of such eminence and historical significance that they do deserve consideration as possible candidates for stamps to be issued in their honor.

Part III. THEMES AND THINGS

STATES AND STATEHOOD

15 Objects, Topics, Themes, and Things on Stamps

Chapter 3 pointed out that the 1,355 stamps could be classified into two groups, person stamps and subject stamps. Person stamps are those that depict or honor one or more identifiable persons, and subject stamps are those that do not depict or honor any identifiable person. Of the 1,355 stamps, there are 585 (43 percent) which depict or honor identifiable persons and 770 (57 percent) which are considered as subject stamps.

Even though 585 stamps were classified as person stamps, the majority include objects and things in their designs or are related to a topic or theme. Very few stamps portray only a person, containing no other object or thing in the design. A few examples of this kind of person stamp can be found in the Presidential Issue of 1938 (Scott Numbers 804, 811, 812, and 819) and in the Prominent Americans Issue of 1965-75 (Scott Numbers 1278, 1279, 1281, 1283, and 1286). A large majority of the person stamps, however, do include objects and things in their designs.

As far as this author could determine, no previous indexes exist either to the identifiable persons on U.S. stamps or to the objects, topics, themes, and things that can be found in the designs of U.S. stamps. Such indexes facilitate or make possible the location of particular stamps about which a minimum is known and a search in a collection of stamps, a catalog, or other philatelic publication. For example, if one recalls that there is a stamp depicting a submarine, but does not know the catalog number or when it was issued it would be time-consuming to look through all the stamps to locate it. But if an index to the objects, topics, themes, and things existed, it would be a simple matter to check the index under the heading, Submarines, to determine that Scott Number 1128 (Minkus Number CM437) depicts a submarine. The same need exists for an index to determine which stamps depict or honor a specific individual. An example of what may result from the lack of an adequate index occurred in the description of a stamp portraying Benjamin Franklin (Scott Number 1393D), appearing in a publication of the United States Postal Service where it was stated, "Only Washington and Lincoln have appeared more frequently on postage stamps than Franklin."[1] However, before this stamp was issued in 1972, George Washington had been honored on sixty-seven stamps, Abraham Lincoln had appeared on twenty stamps, and Benjamin Franklin had already been honored on thirty-three stamps (see Appendix II). If a complete index to U.S. postage stamps had been available at that time, such an erroneous statement would not have been made.

The *Scott Specialized Catalogue of United States Stamps* and the U.S. Postal Service's *Stories & Stamps* contain abbreviated indexes which are inadequate and inconsistent.[2] The *Minkus New American Stamp Catalog* does not contain any kind of index to the stamps that it lists.[3] These publications would be much more valuable to the collector if they contained indexes to the persons, objects, topics, themes, and things on the stamps listed therein.

Without proper indexes, it is difficult and time-consuming to search a catalog or other source in an attempt to locate or identify the stamps that contain a certain item or that have a related topic or theme. An index to the objects, topics, themes, and things on U.S. stamps would be both a great convenience and a real timesaver for philatelists and others attempting to find a specific stamp in a catalog or other source for which the catalog number is not known. Also, topical collectors would benefit greatly from such an index. Topical collecting relates to the gathering of stamps according to a specific topic, theme, or object represented on stamps. Jerome Husak, founder and executive secretary of the American Topical Association, has written about this aspect of philately:

Topical stamp collecting is *the* hobby of the day. No other hobby allows the collector to develop his individuality to such an extent or through such a wide range. Topicals are economical, procurable, and one's collection original-assembled is the only one of its kind! Collecting topicals offers barrels of fun on a small budget, fits in perfectly with vocation or hobbies, affords opportunity for research, encourages delightful correspondence with collectors in distant places, and adds joy and zest to living.[4]

If topical collectors had an index to all objects, topics, themes, and things that have been on U.S. stamps, it would be an easy task to identify the stamps relating to their areas of specialization without examining each stamp individually. Therefore, this author has attempted to compile a comprehensive index of all objects, topics, themes, and things that have appeared on the 1,355 stamps covered by this study.

The purposes of this index are: (1) to help collectors identify stamps when only a single detail is known, (2) to determine if there are stamps whose designs contain a specific item or object and to identify those stamps that may have that item or object, and (3) to specify for topical collectors those stamps which are related to their areas of specialization. This index to the objects, topics, themes, and things on U.S. postage stamps comprises Appendix III at the end of this publication. The index was compiled by carefully examining each of the 1,355 stamps (or reproductions thereof) with a magnifying glass and a small microscope to identify all elements and details in the designs. Then the Scott Number for each stamp containing that element or detail was listed under the appropriate heading.

The index consists of 1,309 headings and 782 subheadings under which 9,177 Scott Numbers are listed. There are many cross references, in addition to the 2,091 headings and subheadings. There are two types of references included in this index, namely, *see* and *see also* references. The *see* references direct the reader from terms not selected as headings, either because of their ambiguity, lack of precise meaning, or because they were synonymous with other terms chosen as headings. The index contains 150 *see* references which direct the user to 368 terms used as headings. Examples of this type of reference are: (1) District of Columbia. *See* Washington, D.C.; (2) Muskets. *See* Rifles and muskets; (3) Pollution. *See* Environmental protection; and (4) Wildlife. *See* Animals; Birds and poultry; Conservation; Fish. The *see also* references indicate other terms and headings of related interest. Some examples of this type of reference are: (1) Boxes, crates, and packages. *See also* Ballot boxes; Barrels; Baskets; Sacks; Trunks, suitcases, and bags; (2) Ballot boxes. *See also* Voting; (3) Trunks, suitcases, and bags. *See also* Briefcases; Sacks; (4) Buckets. *See also* Kettles; Ladles; (5) Kettles. *See also* Coffeepots; Ladles; Teapots and teakettles; (6) Ladles. *See also* Kettles; and (7) Constitution of the United States. *See also* Articles of Confederation; Bill of Rights. Appendix III lists a total of 527 *see also* references to other index terms to assist the reader in locating related topics.

SUMMARY

Most "person" or "subject" stamps include objects and things of one kind or another in their designs. Very few stamps portray a person without an object or some other thing included in the design. Due to the lack of a comprehensive index to the objects, topics, themes, and things that can be found on U.S. stamps, it is often difficult to find a particular stamp in a catalog or in a collection. An index would greatly facilitate the identification of a stamp by either the Scott Number or the Minkus Number. In addition, topical collectors need an extensive and encyclopedic index in order to identify the stamps whose designs include the subjects of their specializations. Just such an index has been compiled by this author, and it is appended at the end of this publication. It is hoped that this index will fulfill its intended purpose: helping collectors identify stamps when only a single detail is known and showing topical collectors which stamps contain the items and subjects related to their areas of specialization.

NOTES

1. U.S., Postal Service, Philatelic Affairs Division, *United States Postage Stamps: An Illustrated Description of all United States Postage and Special Service Stamps* (Washington, D.C.: U.S. Government Printing Office, 1972-), p. 246.

2. *Scott Specialized Catalogue of United States Stamps, 1981* (New York: Scott Publishing Company, 1980), pp. iv-vi; U.S., Postal Service, *Stamps & Stories: The Encyclopedia of U.S. Stamps* (Washington, D.C.: U.S. Postal Service, 1980), pp. 261-64.

3. *Minkus New American Stamp Catalog* 1981 edition (New York: Minkus Publications, Inc., [1980]), 390 pp.

4. Husak, Jerome, Foreword in *Topical Stamp Collecting* by M. W. Martin (New York: Arco Publishing Company, c1975), p. ix.

16 States and Statehood on Stamps

Many stamps feature happenings, occurrences, historical events, places, scenes, or other aspects related to the fifty states of the United States, as well as to the District of Columbia, Puerto Rico, American Samoa, and the Virgin Islands. These places are presented in Table 57 in rank order according to the number of stamps listed under each in Appendix III. All stamps listed under each state or other area have topics that relate in one way or another to these fifty-four geographic localities.

New York is the state featured most frequently on stamps; it has been represented almost twice as many times as the second ranking state, Massachusetts. These are followed by Virginia, California, and Pennsylvania, all of which had leading roles in the formation and development of the United States as a nation. New York, Massachusetts, Virginia, and Pennsylvania were the scenes of many important events of the Revolutionary War and the early years of the republic. California was significant in the movement westward and the growth of the country as it expanded and grew from coast to coast.

All fifty states have been featured on at least two stamps, one of which in each case was the representation of the state flag in the American Bicentennial Issue of 1976 (Scott Numbers 1633-1682). Each stamp of this commemorative sheet of fifty stamps depicted a different state flag; they were arranged on the sheet according to the year of admission to the Union, that is, from Delaware to Hawaii.

Table 57

The Fifty States, the District of Columbia, Puerto Rico, American Samoa, and the Virgin Islands and the Number of Stamps on Which Each Has Been Featured

Place	Number of Stamps	Place	Number of Stamps
New York	45	Kansas	5
Massachusetts	24	Maine	5
Virginia	21	Montana	5
California	18	Nebraska	5
Pennsylvania	17	Nevada	5
District of Columbia	14	Oklahoma	5
North Carolina	11	Oregon	5
Illinois	10	Rhode Island	5
Michigan	10	Alabama	4
Texas	10	Connecticut	4
Arizona	9	Idaho	4
Hawaii	9	Missouri	4
Washington (state)	9	New Hampshire	4
New Mexico	8	South Dakota	4
Alaska	7	Utah	4
Florida	7	Vermont	4
Indiana	7	Arkansas	3
New Jersey	7	Iowa	3
Tennessee	7	Kentucky	3
Wyoming	7	Louisiana	3
Maryland	6	Mississippi	3
Minnesota	6	North Dakota	3
Ohio	6	Puerto Rico	3
South Carolina	6	Delaware	2
Wisconsin	6	Virgin Islands	2
Colorado	5	West Virginia	2
Georgia	5	American Samoa	1

The authors of the Constitution of the United States included as Article VII the stipulation that nine of the thirteen states had to ratify the Constitution before it would be in force. Three states ratified it in 1787, and five more in 1788 before the ninth state, New Hampshire, ratified it on June 21, 1788. Two more states ratified it later in 1788, one in 1789, and the thirteenth state, Rhode Island, ratified it in 1790. There have never been any stamps commemorating the centennials or sesquicentennials of the thirteen original states. However, on June 21, 1938 a stamp was issued commemorating the sesquicentennial of the ratification of the Constitution of the United States (Scott Number 835). This is the only stamp related to the statehood of any of the thirteen states that ratified the Constitution from

1787 to 1790. Even though no stamps have been issued commemorating the statehood of the first thirteen states, stamps have been issued commemorating the early settlements, colonization, or founding of twelve of the thirteen original states (see Table 58). New Hampshire is the only one of the original states for which no stamp has been issued to celebrate or honor its founding, early settlements, or its statehood.

Stamps honoring early settlements in Virginia, Massachusetts, New York, South Carolina, Pennsylvania, Georgia, Maryland, and Connecticut were issued between 1907 and 1935. These eight stamps all came out before the first of the statehood centennial stamps was issued on November 1, 1935 honoring the statehood centennial of Michigan (Scott Number 775). Stamps honoring early settlements in Rhode Island, North Carolina, and Delaware were issued in 1936, 1937, and 1938 respectively. The tercentenary of the arrival of Philip Carteret and the English colonization of New Jersey was commemorated on a stamp that came out in 1964.

During the period, 1891 to 1921, eleven states completed 100 years of statehood, but no stamp was issued to honor any of these centenaries. It was not until 1941 that the first of these eleven states, Vermont, was honored with a sesquicentennial stamp (Scott Number 903). The series of

Table 58
The Thirteen Original States and the First Stamps Issued to Commemorate Their Early Settlements, Colonization, or Founding

State	Year Admitted to Union	Event Honored	Scott Number	Year Issued
Delaware	1787	Arrival of Finns and Swedes, 1638	836	1938
Pennsylvania	1787	Colony founded by William Penn, 1682	724	1932
New Jersey	1787	Landing of Philip Carteret, 1664	1247	1964
Georgia	1788	Arrival of James Oglethorpe, 1733	726	1933
Connecticut	1788	Settlement by Puritans, 1635	772	1935
Massachusetts	1788	Landing of the Pilgrims, 1620	548-550	1920
Maryland	1788	Arrival of Leonard Calvert, 1634	736	1934
South Carolina	1788	Founding of Charles Town, 1680	683	1930
New Hampshire	1788	(none)		
Virginia	1788	Founding of Jamestown, 1607	328-330	1907
New York	1788	Landing of Dutch at Fort Orange, 1624	615	1924
North Carolina	1789	Arrival of English settlers and birth of Virginia Dare, 1587	796	1937
Rhode Island	1790	Settlement established by Roger Williams, 1636	777	1936

sesquicentennial stamps for these eleven states was begun only after the centenary stamps for Michigan and Arkansas (Scott Numbers 775 and 782) had already been issued. The stamps celebrating the sesquicentennials of the eleven states admitted to the Union between 1791 and 1821 came out in the years 1941 and 1971. Beginning in 1935, stamps were issued for each state as it completed either 100 or 150 years of statehood (see Tables 59 and 60).

As mentioned earlier, the first statehood centennial stamp was issued for the state of Michigan on November 1, 1935. The actual date, however, when Michigan was admitted to the Union as the twenty-sixth state, was January 26, 1837; but Michigan had drafted a state constitution, elected officials, and set up a state government in 1835. Arkansas was granted statehood in 1836 and in 1936 a centennial stamp was issued to commemorate its statehood. These two stamps were the beginning of the series of statehood centennial and anniversary stamps. Between 1935 and 1977, fifteen stamps were issued to honor the anniversaries of the fourteen states admitted to the Union between 1836 and 1876. Colorado is the only state to be honored with a stamp commemorating the seventy-fifth anniversary of its statehood as well as one for its centennial. Table 60 lists these fourteen states, the years they were admitted to the Union, and the Scott Numbers and the years of issuance of their anniversary stamps.

Ten states were given statehood between 1889 and 1912, and all but one of these states have had stamps issued for their quinquagenary celebrations between 1939 and 1962 (see Table 61). Utah is the only one of the thirty-seven states that joined the Union between 1791 and 1959 for which no stamp honoring its statehood has been issued. Utah, which was originally intended to be called "Deseret" (meaning honeybee), was first settled in 1847, and a stamp was issued in 1947 to commemorate the arrival and settlement of the Mormons (Scott Number 950). North Dakota, South Dakota, Montana, and Washington were all admitted to the Union between November 2 and 9, 1889; on November 2, 1939 one stamp was issued to commemorate the fiftieth anniversary of these four states (Scott Number 858). Other states have celebrated the same anniversary in the same year, but in all other cases a separate stamp was issued for each state. Examples of this are Florida and Texas which were admitted to the Union in 1845, Idaho and Wyoming gained statehood just a week apart in July 1890, and New Mexico and Arizona joined the Union in 1912.

Alaska and Hawaii became states in 1959 and stamps to honor their statehood were issued on the very day each was given statehood. It is worth noting that Alaska and Hawaii are unique in that stamps honoring their statehood were issued at the time they became states. In addition, the statehood stamps of these two states are the only air mail stamps issued to honor statehood (Scott Numbers C53 and C55). This is probably due to the fact that in 1959 there still existed a separate postage category for domestic air mail, and the distance of these two states from the other forty-eight meant that air mail stamps would have been the most appropriate and the most commonly used for mail from these two states.

Table 59
Sesquicentennial Statehood Issues

State	Year Admitted to the Union	Scott Number	Year Issued
Vermont	1791	903	1941
Kentucky	1792	904	1942
Tennessee	1796	941	1946
Ohio	1803	1018	1953
Louisiana	1812	1197	1962
Indiana	1816	1308	1966
Mississippi	1817	1337	1967
Illinois	1818	1339	1968
Alabama	1819	1375	1969
Maine	1820	1391	1970
Missouri	1821	1426	1971

Table 60
Centennial and Seventy-Fifth Anniversary Statehood Issues

State	Year Admitted to the Union	Scott Number	Year Issued
Arkansas	1836	782	1936
Michigan	1837	775	1935
Florida	1845	927	1945
Texas	1845	938	1945
Iowa	1846	942	1946
Wisconsin	1848	957	1948
California	1850	997	1950
Minnesota	1858	1106	1958
Oregon	1859	1124	1959
Kansas	1861	1183	1961
West Virginia	1863	1232	1963
Nevada	1864	1248	1964
Nebraska	1867	1328	1967
Colorado	1876	1001	1951
Colorado	1876	1711	1977

Table 61
Quinquagenary Statehood Issues

State	Year Admitted to the Union	Scott Number	Year Issued
North Dakota	1889	858	1939
South Dakota	1889	858	1939
Montana	1889	858	1939
Washington	1889	858	1939
Idaho	1890	896	1940
Wyoming	1890	897	1940
Utah	1896	—	—
Oklahoma	1907	1092	1957
New Mexico	1912	1191	1962
Arizona	1912	1192	1962

SUMMARY

All fifty states, the District of Columbia, Puerto Rico, American Samoa, and the Virgin Islands have been honored on U.S. stamps. New York is the most honored state, followed by Massachusetts, Virginia, California, and Pennsylvania. The other forty-five states have been honored on at least two stamps each. Early settlements, the colonization, or the founding of twelve of the thirteen colonies have been commemorated on stamps, but no stamps celebrating their centennials or sesquicentennials have been issued. Perhaps these states will be honored with bicentennial stamps beginning in 1987. New Hampshire is the only one of the thirteen original states for which no stamp was ever issued honoring an early settlement, its founding, or its statehood. The eleven states admitted to the Union from 1791 to 1821 were all honored with sesquicentennial stamps between 1941 and 1971. From 1935 to 1977, centennial stamps came out for the fourteen states granted statehood from 1836 to 1876. Colorado is the only state with a stamp honoring its seventy-fifth anniversary. Ten states came into the Union during the twenty-four year period, 1889-1912, and stamps honoring the statehood quinquagenary of nine of these ten states were issued from 1939 to 1962. Utah is the only state admitted to the Union since 1791 for which no statehood stamp was ever issued. Alaska and Hawaii are the only states for which statehood stamps were issued at the time they became states; all other states have had to wait a minimum of fifty years.

17 Things on Stamps
Common and Uncommon

Stamps of the United States have depicted or honored a wide variety of objects, topics, themes, and things. There are 2,091 headings and sub-headings (1,309 headings and 782 subheadings) listed in Appendix III. This large number of headings points out the great diversity of things that can be found in the designs of U.S. stamps. Some items are found on many stamps, whereas others are unique and found on a single stamp.

The top-ranking object is the male person, which includes both identifiable and unidentifiable men, boys, and male figures. There are 722 stamps (53.28 percent of the 1,355 stamps) which depict males, but only 188 stamps (13.87 percent) contain females. In fact, there are fewer stamps depicting females than those depicting trees, headgear, or flags. The predominance of the male figure is even more evident when one notices that neckties are on 178 stamps and beards and moustaches are on 134 stamps. Appendix III, however, only lists five stamps under brooches and eleven under necklaces.

Headgear is the second-ranking object included in stamp designs; female, male, and military headgear are found 327 times. Trees rank third and are depicted on 227 (16.75 percent) of the stamps. Flags are fourth and have appeared 193 times. The most common flag, of course, is our national flag which has been represented eighty-three times. Flags of the Revolutionary War have appeared eleven times, and flags of the fifty states have been on fifty-six stamps. Foreign flags have been depicted forty times. The other three flags are those of the U.S. Coast and Geodetic Survey, the Red Cross, and the United Nations.

Only four kinds of common wearing apparel are listed in Appendix III, namely, headgear, footwear, neckties, and aprons. Shirts, pants, and dresses were not included, as these are found in almost all cases on the same stamps depicting male and female figures. Male civilian headgear, male and female footwear, and neckties are depicted on more than 13 percent of the 1,355 stamps. Aprons are found on just eleven stamps.

The star is the most widely used decorative and symbolic figure in the designs of U.S. stamps; 170 stamps (12.55 percent) included decorative and symbolic stamps. (This number does not include stamps depicting flags, coats of arms, seals, and shields—many of which also contain stars in their designs.)

Watercraft (boats, ships, canoes, rowboats, and submarines) and airplanes are the most common modes of transportation appearing on stamps. Watercraft are on 108 stamps (7.97 percent), and airplanes are depicted on sixty-eight stamps (5.02 percent).

More stamps were issued to celebrate the American Revolution Bicentennial than for any other event; exactly 100 stamps were issued to commemorate the bicentennial of the Revolution. The various events, battles, and occurrences of the Revolutionary War have only been commemorated on seventy-three stamps.

Only three animals have been depicted on twenty-five or more stamps: horses, eagles, and cattle. This is not really surprising when one considers that horses and oxen were commonly used for transportation prior to the twentieth century and that the eagle has been our national emblem since 1782.

Table 62 lists the sixty-eight headings in Appendix III under which twenty-five or more Scott Numbers are listed. The quantity of Scott Numbers does not necessarily indicate the number of different stamps on which that object, topic, theme, or thing may appear. For example, under maps, sixty Scott Numbers are listed under various subheadings, but there are actually only forty-two different numbers. The reason for this is that some maps on a single stamp may include more than one geographic locality, such as the stamp with a map of the Gadsden Purchase (Scott Number 1028). This stamp number is listed under the subheadings, Arizona, California, Gadsden Purchase, New Mexico, and United States—Southwestern states. Thus, the Scott Number 1028 in this case is listed five times under the heading for maps.

The headings chosen for the items listed in Appendix III were as specific as possible; for this reason there are several broad categories which may not be readily discernible without grouping some of the specific topics under general headings. Twenty-five general headings were selected to bring together the various topics that could be grouped under the same broad

Table 62

Headings in Appendix III with Listings of Twenty-five or More Scott Numbers

Heading	Number	Heading	Number
Men, boys, and male figures	722	New York State	45
Headgear	327	Swords	44
Trees	227	Mountains	43
Flags	193	Indians	41
Women, girls, and female figures	188	Rivers	41
Footwear	186	Torches	38
Neckties	178	Christmas	37
Stars (decorative and symbolic)	170	Carriages and other animal-drawn vehicles	36
Beards and moustaches	134	World globe	36
Boats and ships	108	Armed Forces	35
American Revolution Bicentennial	100	Books	35
Houses	83	Great Britain	34
Clouds	82	Letters (correspondence)	34
Children and youths	79	Eyeglasses	33
Laurel leaves and branches	79	Sports	32
Coats of arms, seals, and shields	77	World War II	32
Horses	75	Musical instruments	32
Revolutionary War	73	Conservation	31
Water	72	Postal workers	31
Airplanes	68	Olive leaves and branches	30
Buildings and other structures	68	Medallions, medals, and decorations	29
Rifles and muskets	61	Sun	29
Maps	60	Battles	28
Armed Forces personnel	59	Headlights	28
Postal services	58	Italy	28
Flowers	57	Snow	28
Organizations and associations	57	Canoes and rowboats	27
Eagles	52	Capitols	27
Mottoes	52	Immigrants to the United States	27
Printing styles	52	Wheat	27
Stairs and steps	51	Teeth	26
Quotations	47	Cattle	25
Smoke	46	Chairs	25
		Indian feather headdresses	25
		Quill pens	25

category. These twenty-five categories are listed in Table 63. Each category in Appendix III is listed at the left with the number of its headings and total

Table 63

**The Twenty-five Broad Categories and the Number of Headings and
Scott Numbers Included in Each Category**

Broad Category	Number of Headings	Number of Scott Numbers
Animals	27	174
Arms and weapons	15	193
Birds and poultry	19	118
Buildings, dwellings, and structures	38	369
Communications	13	64
Containers, receptacles, and repositories	31	170
Costume and personal appearance	22	1,015
Education	15	68
Foreign lands	34	202
Furniture	5	59
Government and the governed	51	613
Light, lighting, and illumination	18	215
Mail and postal services	15	175
Medicine and health	20	32
National shrines	14	71
Nature	16	307
Occupations and professions	42	189
People	25	1,197
Plants	33	529
Religion	17	125
Signs, symbols, and symbolic figures	36	569
Tools, implements, instruments, and machinery	29	103
Transportation	20	287
Wars and battles	8	123
Water	12	219
Total	575	7,186

number of Scott Numbers that are listed under those headings at the right.

The following sections consist of these broad categories arranged alphabetically with the various topics that can be classified in that category. The headings from Appendix III are given in rank order under each broad category according to the number of times each topic or item appeared on stamps.

ANIMALS

A total of twenty-seven different kinds of animals (excluding birds and poultry) have been depicted on U.S. stamps. The horse has appeared on

ANIMALS

Coral Reefs USA 15¢

Chalice Coral: American Samoa

EVERGLADES
NATIONAL PARK
3¢

UNITED STATES POSTAGE

USA 15¢

Seeing For Me

WILDLIFE CONSERVATION

WHOOPING
CRANES

U.S. POSTAGE 3¢

RURAL AMERICA

UNITED STATES

AMERICA'S WOOL

Swallowtail

USA 13¢ *Papilio oregonius*

WILDLIFE CONSERVATION

UNITED STATES 6¢

U.S.
POSTAGE
5¢
ANIMALS

WILDLIFE CONSERVATION

KING
SALMON

3¢ UNITED STATES POSTAGE 3¢

GREAT GRAY OWL 15¢

WILDLIFE CONSERVATION·USA

WATERFOWL CONSERVATION

UNITED STATES 6¢

U.S. 6¢

THE AGE OF REPTILES

WILDLIFE CONSERVATION 8¢

POLAR BEAR

UNITED STATES

seventy-five stamps, whereas all the other animals together have only been on ninety-nine stamps. it is curious and worth noting that the cat is the only domestic animal depicted on a single stamp. In addition to the animals listed below, the chimera, a mythical fire-breathing monster, has appeared on three stamps; Pegasus, a mythical winged horse, has been on six stamps; and one stamp portrayed a mermaid.

Horses	75	Bears	3	Crabs	1
Cattle	25	Donkeys	3	Dinosaurs	1
Dogs	13	Elk	3	Dolphins	1
Fish	9	Sheep	3	Elephants	1
Snakes	7	Alligators	1	Foxes	1
Deer	6	Antelopes	1	Mastodon remains	1
Buffaloes	5	Badgers	1	Raccoons	1
Lions	4	Cats	1	Seals	1
Moose	4	Chipmunks	1	Starfish	1

ARMS AND WEAPONS

Warfare and combat have played significant roles in the development of the United States as a nation stretching from coast to coast and in the establishment of the United States as a world power. Therefore, it is not surprising that fifteen different kinds of arms and weapons are found in the designs of U.S. stamps. The fact that so many stamps depict cannons, swords, rifles, and muskets is not astonishing when one considers the large number of stamps related to the battles and other events of the Revolutionary War. It is surprising, however, that such a common weapon as the pistol is only found on five stamps.

Rifles and muskets	61	Spears	8	Pikes	4
Swords	44	Bows and arrows	5	Shields	4
Cannons	23	Pistols	5	Tridents	3
Arrows	15	Cannonballs	4	Tomahawks	2
Bayonets	10	Knives	4	Arrowheads	1

BIRDS AND POULTRY

It is fitting and appropriate that our national emblem, the eagle, is the bird appearing most frequently on our stamps. The eagle is depicted on fifty-two stamps, or 44 percent of the stamps depicting birds and poultry. There are fifteen stamps on which unidentifiable birds are included in the designs, and fourteen that depict the mythical bird, the phoenix. The next-ranking identifiable bird is the dove which is used as a symbol of peace on seven stamps; the dove is followed by the owl which was used on one stamp as a symbol of wisdom and on four stamps to publicize wildlife conservation. The nineteen classes of birds and poultry that appear on stamps are given below.

Eagles	52	Ducks	3	Geese	1
Birds		Gulls	3	Herons	1
(unidentifiable)	15	Pelicans	3	Partridges	1
Phoenix	14	Cardinals	2	Pterosaurs	1
Doves	7	Chickens	2	Whooping cranes	1
Owls	5	Turkeys	2	Yellowhammers	1
Bluejays	3	Condors	1		

BUILDINGS, DWELLINGS, AND STRUCTURES

More than 300 (22 percent) of the 1,355 stamps depict some kind of building, dwelling, or structure. Many stamps depict more than one kind, and therefore the total number of stamps is not as great as the sum of the different categories listed below. The most common of these are houses which are sometimes the main feature of a stamp, but most frequently they are just background in the design. The thirty-eight headings from Appendix III which fall into this broad category are listed below.

Houses	83	Tents and tepees	4
Buildings (not included elsewhere)	56	Water towers	4
Capitols	27	Lighthouses	3
Forts and stockades	22	Schools	3
Churches	16	Stores and shops	3
Presidential homes	16	Huts	2
Post offices	15	Libraries	2
Skylines of cities	15	Oil derricks	2
Bridges	13	Water mills	2
Barns and stables	12	Beacon light towers	1
Universities and colleges	9	Courthouses	1
Factories	8	Hangars	1
Silos	8	Launching towers	1
Windmills	8	Observatories	1
Log cabins	6	Radio transmission towers	1
Museums	6	Sawmills	1
Castles	5	Sod houses	1
Dams	5	Temples	1
Missions (churches)	4	Theaters	1

COMMUNICATIONS

The field of communications is an extensive category, and several types of communication media have been acclaimed through illustrations on stamps. The one most commonly found (excluding mail and postal services) is the printing press and its products, namely, books, newspapers, and broadsides, which have been on forty-five stamps. Even though radio and television are represented on several stamps, no stamp depicts a radio receiver or a television set. The various media included in this category are given below.

Books	35	Sound recording	2
Printing and printing presses	5	Telephony	2
Radio	5	Broadsides	1
Newspapers and newspaper publishing	4	Drumming	1
		Scrolls	1
Telegraphy	4	Smoke signals	1
Satellites	2	Television	1

CONTAINERS, RECEPTACLES, AND REPOSITORIES

A container, receptacle, or repository is anything that contains, or can contain something; they can be any shape or size. The containers, receptacles, and repositories found on stamps range in size from water towers and silos to inkwells and envelopes. The following list includes thirty-one types of containers, receptacles, and repositories found on U.S. stamps.

Boxes, crates, and packages	18	Water towers	4
Inkwells	17	Coffeepots	3
Mailbags	16	Holsters	3
Barrels	13	Teapots and teakettles	3
Powderhorns	13	Trunks, suitcases, and bags	3
Baskets	9	Ballot boxes	2
Silos	8	Buckets	2
Urns, vases, and flowerpots	8	Gasoline cans	2
Bottles and flasks	7	Kettles	2
Earthen pots	5	Briefcases	1
Envelopes	5	Cups	1
Water pitchers	5	Ladles	1
Bowls	4	Mortar and pestle	1
Cornucopias	4	Tea caddies	1
Mailboxes	4	Water glasses	1
Sacks	4		

COSTUME AND PERSONAL APPEARANCE

It is only natural that most stamps have in their designs articles of apparel and other items of personal use and appearance because more than one-half of all U.S. stamps depict human figures. The predominance of the male figure accounts for the many neckties and male footwear and headgear. Many persons depicted on stamps are probably wearing wigs, but only one stamp is listed under this heading because from pictures it is very difficult, if not impossible, to discern real hair from wigs. Twenty-two items listed in Appendix III fall into this broad category of costume and personal appearance. These are listed below with the number of times each appears.

Headgear	327	Phrygian cap	10
Footwear	186	Crowns	8
Neckties	178	Masks	6
Beards and moustaches	134	Brooches	5
Eyeglasses	33	Spacesuits	4
Medallions, medals, and		Goggles	2
decorations	29	Parasols	2
Teeth	26	Umbrellas	2
Indian feather headdresses	25	Wristwatches	2
Walking sticks	12	Gauntlets	1
Aprons	11	Wigs and wig blocks	1
Necklaces	11		

EDUCATION

More stamps depict books than all the other aspects of education combined. Institutions of higher learning are the second-ranking topic in the field of education. Three school buildings are depicted on stamps, but only two stamps include libraries in their designs. The fifteen topics related to education are the following:

Books	35	National Apprenticeship Program	1
Universities and colleges	9	National Education Association	1
Education	8	Parent Teacher Association	1
Schools	3	Reading	1
Libraries	2	United States Military Academy	1
Teachers	2	United States Naval Academy	1
Education for traffic safety	1	Writing ability	1
Higher education	1		

FOREIGN LANDS

Thirty-four foreign lands have been represented on U.S. stamps in various ways. Seventeen countries are symbolized by their flags in stamp designs, and some countries are portrayed by map designs. Some stamps depict objects or scenes located in alien lands, and others portray foreign individuals or honor foreigners by including their names in the designs. Not surprisingly Great Britain tops the list when one considers our history and cultural heritage. Italy and Spain rank second and third due to the fact that the Columbian Exposition Issue of 1893 consisted of sixteen stamps honoring Christopher Columbus and the Spanish monarchs, Isabella and Ferdinand. The foreign places represented on U.S. stamps are listed below with the number of times each appeared.

Great Britain	34	China	2
Italy	28	Hungary	2
Spain	24	India	2
France	19	Mexico	2
Canada	15	Soviet Union	2
Netherlands	11	Switzerland	2
Germany	7	Venezuela	2
Poland	7	Albania	1
Japan	6	Arctic	1
Philippines	5	Austria	1
Finland	4	Brazil	1
Norway	4	Cuba	1
Sweden	4	Denmark	1
Belgium	3	Greece	1
Czechoslovakia	3	Korea	1
Antarctica	2	Luxembourg	1
Argentina	2	Yugoslavia	1

FURNITURE

Very few stamps depict any type of furniture. Of the eighty-three entries under houses, only ten show house interiors. Only thirty-eight different stamps include furniture. The most frequently depicted types of furniture are tables and chairs, which are often found on the same stamps, but no bedroom furniture is found on U.S. stamps. The only stamp that might appear to have a bed in it is the stamp honoring doctors (Scott Number 949): in this stamp, however, the sick little girl is lying on a makeshift bed formed by two chairs and pillows. The five kinds of furniture and the number of stamps on which each appears are given below.

Chairs	25	Stools	2
Tables	24	Sewing cabinets	1
Benches	7		

GOVERNMENT AND THE GOVERNED

Society creates and shapes government, and government controls and directs the actions and affairs of society. Many different topics and themes of U.S. stamps are related to the creation and formation of government, as well as to the effects of government on society through its various functions and services. The rights and responsibilities of citizens are a part of the governmental process and are well represented on stamps. The fifty-one topics found on stamps which relate to government and the society that empowers it are listed below.

Flags	193	Federal Hall	2
Coats of arms, seals, and shields	77	Freedom from want	2
Postal services	58	Freedom of the press	2
Mottoes	52	Law enforcement	2
Armed Forces	35	Palace of the Governors	2
Capitols	27	Articles of Confederation	1
International agreements		Carolina Charter	1
and treaties	20	Carpenters' Hall	1
Champions of Liberty	19	Charter Oak	1
Independence Hall	9	Coast and Geodetic Survey	1
Liberty (symbolic figure)	9	Courthouses	1
Bill of Rights	8	Freedom from fear	1
Declaration of Independence	8	Freedom from hunger	1
Laws, acts, and programs	8	Freedom (symbolic figure)	1
Scales of justice	8	Freedom to read	1
White House	7	Inauguration of	
E Pluribus Unum	6	George Washington	1
Great Seal of the United States	6	Liberty under law	1
In God We Trust	6	Lincoln-Douglas debates	1
Voting	6	Magna Carta	1
Justice (symbolic figure)	5	Mayflower Compact	1
Constitution of the United States	4	National Park Service	1
Freedom of religion	3	Right to assemble	1
Freedom of speech	3	Right to petition for redress	1
Of the people, by the people,		Savings bonds	1
for the people	3	Supreme Court Building	1
Continental Congress	2	Veterans Administration	1

LIGHT, LIGHTING, AND ILLUMINATION

Both artificial and natural light are evident on stamps in many different forms. The following list of topics includes light itself, as well as devices used for illumination. The most common is the torch which is also used as a symbol of enlightenment or learning. There are eighteen headings in Appendix III which fall into this broad category.

Torches	38	Lamps and lanterns	22
Sun	29	Fire and flames	18
Headlights	28	Rays of sunshine	17

Moon	15	Halos	4
Stars (celestial)	13	Candelabra and candlesticks	3
Lightning	6	Lighthouses	3
Candles	5	Streetlights	2
Light and lights	5	Beacon light towers	1
Light bulbs	5	Traffic signals	1

MAIL AND POSTAL SERVICES

Sixty-seven different stamps contain one or more elements relating to mail, its transport, handling, and delivery. Thirty-four, or more than one-half of these stamps, depict letters; and fourteen, or almost one-fourth of the stamps in this category portray letter carriers. Fifteen stamps show either the interior or exterior of post offices. Only thirteen stamps have postage stamps in their designs. The various objects and aspects of mail and postal service that appear in the sixty-seven stamps are listed below followed by the number of times each is shown on stamps.

Letters	34	Special delivery service	9
Postal workers	31	Air mail service	6
Mailbags	16	Mailboxes	4
Post offices	15	Pony express service	4
Letter carriers	14	Parcel post service	3
Postage stamps	13	Mailgram transmission	1
Surface mail transport	13	Zip code	1
Universal Postal Union	11		

MEDICINE AND HEALTH

Few stamps contain themes or elements related to medicine and health. The most common elements are medical emblems, namely, the Bowl of Hygeia, the Caduceus, and the Staff of Aesculapius. Four diseases (cancer, malaria, poliomyelitis, and tuberculosis) have been included in the themes of five different stamps. The specific topics of medicine and health and the number of stamps on which each has appeared are given below.

Red Cross	4	Bowl of Hygeia	1
Caduceus	3	Dental health	1
Blind persons	2	Doctors	1
Cancer	2	Malaria	1
Crippled persons	2	Osteopathic medicine	1
Nurses and nursing	2	Pharmacy	1
Physical fitness	2	Poliomyelitis	1
Retarded children	2	Prevent drug abuse	1
Staff of Aesculapius	2	Pure Food and Drug Act	1
Blood donations	1	Tuberculosis	1

MEDICINE AND HEALTH

NATIONAL SHRINES

Many places and objects important in the history of the United States are so esteemed and venerated that they could be considered as national shrines. However, fourteen monuments, memorials, edifices, and objects that have appeared seventy-one times on U.S. stamps are indubitably among the most cherished and revered.

Capitol of the United States	15	Mount Rushmore National	
Statue of Liberty	14	Memorial	2
Independence Hall	9	Mount Vernon	2
White House	7	Statue of Freedom	2
Washington Monument	6	Carpenters' Hall	1
Liberty Bell	5	Lincoln Memorial	1
Jefferson Memorial	4	Monticello	1
Federal Hall	2		

NATURE

Elements of nature are prevalent in the designs of stamps. The most common is water which is so widespread and appears in so many forms that it is listed as a separate category later in this chapter. The elements included here can be divided into two groups: celestial elements and earthly elements. The celestial elements are clouds, lightning, moon, planets (except Earth), rainbows, rays of sunshine, stars, sun, and wind; these nine have appeared a total of 169 times. The seven earthly elements consist of coral reefs, the planet Earth, fire and flames, minerals, mountains, rock formations, and smoke; these are shown on 138 stamps. The sixteen elements of nature and the number of stamps on which earth has appeared are given below.

Clouds	82	Stars (celestial)	13
Smoke	46	Rock formations	8
Mountains	43	Lightning	6
Sun	29	Coral reefs	4
Fire and flames	18	Minerals	4
Rays of sunshine	17	Planets	4
Earth (planet)	15	Rainbows	2
Moon	15	Wind	1

OCCUPATIONS AND PROFESSIONS

Many occupations and professions have been honored or represented on U.S. stamps throughout the course of U.S. postage stamp history. The occupations and professions of all identified persons were listed and discussed in Chapter 11 and are not included here or in Appendix III. This section deals only with the occupations and professions specifically honored on stamps, as well as those represented by unidentifiable figures of persons included in the designs of stamps. Forty-two professions have been honored or represented 189 times. The most common is for Armed Forces personnel, who are represented fifty-nine times and account for almost one-third of those listed in this category. The second-ranking occupation is that of persons employed in the various postal services who appear on thirty-one stamps and make up almost 17 percent of the stamps in this category. Farmers and agricultural workers are included in eighteen, or almost 10 percent, of the 185 stamps honoring or containing figures of persons representing occupations and professions. The three groups mentioned above (Armed Forces personnel, postal workers, and farmers) appear a total of 108 times and account for more than 58 percent of all the stamps representing the forty-two occupations and professions included here. The occupations and professions honored on stamps or represented by unidentifiable figures are listed below in rank order.

Armed Forces personnel	59	Chemists	1
Postal workers	31	Dentists	1
Farmers	18	Doctors	1
Airplane pilots	8	Druggists	1
Miners	8	Engineers	1
Cowboys	6	Firefighters	1
Astronauts	4	Glassblowers	1
Clergy and missionaries	4	Hatmakers	1
Dancers	4	Homemakers	1
Pony express riders	4	Jockeys	1
Fishermen	3	Lawyers	1
Industrial workers	3	Leatherworkers	1
Blacksmiths	2	Newspaperboys	1
Clowns	2	Photographers	1
Nurses	2	Policemen	1
Printers	2	Railroad engineers	1
Stagecoach drivers	2	Seamstresses	1
Streetcar drivers	2	Silversmiths	1
Teachers	2	Truckers	1
Architects	1	Wheelwrights	1
Bankers	1	Wigmakers	1

PEOPLE

More than one-half of all U.S. stamps portray people. Many are just of figures representing persons, and others are portrayals of real persons. Some figures represent specific occupations and professions, and other symbolize different classes or types of persons. There are twenty-five groups of persons listed in Appendix III under headings completely unrelated to any occupation or profession. These are given below with the number of times each appears.

Men, boys, and male figures	722	Mothers	4
Women, girls, and		Pilgrims	4
female figures	188	Huguenots	3
Children and youths	79	Walloons	3
Indians	41	Blind persons	2
Immigrants to the United States	27	Crippled persons	2
Black Americans	22	Puritans	2
Champions of Liberty	19	Refugees	2
Infants	19	Retarded children	2
Pioneers	19	Gold Star Mothers	1
Nude figures	14	Green Mountain Boys	1
Biblical personages	10	Minutemen	1
Veterans	9	Vikings	1

PLANTS

More than 400 stamps depict one or more kinds of plants, fruits, and other forms of vegetation. The tree is the most common plant found in the designs of stamps. Trees are found on 227, or one-sixth of all U.S. stamps. Laurel, oak, olive, and palm leaves are depicted on 143 stamps, or 10.55 percent of the 1,355 stamps. Several kinds of flowers are found fifty-seven times on forty-nine different stamps. The various plants and their fruits that appear on stamps are given below.

Trees	227	Citrus fruits	2
Laurel leaves and branches	79	Holly	2
Flowers	57	Tobacco	2
Olive leaves and branches	30	Buckeye leaf	1
Wheat	27	Cantaloupes	1
Oak leaves and branches	23	Clover	1
Corn	19	Cotton	1
Fruits and vegetables	13	Indigo	1
Palm fronds	11	Maple leaf	1
Grapes	5	Mistletoe	1
Pine cones	4	Pears	1
Forests and forestry	3	Pumpkins	1
Leaves (unidentifiable)	3	Rice	1
Wreaths	3	Sagebrush	1
Acorns	2	Seaweed	1
Apples	2	Spanish moss	1
Cactuses	2		

RELIGION

The First Amendment to the Constitution prohibits the government from interfering with the religious practices of the American people and it cannot establish a state-supported church or favor one religion over another. In view of this, it is not surprising that Christmas stamps are the only U.S. stamps having a purely religious theme, and only fourteen of the thirty-seven Christmas stamps are strictly religious. Ten of these depict Mary and the Baby Jesus; of these ten, only three also include Joseph, the husband of Mary. Three religious Christmas stamps portray angels, and the fourteenth one is a scene showing people arriving at a church. The other twenty-three Christmas stamps have nonreligious themes. Just three stamps depict identifiable clergymen (see Chapter 11), but there are four with unidentified clergymen. Although many stamps depict persons of non-Christian religions, only five stamps contain religious elements unrelated to Christianity. These five elements are gods and goddesses: four Roman and one Polynesian. The seventeen headings related to religion listed in Appendix III are given below.

Christmas	37	Missions	4
Churches	16	Bible	3
Angels and cherubim	11	Christmas trees	3
Crosses	11	Freedom of religion	3
Biblical personages	10	Wreaths	3
God	7	Biblical quotations	2
Gods and goddesses	5	Salvation Army	1
Clergy and missionaries	4	Temples	1
Halos	4		

SIGNS, SYMBOLS, AND SYMBOLIC FIGURES

Many objects have appeared on U.S. stamps as symbols of concepts and ideas that are intangible or spiritual, such as the Phrygian cap used as a symbol of liberty. Other objects are used symbolically to indicate honor, veneration, high esteem, or authority, such as halos or the fasces. Some items have become so closely associated with an idea or another thing that they are used almost interchangeably; examples of these are the eagle as a symbol of the United States and the cross which symbolizes Christianity. Signs are conventional marks which may represent a word or words and are used as abbreviations in many cases, such as the ampersand and the equal sign.

Stars are the most common figures found on U.S. stamps; second are leaves. Six kinds of leaves are used symbolically on the stamps, namely, laurel, oak, olive, palm, buckeye, and maple. Laurel and oak leaves are used to indicate honor, glory, or veneration. Olive branches signify peace and often appear with doves. Palm fronds are emblems of victory or success. The maple leaf was used on one stamp as a symbol of Canada, and the buckeye leaf represented Ohio on its sesquicentennial stamp. More than 500 stamps have included in their designs different signs, symbols, and symbolic figures representing many concepts, ideas, and other objects. The thirty-six signs, symbols, and symbolic figures found on U.S. stamps are listed below with the number of stamps on which each may be found.

Stars (decorative and symbolic)	170	Justice (symbolic figure)	5
Laurel leaves and branches	79	Ampersands	4
Eagles	52	Halos	4
Torches	38	Arrows (symbols)	2
Olive leaves and branches	30	Statue of Freedom	2
Oak leaves and branches	23	Buckeye leaf	1
Hands (symbolic figures)	20	Divine Inspiration	
Wings (symbolic figures)	18	(symbolic figure)	1
Chains	17	Double-barred cross	1
Statue of Liberty	14	Equal sign	1
Crosses (Christian emblems)	11	Exclamation mark	1
Palm fronds	11	Female symbol	1
Phrygian cap	10	Freedom (symbolic figure)	1
Liberty (symbolic figure)	9	Gauntlets	1
Cogwheel (industrial symbol)	9	Maple leaf	1
Crowns	8	Truth (symbolic figure)	1
Fasces	8	Vision (symbolic figure)	1
Doves	7	Wisdom (symbolic figure)	1
Medical emblems	6		

TOOLS, IMPLEMENTS, INSTRUMENTS, AND MACHINERY

U.S. stamps have depicted twenty-nine different types of tools, implements, instruments, and machinery. The most frequently depicted is the plow which is often used to represent farming. The second-ranking item in this category is the pickaxe, often used as a symbol of mining. The various tools, implements, instruments, and machinery are listed below with the number of times each has appeared.

Plows	16	Scythes	4
Pickaxes	13	Harvesting machinery	2
Hammers	11	Hoes	2
Shovels	11	Pans for placer mining	2
Mallets and mauls	6	Scales for weighing	2
Axes	5	Tractors	2
Chisels	5	Alidades	1
Anvils	4	Armillary spheres	1
Microscopes	4	Drill presses	1

Fire irons	1	Spinning wheels	1
Magnifying glasses	1	Stethoscopes	1
Micrometers	1	Telescopes	1
Mortar and pestle	1	Tongs	1
Pitchforks	1	Wrenches	1
Slickers	1		

TRANSPORTATION

Among the twenty different modes of transportation depicted on U.S. stamps the most common are watercraft. Watercraft (boats, ships, canoes, rowboats, and submarines) are found on 108 different stamps, and several stamps depict more than one kind of watercraft. Land vehicles are on ninety-one stamps; aircraft (airplanes, balloons, and dirigibles) appear on seventy-three stamps; and spacecraft on eleven stamps. Animal-drawn vehicles are depicted on thirty-six, or almost 40 percent, of the stamps illustrating land transportation. The most common is the covered wagon which is on nineteen stamps and accounts for more than one-half of the thirty-six stamps depicting animal-drawn vehicles. The various modes of transportation and the number of times each is depicted appear below.

Boats and ships	108	Dirigibles	4
Airplanes	68	Motorcycles	4
Covered wagons	19	Bicycles	2
Trains	19	Sleighs	2
Automobiles	15	Stagecoaches	2
Spacecraft	14	Balloons	1
Trucks	10	Dog sleds	1
Buggies	5	Jeeps	1
Buses and streetcars	5	Lunar rover	1
Carts	5	Submarines	1

WARS AND BATTLES

Events, battles, and other occurrences related to eight different wars have been depicted or commemorated on 123 different stamps. More stamps commemorating events of the Revolutionary War have been issued than for all the other wars together; in fact, seventy-three stamps, or 59 percent of the 123 stamps in this category are related to the Revolution. Fourteen battles of the Revolution have been commemorated on eighteen stamps— more than for all the other wars combined. Four Civil War battles, two of World War II, and one battle of the War of 1812 have also been commemorated on stamps. No battle of the French and Indian War, the Spanish-American War, World War I, or the Vietnam War has been commemorated on U.S. stamps. Only two stamps have been issued to commemorate the end of a war: the Victory stamp of 1919 (Scott Number 537) acclaimed the Allied victory in World War I, and the Appomattox stamp of 1965 (Scott Number 1182) marked the centennial of Lee's surrender to Grant in a farmhouse near the small town of Appomattox Court House, Virginia on April 9, 1865. The eight wars and the number of stamps related to each are given below.

Revolutionary War	73	French and Indian War	2
World War II	32	Spanish-American War	1
Civil War	7	Vietnam War	1
War of 1812	6	World War I	1

WATER

Water is the most common natural element found on stamps. The planet Earth is also known as the water planet because approximately three-fourths of its surface is covered by water (oceans, lakes, rivers, and icecaps), and so it seems quite natural that many stamps would include water in their designs. The most common mode of transportation found on stamps is watercraft; the stamps depicting watercraft naturally include water. Water appears in many forms and often is an unidentified body of water, nevertheless, it is water. However, more than one-half of the stamps depicting water in one form or another contain bodies and streams of water that are identifiable and have proper names. The types of bodies and streams of water and the various other forms in which water appears are listed below in rank order.

Water (unidentifiable)	72	Canals	6
Rivers	41	Waterfalls	6
Snow	28	Ice	4
Bays and harbors	23	Geysers	2
Oceans	23	Tidal Basin	2
Lakes	11	Rain	1

SUMMARY

The sixty-eight topics and items listed in Table 62 are those that have appeared on stamps at least twenty-five times and are therefore the most common elements included in the designs of U.S. stamps. The total sum of Scott Numbers listed under these sixty-eight headings is 5,065. A total of 1,309 headings appear in Appendix III with the listings of 9,177 Scott Numbers for the 1,355 stamps included in this study. This means that there is an average of almost seven entries for each of the 1,355 stamps. The sixty-eight headings in Table 62 represent only 5.2 percent of the 1,309 headings in Appendix III, but they account for 55.2 percent of the 9,177 Scott Numbers listed in Appendix III.

TRANSPORTATION

An analysis of the data in Table 63 shows that there are eleven categories with 200 or more Scott Numbers: (1) Buildings, dwellings, and structures, (2) Costume and personal appearance, (3) Foreign lands, (4) Government and the governed, (5) Light, lighting, and illumination, (6) Nature, (7) People, (8) Plants, (9) Signs, symbols, and symbolic figures, (10) Transportation, and (11) Water. These eleven categories combined have a total of 5,522 Scott Numbers, or almost 77 percent of the 7,186 Scott Numbers included in the twenty-five broad categories listed in Table 63. Just two of these broad categories (Costume and personal appearance, and People) have 2,212 Scott Numbers or 24 percent of the 9,177 Scott Numbers listed in Appendix III.

Each broad category lists many items which are only found on one or two stamps; in fact, of the 575 headings listed under the twenty-five categories, there are 90 headings for items found only on two stamps and 174 headings for items which are unique and just found on one stamp. Appendix III includes many more found just on one or two stamps.

The items listed in Tables 62 and 63 and the headings included under each of the twenty-five broad categories demonstrate that some things are quite common in the designs of stamps and other things are most uncommon and found only in the design of a single stamp.

APPENDIX I The Stamps

The numbers listed below indicate the stamps selected according to the criteria given in Chapter 2 and covered by this study. They are listed numerically by Scott Numbers and accompanied by the corresponding Minkus Numbers.

REGULAR ISSUES AND COMMEMORATIVE STAMPS

Scott Number	Minkus Number	Scott Number	Minkus Number	Scott Number	Minkus Number
1	1	68	51	118	92
2	2	69	52	120	94
5	3	70	55	121	95
10	10	71	57	122	96
12	12	72	58	145	108
13	13	73	44	146	109
17	17	77	53	147	110
37	40	112	86	148	111
38	41	113	87	149	112
39	42	114	88	150	113
63	43	115	89	151	114
64	45	116	90	152	115
67	47	117	91	153	116

Scott Number	Minkus Number	Scott Number	Minkus Number	Scott Number	Minkus Number
154	117	293	CM25	398	CM48
155	118	294	CM26	399	CM49
179	123	295	CM27	400	CM50
205	154	296	CM28	405	297
210	150	297	CM29	406	298
211	152	298	CM30	407	279
212	149	299	CM31	414	305
219	156	300	211	415	306
220	158	301	212	416	307
221	159	302	213	417	308
222	160	303	214	418	309
223	161	304	215	419	310
224	162	305	216	420	311
225	163	306	217	421	312
226	164	307	218	423	314
227	165	308	219	434	325
228	166	309	220	513	393
229	167	310	221	523	400
230	CM1	311	222	524	402
231	CM2	312	223	537	CM56
232	CM3	313	224	548	CM57
233	CM4	319	231	549	CM58
234	CM5	323	CM32	550	CM59
235	CM6	324	CM33	551	418
236	CM7	325	CM34	552	419
237	CM8	326	CM35	553	420
238	CM9	327	CM36	554	421
239	CM10	328	CM37	555	422
240	CM11	329	CM38	556	423
241	CM12	330	CM39	557	424
242	CM13	331	237	558	425
243	CM14	332	238	559	426
244	CM15	333	239	560	427
245	CM16	334	240	561	428
260	182	335	241	562	429
261	183	336	242	563	430
262	185	337	243	564	431
263	186	338	244	565	433
285	CM17	339	245	566	434
286	CM18	340	246	567	436
287	CM19	341	247	568	437
288	CM20	342	248	569	438
289	CM21	367	CM40	570	439
290	CM22	370	CM43	571	440
291	CM23	372	CM45	572	441
292	CM24	397	CM47	573	442

Scott Number	Minkus Number	Scott Number	Minkus Number	Scott Number	Minkus Number
610	CM60	714	CM108	793	CM180
614	CM64	715	CM109	794	CM181
615	CM65	716	CM110	795	CM182
616	CM66	717	CM111	796	CM183
617	CM67	718	CM112	798	CM185
618	CM68	719	CM113	799	CM186
619	CM69	720	518	800	CM187
620	CM70	724	CM114	801	CM188
621	CM71	725	CM115	802	CM189
622	432	726	CM116	803	524
623	435	727	CM117	804	525
627	CM72	728	CM118	805	526
628	CM73	729	CM119	806	527
629	CM74	732	CM122	807	528
643	CM76	733	CM123	808	529
644	CM77	734	CM124	809	530
645	CM78	736	CM126	810	531
646	CM81	737	CM127	811	532
647	CM79	739	CM129	812	533
648	CM80	740	CM130	813	534
649	CM82	741	CM131	814	535
650	CM83	742	CM132	815	536
651	CM84	743	CM133	816	537
654	CM85	744	CM134	817	538
657	CM88	745	CM135	818	539
680	CM89	746	CM136	819	540
681	CM90	747	CM137	820	541
682	CM91	748	CM138	821	542
683	CM92	749	CM139	822	543
684	517	772	CM162	823	544
685	519	773	CM163	824	545
688	CM93	774	CM164	825	546
689	CM94	775	CM165	826	547
690	CM95	776	CM166	827	548
702	CM96	777	CM167	828	549
703	CM97	782	CM169	829	550
704	CM98	783	CM170	830	551
705	CM99	784	CM171	831	552
706	CM100	785	CM172	832	553
707	CM101	786	CM173	833	554
708	CM102	787	CM174	834	555
709	CM103	788	CM175	835	CM190
710	CM104	789	CM176	836	CM191
711	CM105	790	CM177	837	CM192
712	CM106	791	CM178	838	CM193
713	CM107	792	CM179	852	CM194

Scott Number	Minkus Number	Scott Number	Minkus Number	Scott Number	Minkus Number
853	CM195	898	CM240	943	CM285
854	CM196	899	CM241	944	CM286
855	CM197	900	CM242	945	CM287
856	CM198	901	CM243	946	CM288
857	CM199	902	CM244	947	CM289
858	CM200	903	CM245	949	CM291
859	CM201	904	CM246	950	CM292
860	CM202	905	CM247	951	CM293
861	CM203	906	CM248	952	CM294
862	CM204	907	CM249	953	CM295
863	CM205	908	CM250	954	CM296
864	CM206	909	CM251	955	CM297
865	CM207	910	CM252	956	CM298
866	CM208	911	CM253	957	CM299
867	CM209	912	CM254	958	CM300
868	CM210	913	CM255	959	CM301
869	CM211	914	CM256	960	CM302
870	CM212	915	CM257	961	CM303
871	CM213	916	CM258	962	CM304
872	CM214	917	CM259	963	CM305
873	CM215	918	CM260	964	CM306
874	CM216	919	CM261	965	CM307
875	CM217	920	CM262	966	CM308
876	CM218	921	CM263	967	CM309
877	CM219	922	CM264	968	CM310
878	CM220	923	CM265	969	CM311
879	CM221	924	CM266	970	CM312
880	CM222	925	CM267	971	CM313
881	CM223	926	CM268	972	CM314
882	CM224	927	CM269	973	CM315
883	CM225	928	CM270	974	CM316
884	CM226	929	CM275	975	CM317
885	CM227	930	CM271	976	CM318
886	CM228	931	CM272	977	CM319
887	CM229	932	CM273	978	CM320
888	CM230	933	CM274	979	CM321
889	CM231	934	CM276	980	CM322
890	CM232	935	CM277	981	CM323
891	CM233	936	CM278	982	CM324
892	CM234	937	CM280	983	CM325
893	CM235	938	CM281	984	CM326
894	CM236	939	CM279	985	CM327
895	CM237	940	CM282	986	CM328
896	CM238	941	CM283	987	CM329
897	CM239	942	CM284	988	CM330

Scott Number	Minkus Number	Scott Number	Minkus Number	Scott Number	Minkus Number
989	CM331	1033	572	1083	CM395
990	CM332	1034	594	1084	CM396
991	CM333	1035	573	1085	CM397
992	CM334	1036	574	1086	CM398
993	CM335	1037	595	1087	CM399
994	CM336	1038	575	1088	CM400
995	CM337	1039	576	1089	CM401
996	CM338	1040	577	1090	CM402
997	CM339	1041	578	1091	CM403
998	CM340	1042	591	1092	CM404
999	CM341	1042A	602	1093	CM405
1000	CM342	1043	579	1094	CM406
1001	CM343	1044	580	1095	CM407
1002	CM344	1044A	601	1096	CM408
1003	CM345	1045	596	1097	CM409
1004	CM346	1046	592	1098	CM410
1005	CM347	1047	581	1099	CM411
1006	CM348	1048	593	1100	CM412
1007	CM349	1049	582	1104	CM413
1008	CM350	1050	583	1105	CM414
1009	CM351	1051	584	1106	CM415
1010	CM352	1052	585	1107	CM416
1011	CM353	1053	586	1108	CM417
1012	CM354	1060	CM372	1109	CM418
1013	CM355	1061	CM373	1110	CM419
1014	CM356	1062	CM374	1111	CM420
1015	CM357	1063	CM375	1112	CM421
1016	CM358	1064	CM376	1113	CM430
1017	CM359	1065	CM377	1114	CM431
1018	CM360	1066	CM378	1115	CM422
1019	CM361	1067	CM379	1116	CM432
1020	CM362	1068	CM380	1117	CM423
1021	CM363	1069	CM381	1118	CM424
1022	CM364	1070	CM382	1119	CM425
1023	CM365	1071	CM383	1120	CM426
1024	CM366	1072	CM384	1121	CM427
1025	CM367	1073	CM385	1122	CM428
1026	CM368	1074	CM386	1123	CM429
1027	CM369	1076	CM387	1124	CM433
1028	CM370	1077	CM389	1125	CM434
1029	CM371	1078	CM390	1126	CM435
1030	569	1079	CM391	1127	CM436
1031	570	1080	CM392	1128	CM437
1031A	599	1081	CM393	1129	CM438
1032	571	1082	CM394	1130	CM439

Scott Number	Minkus Number	Scott Number	Minkus Number	Scott Number	Minkus Number
1131	CM440	1176	CM485	1241	CM526
1132	CM441	1177	CM486	1242	CM527
1133	CM442	1178	CM487	1243	CM528
1134	CM443	1179	CM488	1244	CM529
1135	CM444	1180	CM489	1245	CM530
1136	CM445	1181	CM490	1246	CM531
1137	CM446	1182	CM491	1247	CM532
1138	CM447	1183	CM492	1248	CM533
1139	CM448	1184	CM493	1249	CM534
1140	CM449	1185	CM494	1250	CM535
1141	CM450	1186	CM495	1251	CM536
1142	CM451	1187	CM496	1252	CM537
1143	CM452	1188	CM497	1253	CM538
1144	CM453	1189	CM498	1254	610
1145	CM454	1190	CM499	1255	611
1146	CM455	1191	CM500	1256	612
1147	CM456	1192	CM501	1257	613
1148	CM457	1193	CM502	1258	CM539
1149	CM458	1194	CM503	1259	CM540
1150	CM459	1195	CM504	1260	CM541
1151	CM460	1196	CM505	1261	CM542
1152	CM461	1197	CM506	1262	CM543
1153	CM462	1198	CM507	1263	CM544
1154	CM463	1199	CM508	1264	CM545
1155	CM464	1200	CM509	1265	CM546
1156	CM465	1201	CM510	1266	CM547
1157	CM466	1202	CM511	1267	CM548
1158	CM467	1203	CM512	1268	CM549
1159	CM468	1205	603	1269	CM550
1160	CM469	1206	CM514	1270	CM551
1161	CM470	1207	CM515	1271	CM552
1162	CM471	1208	606	1272	CM553
1163	CM472	1209	607	1273	CM554
1164	CM473	1213	604	1274	CM555
1165	CM474	1230	CM516	1275	CM556
1166	CM475	1231	CM517	1276	615
1167	CM476	1232	CM518	1278	616
1168	CM477	1233	CM519	1279	617
1169	CM478	1234	CM520	1280	618
1170	CM479	1235	CM521	1281	619
1171	CM481	1236	CM522	1282	620
1172	CM480	1237	CM523	1283	621
1173	CM482	1238	CM524	1284	622
1174	CM483	1239	CM525	1285	623
1175	CM484	1240	609	1286	624

Scott Number	Minkus Number	Scott Number	Minkus Number	Scott Number	Minkus Number
1286A	624A	1340	CM588	1385	CM630
1287	625	1341	648	1386	CM631
1288	626	1342	CM589	1387	CM632
1289	627	1343	CM590	1388	CM633
1290	628	1344	CM591	1389	CM634
1291	629	1345	CM592	1390	CM635
1292	630	1346	CM593	1391	CM636
1293	631	1347	CM594	1392	CM637
1294	632	1348	CM595	1393	652
1295	633	1349	CM596	393D	669
1305	637	1350	CM597	1394	663
1306	CM557	1351	CM598	1396	665
1307	CM558	1352	CM599	1397	668
1308	CM559	1353	CM600	1398	660
1309	CM560	1354	CM601	1399	681
1310	CM561	1355	CM602	1400	673
1312	CM563	1356	CM603	1405	CM638
1313	CM564	1357	CM604	1406	CM639
1314	CM565	1358	CM605	1407	CM640
1315	CM566	1359	CM606	1408	CM641
1316	CM567	1360	CM607	1409	CM642
1317	CM568	1361	CM608	1410	CM643
1318	CM569	1362	CM609	1411	CM644
1319	CM570	1363	649	1412	CM645
1320	CM571	1364	CM610	1413	CM646
1321	644	1365	CM611	1414	659
1322	CM572	1366	CM612	1415	655
1323	CM573	1367	CM613	1416	656
1324	CM574	1368	CM614	1417	657
1325	CM575	1369	CM615	1418	658
1326	CM576	1370	CM616	1419	CM647
1327	CM577	1371	CM617	1420	CM648
1328	CM578	1372	CM618	1421	CM649
1329	CM579	1373	CM619	1422	CM650
1330	CM580	1374	CM620	1423	CM651
1331	CM581	1375	CM621	1424	CM652
1332	CM582	1376	CM622	1425	CM653
1333	CM583	1377	CM623	1426	CM654
1334	CM584	1378	CM624	1427	CM655
1335	CM585	1379	CM625	1428	CM656
1336	645	1380	CM626	1429	CM657
1337	CM586	1381	CM627	1430	CM658
1338	647	1382	CM628	1431	CM659
1338F	661	1383	CM629	1432	CM660
1339	CM587	1384	651	1433	CM663

Scott Number	Minkus Number	Scott Number	Minkus Number	Scott Number	Minkus Number
1434	CM661	1480	CM717	1538	CM743
1435	CM662	1481	CM718	1539	CM745
1436	CM664	1482	CM719	1540	CM742
1437	CM665	1483	CM720	1541	CM744
1438	CM666	1484	CM704	1542	CM746
1439	CM667	1485	CM724	1543	CM747
1440	CM668	1486	CM726	1544	CM749
1441	CM669	1487	CM727	1545	CM750
1442	CM670	1488	CM705	1546	CM748
1443	CM671	1489	CM706	1547	CM753
1444	667	1490	CM707	1548	CM754
1445	666	1491	CM708	1549	CM755
1446	CM672	1492	CM709	1550	685
1447	CM673	1493	CM710	1551	683
1448	CM675	1494	CM711	1552	684
1449	CM676	1495	CM712	1553	CM756
1450	CM677	1496	CM713	1554	CM765
1451	CM678	1497	CM714	1555	CM766
1452	CM679	1498	CM715	1556	CM757
1453	CM674	1499	CM716	1557	CM763
1454	CM680	1500	CM721	1558	CM758
1455	CM681	1501	CM722	1559	CM759
1456	CM682	1502	CM723	1560	CM760
1457	CM683	1503	CM725	1561	CM761
1458	CM684	1504	CM728	1562	CM762
1459	CM685	1505	CM751	1563	CM764
1460	CM686	1506	CM752	1564	CM767
1461	CM687	1507	674	1565	CM768
1462	CM688	1508	675	1566	CM769
1463	CM689	1509	676	1567	CM770
1464	CM690	1510	678	1568	CM771
1465	CM691	1511	680	1569	CM772
1466	CM692	1518	682	1570	CM773
1467	CM693	1525	CM729	1571	CM775
1468	CM694	1526	CM730	1572	CM776
1469	CM695	1527	CM731	1573	CM777
1470	CM696	1528	CM732	1574	CM778
1471	671	1529	CM733	1575	CM779
1472	670	1530	CM738	1576	CM774
1473	CM697	1531	CM739	1577	CM780
1474	CM698	1532	CM740	1578	CM781
1475	CM699	1533	CM741	1579	687
1476	CM700	1534	CM734	1580	686
1477	CM701	1535	CM735	1581	710
1478	CM702	1536	CM736	1582	711
1479	CM703	1537	CM737	1584	712

Scott Number	Minkus Number	Scott Number	Minkus Number	Scott Number	Minkus Number
1585	713	1653	CM806	1688d	CM841d
1591	688	1654	CM807	1688e	CM841e
1592	708	1655	CM808	1689a	CM842a
1593	689	1656	CM809	1689b	CM842b
1595	695	1657	CM810	1689c	CM842c
1596	691	1658	CM811	1689d	CM842d
1598	722	1659	CM812	1689e	CM842e
1599	715	1660	CM813	1690	CM843
1603	692	1661	CM814	1691	CM844
1604	726	1662	CM815	1692	CM845
1605	717	1663	CM816	1693	CM846
1606	732	1664	CM817	1694	CM847
1608	733	1665	CM818	1695	CM848
1610	730	1666	CM819	1696	CM849
1611	729	1667	CM820	1697	CM850
1612	731	1668	CM821	1698	CM851
1613	736	1669	CM822	1699	CM852
1614	701	1670	CM823	1700	CM853
1615	698	1671	CM824	1701	700
1615C	725	1672	CM825	1702	699
1622	690	1673	CM826	1704	CM854
1623	703	1674	CM827	1705	CM855
1629	CM782	1675	CM828	1706	CM856
1630	CM783	1676	CM829	1707	CM857
1631	CM784	1677	CM830	1708	CM858
1632	CM785	1678	CM831	1709	CM859
1633	CM786	1679	CM832	1710	CM860
1634	CM787	1680	CM833	1711	CM861
1635	CM788	1681	CM834	1712	CM862
1636	CM789	1682	CM835	1713	CM863
1637	CM790	1683	CM836	1714	CM864
1638	CM791	1684	CM837	1715	CM865
1639	CM792	1685	CM838	1716	CM866
1640	CM793	1686a	CM839a	1717	CM867
1641	CM794	1686b	CM839b	1718	CM868
1642	CM795	1686c	CM839c	1719	CM869
1643	CM796	1686d	CM839d	1720	CM870
1644	CM797	1686e	CM839e	1721	CM871
1645	CM798	1687a	CM840a	1722	CM872
1646	CM799	1687b	CM840b	1723	706
1647	CM800	1687c	CM840c	1724	707
1648	CM801	1687d	CM840d	1725	CM873
1649	CM802	1687e	CM840e	1726	CM874
1650	CM803	1688a	CM841a	1727	CM875
1651	CM804	1688b	CM841b	1728	CM876
1652	CM805	1688c	CM841c	1729	705

Scott Number	Minkus Number	Scott Number	Minkus Number	Scott Number	Minkus Number
1730	704	1761	CM897	1797	CM934
1731	CM877	1762	CM898	1798	CM935
1732	CM878	1763	CM899	1799	735
1733	CM879	1764	CM900	1800	734
1734	714	1765	CM901	1801	CM929
1735	718	1766	CM902	1802	CM930
1737	724	1767	CM903	1803	CM931
1738	737	1768	728	1804	CM936
1739	738	1769	727	1805	CM937
1740	739	1770	CM904	1806	CM938
1741	740	1771	CM905	1807	CM939
1742	741	1772	CM906	1809	CM941
1744	CM880	1773	CM907	1813	744
1745	CM881	1774	CM908	1821	CM943
1746	CM882	1775	CM909	1822	743
1747	CM883	1776	CM910	1823	CM944
1748	CM884	1777	CM911	1824	CM945
1749	CM885	1778	CM912	1825	CM946
1750	CM886	1779	CM913	1826	CM947
1751	CM887	1780	CM914	1827	CM948
1752	CM888	1781	CM915	1828	CM949
1753	CM889	1782	CM916	1829	CM950
1754	CM890	1783	CM917	1830	CM951
1755	CM891	1784	CM918	1831	CM952
1756	CM894	1785	CM919	1832	CM953
1757a	CM892a	1786	CM920	1833	CM954
1757b	CM892b	1787	CM921	1834	CM955
1757c	CM892c	1788	CM922	1835	CM956
1757d	CM892d	1789	CM924	1836	CM957
1757e	CM892e	1790	CM923	1837	CM958
1757f	CM892f	1791	CM925	1838	CM959
1757g	CM892g	1792	CM926	1839	CM960
1757h	CM892h	1793	CM927	1840	CM961
1758	CM893	1794	CM928	1841	CM962
1759	CM895	1795	CM932	1842	746
1760	CM896	1796	CM933	1843	745
				1851	747

AIR MAIL STAMPS

Scott Number	Minkus Number	Scott Number	Minkus Number	Scott Number	Minkus Number
C1	A1	C3	A3	C5	A5
C2	A2	C4	A4	C6	A6

Scott Number	Minkus Number	Scott Number	Minkus Number	Scott Number	Minkus Number
C7	A7	C36	A37	C71	A71
C8	A8	C38	A38	C72	A72
C9	A9	C39	A39	C74	A74
C10	A10	C40	A41	C75	A75
C11	A11	C42	A42	C76	A76
C12	A12	C43	A43	C77	A77
C13	A13	C44	A44	C78	A78
C14	A14	C45	A45	C79	A85
C15	A15	C46	A46	C80	A80
C17	A18	C47	A47	C81	A81
C18	A19	C48	A48	C84	A82
C19	A17	C49	A49	C85	A83
C20	A21	C50	A50	C86	A84
C21	A20	C51	A51	C87	A87
C22	A22	C53	A53	C88	A88
C23	A23	C54	A54	C89	A89
C24	A24	C55	A56	C90	A90
C25	A25	C56	A55	C91	A91
C26	A26	C57	A57	C92	A92
C27	A27	C58	A58	C93	A93
C28	A28	C59	A59	C94	A94
C29	A29	C62	A63	C95	A96
C30	A30	C64	A64	C96	A97
C31	A31	C66	A66	C97	A95
C32	A32	C67	A67	C98	A98
C33	A33	C68	A68	C99	A99
C34	A35	C69	A69	C100	A100
C35	A36	C70	A70		

AIR MAIL SPECIAL DELIVERY STAMP

Scott Number	Minkus Number
CE1	ASD1

SPECIAL DELIVERY STAMPS

Scott Number	Minkus Number	Scott Number	Minkus Number
E1	SD1	E12	SD12
E2	SD2	E13	SD13
E6	SD6	E14	SD14
E7	SD7	E17	SD16

Scott Number	Minkus Number	Scott Number	Minkus Number
E18	SD18	E22	SD22
E20	SD20	E23	SD23
E21	SD21		

PARCEL POST STAMPS

Scott Number	Minkus Number	Scott Number	Minkus Number
Q1	PP1	Q7	PP7
Q2	PP2	Q8	PP8
Q3	PP3	Q9	PP9
Q4	PP4	Q10	PP10
Q5	PP5	Q11	PP11
Q6	PP6	Q12	PP12

APPENDIX II   The Individuals

Every identified individual who was honored on United States postage stamps issued between July 1, 1847 and December 31, 1980 is listed below in alphabetical order. The names of the individuals are accompanied by birth and death dates, and these are followed by the Scott Numbers for the stamps on which that person was honored.

Adams, John (1735-1826), 120, 806, 854, 1687, 1692
Adams, John Quincy (1767-1848), 811
Adams, Samuel (1722-1803), 120, 1691
Addams, Jane (1860-1935), 878
Albers, Josef (1888-1976), 1833
Alcott, Louisa May (1832-88), 862
Allen, Ethan (1738-89), 1071
Anthony, Susan Brownell (1820-1906), 784, 1051
Appleseed, Johnny (1774-1845), 1317
Armstrong, Neil Alden (1930-   ), C76
Arthur, Chester Alan (1829-86), 826
Audubon, John James (1785-1851), 874, 1241, C71
Austin, Stephen Fuller (1793-1836), 776

Balboa, Vasco Núñez de (1475-1519), 235, 397
Baldwin, Abraham (1754-1807), 798
Banneker, Benjamin (1731-1806), 1804
Barbé-Marbois, François de (1745-1837), 1020
Barry, John (1745-1803), 790
Bartlett, Josiah (1729-95), 120, 1691
Barton, Clara (1821-1912), 967
Bassett, Richard (1745-1815), 798
Bedford, Gunning (1747-1812), 798
Bell, Alexander Graham (1847-1922), 893, 1683
Benton, Thomas Hart (1889-1975), 1426
Biglin, Bernard (1840-1924), 1335

APPENDIX III Objects, Topics, Themes, and Things

The following list is an alphabetical index to the identifiable objects, topics, themes, and things that have appeared on U.S. stamps. Each entry is followed by the Scott Numbers of the stamps featuring that detail. Every effort was exerted to identify all elements contained in the designs of the 1,355 stamps included in this study and to compile a list that would be as comprehensive and exhaustive as possible.

This index to the objects, topics, themes, and things on U.S. postage stamps has two basic purposes. The first purpose is to provide a subject guide enabling the user to determine the Scott Number of a stamp by means of any known detail or element contained in the design. This serves thus as a supplementary index to the *Scott Specialized Catalogue of United States Stamps*. The second purpose is to help topical collectors identify the U.S. stamps that feature the subjects of their specializations. This index does not pretend to include each and every element in the 1,355 stamps covered by this study; instead the index provides an indispensable basic list which the topical collector may use as a starting point.

Many topics and objects have multiple entries. Geographic designations and special events of all kinds are listed under their own names, as well as under the country, state, or other area where they are located, took place, or to which they are related in one way or another. An example of this is the stamp issued to publicize the Winter Olympic Games held in Sapporo, Japan in 1972 (Scott Number 1461); entries for this stamp are: (1) Japan, (2) Sapporo, Japan, (3) Olympic Games, (4) Sleds, (5) Sports: Bobsled racing, and (6) Bobsled racing. Many objects are listed under a specific name and also under a general category or generic term; for example, all bridges are listed under Bridges, and those which are identifiable and have names are also listed under their own names, such as the Verrazano-Narrows Bridge and the San Francisco-Oakland Bay Bridge.

Numerous items which are inherent parts or aspects of another object are not listed separately in this index; instead, cross references are made to the object of which those items are integral parts. One example is the Great Seal of the United States depicting an eagle with arrows clutched in its left talon and an olive branch in its right one, a shield, and the motto, *E Pluribus Unum*. Under the entries, Arrows, Olive leaves and branches, *E Pluribus Unum*, and Coats of arms, seals, and shields, references direct the reader to *see also* the heading, Great Seal of the United States. Another example is the Statue of Liberty wearing a crown and holding a book in her left arm and a torch in her right hand; under the headings, Books, Crowns, and Torches, there are cross references to the entry, Statue of Liberty. Following the heading, Snakes, only one Scott Number is given, but a cross reference informs the reader to *see also* Medical emblems because snakes are an inherent aspect of all medical emblems on the stamps given under that heading. Thus many items which are inseparable parts of another object may be found easily by consulting the headings in the cross references given at the end of many index entries.

Occupations and professions are listed in this index only when figures in the design of the stamps do not represent real persons or when the occupation or profession itself is honored. The occupations and professions of real persons portrayed or honored on stamps may be found in Chapter 11 and have been excluded here to avoid unnecessary duplication.

This alphabetical index is comprised of 1,309 headings and 782 subheadings with listings of 9,172 Scott Numbers. In addition to the 2,091 headings and subheadings, there are 150 terms not used as entries because they are either synonymous with or very similar to those terms selected for headings, or because of their ambiguity and lack of precise meaning. The reader is referred from these terms to 368 other terms actually used as headings. Some examples of this type of entry are (1) Glasses. *See* Eyeglasses; Goggles; Water glasses, (2) Military. *See* Armed Forces, (3) Railroads. *See* Trains, and (4) Watches. *See* Clocks; Wristwatches. There are 527 entries listed as cross references at the end of many entries to assist the reader in finding topics and objects related to the one consulted. Examples of this kind of reference are: (1) Chairs. *See also* Benches; Stools; Tables; Wheelchairs, (2) Light bulbs. *See also* Candles; Electricity; Lamps and lanterns, and (3) Spacecraft. *See also* Rockets; Satellites; Space exploration.

Selected References

This list of selected references consists of the most frequently consulted sources used in the preparation of this guide. Biographical and historical data were gathered from standard reference works, namely, biographical dictionaries and directories, general and specialized encyclopedias, histories, biographies, indexes, newspapers, periodicals, and publications of the U.S. government.

Brookman, Lester G. *The 19th Century Postage Stamps of the United States*. New York: H. L. Lindquist, 1947. 2 vols.

Cabeen, Richard M. *Standard Handbook of Stamp Collecting*. New revised edition. New York: Thomas Y. Crowell, 1979. 630 pp.

Cullinan, Gerald. *The Post Office Department*. Foreword by James A. Farley. New York: Frederick A. Praeger, 1968. 272 pp.

Fuller, Wayne E. *The American Mail: Enlarger of the Common Life*. Chicago: University of Chicago Press, 1972. 378 pp.

Johl, Max G. *The United States Commemorative Stamps of the Twentieth Century*. New York: H. L. Lindquist, 1947. Vol. 1.

Kelly, Clyde. *United States Postal Policy*. New York: Appleton, 1932. 320 pp.

Martin, M. W. *Topical Stamp Collecting*. New York: Arco, 1975. 159 pp.

Minkus New American Stamp Catalog. 1981 edition. New York: Minkus Publications, 1980. 390 pp.

Minkus Stamp & Coin Journal. New York: Minkus Publications, 1980-.

Minkus Stamp Journal. New York: Minkus Publications, Inc. 1966-80

Mueller, Barbara R. *United States Postage Stamps: How To Collect, Understand, and Enjoy Them*. Princeton, N.J.: Van Nostrand, 1958. 343 pp.

Petersham, Maud and Miska. *America's Stamps: The Story of One Hundred Years of U.S. Postage Stamps.* New York: Macmillan, 1947. 144 pp.

Reinfeld, Fred. *Commemorative Stamps of the U.S.A.: An Illustrated History of Our Country.* New York: Thomas Y. Crowell, 1954. 344 pp.

Schenk, Gustav. *The Romance of the Postage Stamp.* Translated from the German by Mervyn Savill. Garden City, N.Y.: Doubleday, 1962. 231 pp.

Scott Specialized Catalogue of United States Stamps, 1981. 59th edition. New York: Scott Publishing Company, 1980. 762 pp.

Scott's Monthly Stamp Journal. New York: Scott Publishing Company, 1920-.

United States Postal Service. *Stamps & Stories: The Encyclopedia of U.S. Stamps.* Washington, D.C.: U.S. Postal Service, 1980. 264 pp.

United States Postal Service. Philatelic Affairs Division. *United States Postage Stamps: An Illustrated Description of All United States Postage and Special Service Stamps.* Washington, D.C.: U.S. Government Printing Office, 1972-.

Index

About the Author

DONALD J. LEHNUS is Associate Professor in the Graduate School of Library and Information Science at the University of Mississippi. Among his earlier publications are *Who's on TIME?* and *Book Numbers.*